Adam

Smith

Reviewed

Adam

Smith

Reviewed

edited by
PETER JONES and ANDREW S. SKINNER

EDINBURGH UNIVERSITY PRESS

© Edinburgh University Press, 1992
Edinburgh University Press
22 George Square, Edinburgh

Typeset in Linotron Baskerville 2
by Photoprint, Torquay, and
printed in Great Britain by
the University Press, Cambridge

A CIP record for this book is available from the British Library

ISBN 0 7486 0346 8

Contents

Contributors

John C. Bryce is Emeritus Bradley Professor of English Literature at the University of Glasgow.

John W. Cairns is Senior Lecturer in Scots Law at The University of Edinburgh.

Robin S. Downie is Professor of Moral Philosophy at the University of Glasgow.

John Dwyer is the Canada Research Fellow in the Department of History, York University, Ontario.

Peter Jones is Director of the Institute for Advanced Studies in the Humanities, and Professor of Philosophy, University of Edinburgh.

H. Christopher Longuet-Higgins is Professor Emeritus at the University of Sussex.

Frans Plank is Professor of Linguistics at the Universitat Konstanz.

David D. Raphael is Emeritus Professor of Philosophy, University of London.

Andrew S. Skinner is Daniel Jack Professor of Political Economy, and Vice-Principal, University of Glasgow.

Abbreviations

All references are to the Glasgow Edition of the works and correspondence of Adam Smith, published by the Clarendon Press, Oxford, 1976–1983.

Works of Adam Smith

Corr.	*Correspondence*
EPS	*Essays on Philosophical Subjects,* included among which are:
Ancient Logics	'The History of the Ancient Logics and Metaphysics'
Ancient Physics	'The History of the Ancient Physics'
Astronomy	'The History of Astronomy'
English and Italian Verses	'Of the Affinity between certain English and Italian Verses'
External Senses	'Of the External Senses'
Imitative Arts	'Of the Nature of that Imitation which takes place in what are called the Imitative Arts'
Stewart	Dugald Stewart, 'Account of the Life and Writings of Adam Smith, LL.D.'
Languages	*Considerations Concerning the First Formation of Languages*
TMS	*The Theory of Moral Sentiments*
WN	*The Wealth of Nations*

LJ (A)	*Lectures on Jurisprudence*, Report of 1762–3
LJ (B)	*Lectures on Jurisprudence*, Report dated 1766
LRBL	*Lectures on Rhetoric and Belles Lettres*

References are given to page, to number of the letter, or to section and paragraph, as appropriate.

In the Glasgow edition, WN was edited by R. H. Campbell, A. S. Skinner and W. B. Todd (1976); TMS, by D. D. Raphael and A. L. Macfie (1976); Corr., by E. C. Mossner and I. S. Ross (1977); EPS, by W. P. D. Wightman (1980); and LRBL by J. C. Bryce (1983). LJ (A), and LJ (B), by R. L. Meek, D. D. Raphael and P. G. Stein (1978).

Associated volume

EAS	*Essays on Adam Smith*, edited by Andrew S. Skinner and Thomas Wilson (1975)

Introduction

PETER JONES

Adam Smith died on 17 July 1790. Many events were arranged to commemorate the bicentennial of his death, including an exhibition in the Royal Museum of Scotland, entitled 'Morals, Motives and Markets: Adam Smith 1723–1790'. That exhibition, devised by Jean Jones, and opened by ten Nobel Laureates in Economics who gathered for the occasion, considered the full range of Smith's interests and achievements, and showed how his economic theories were based on his ideas about human nature and human motives. This book is also designed to describe and assess the range of Smith's thought, from astronomy to aesthetics, from economics to jurisprudence, from rhetoric to moral philosophy. The contributors are not concerned to establish a hagiography. Rather, they seek both to recreate the context in which Smith was writing, since he was necessarily a man of his times, and to assess the cogency and value of his ideas from the perspective of today.

The book opens with a chapter by J. C. Bryce, in which he outlines the context of Smith's lectures on rhetoric, first delivered in Edinburgh in 1748. For Smith, who continued to lecture on these subjects after taking up his chair at the University of Glasgow, the nature of effective communication and the structure of language were both matters of ethical concern and taste. Unlike his close friend David Hume, however, Smith presented no epistemological basis to his reflections. Frans Plank develops Bryce's reflections by an analysis of Smith's third lecture on rhetoric, published in 1761 under the title *Considerations Concerning the First Formation of Languages, and the Different Genius of Original and Compounded*

Languages. As a 'conjectural historian' Smith sought to confirm the seniority of ancient over modern languages, by tracing the structural mechanisms of ancient languages further back in time. Plank argues that the typological significance of Smith's reflections on the origins and nature of grammatical structures lies in the subtle details of his analysis, and not in the generally accepted generalisation that language could be grossly classified as inflecting or non-inflecting. His aim was to explain structural classes as successive stages in linguistic, cognitive and social evolution.

Smith's writing on aesthetics has attracted even less attention than his views on language, not least because his essay 'Of the Nature of that Imitation which takes place in what are called the Imitative Arts' was published only posthumously. Peter Jones begins with the context and sources of Smith's views. Although he had read contemporary theories of music, Smith anchored most of his reflections to literature, as did his friend Hume, whose views he largely followed. But whereas Hume stresses the ineradicable role of context in making critical judgements of art, Smith underlines the implication of that point by stressing that our overriding concern is with the meaning of such works. Like most of his contemporaries, Smith fails to grasp the roles of conventions in representation and interpretation, although, like his friend Allan Ramsay, he held that fashion and custom were the two most dominant influences on taste.

Christopher Longuet-Higgins asks whether Smith's essay on 'The History of Astronomy' harmonises with modern ideas about the methods of science or the structure of scientific revolutions. He points out that Smith's emphasis on surprise and wonder as motives to enquiry leaves it unclear whether imagination is led thereby towards, or away from, new systems of thought. In any case, the author argues that Smith did not sufficiently recognise either the predictive character of scientific theories or the need for testability.

There follow three chapters on moral philosophy, broadly conceived. D. D. Raphael shows how Smith, by reference to sympathy, tried to remedy the defect in earlier theories which failed to indicate how propriety is to be measured. This move fails, however, to harmonise with Smith's own distinctions between propriety and virtue. Andrew Skinner extends the discussion by showing that propriety is the central concept in Smith's account of how we judge the behaviour of ourselves and others. An understanding of such behaviour, the psychological dimensions of which are explored in *The Theory of Moral Sentiments*, itself underlies a grasp of the main political and economic issues Smith addresses. R. S. Downie looks at the nature and roles of casuistry in Smith's day and in our own. Smith's rejection of casuistry was orthodox for the times, on the general grounds that casuists try to impose rules too rigidly on particular cases. Smith's rejection needs interpretation, however, since he admits that writers on jurisprudence, such as Locke and Grotius, simultaneously adopted, whilst denying, the mantle of casuistry. Downie concludes by considering whether, today, casuistry is possible, desirable or legitimate as a part of moral philosophy.

The next two chapters address issues in jurisprudence and the political context. John Cairns shows that by 1750 the natural law approach to the basis of both moral and legal obligations had become institutionalised in the teaching of moral philosophy, and public law and the Law of Nature and Nations. The Faculty of Advocates insisted in the 1760s that their students study natural law, possibly because Smith's Lectures on Jurisprudence showed how law could be taught as a dynamic historical process. John Dwyer attempts to show how Smith, in *The Wealth of Nations*, whilst developing his social and economic vision, nevertheless retained a civic programme of recognisably Harringtonian origins. Smith's model of a society of prudent farmers was tied to his views about man's natural attachment to the land, and that ownership of land encouraged independent thought and personal development. Such an interpretation supports those economic historians who argue that modern capitalism originated in an agrarian context, characterised by rent-paying tenants operating small family farms.

In the final chapter Andrew Skinner sets Smith's economic ideas against the background of Hume and Sir James Steuart. A distinctive feature of Smith's thought, appreciated by contemporaries such as Dugald Stewart, was his *system*, but his subsequent success lay as much in the broad advocacy of free trade, which inspired a new classical orthodoxy.

The editors of this volume are confident that, as a result of their new interpretations, assessment and contextual identification, these essays will provoke further interest in the range and value of Smith's work.

1

Lectures on rhetoric and belles lettres

J. C. BRYCE

I

A student of the traditional rhetoric who reads Smith's *Lectures on Rhetoric* as he runs (or – as Smith would put it – 'one partly asleep'), may possibly, as he encounters familiar topics, concepts and terminology, conclude that this is the well-worn old story, a story told often in the past, a dreary one. Smith, in speaking of the many systems of rhetoric both ancient and modern, observed that they were generally 'a very silly set of books and not at all instructive' (LRBL i. v. 59). Such a reader will have missed the motive which gives unity and direction to the lectures and the framework of thought which transforms the old discipline: above all, he will be ignoring the delight which informs the whole and its details.

Smith began lecturing at a time when the study of rhetoric was turning increasingly, especially in Scotland, to the study of taste. Hugh Blair opens the *Lectures on Rhetoric and Belles Lettres* which he first delivered in 1759 by summing up their twofold aim: 'Whatever enables genius to execute well, will enable taste to criticise justly.' Smith was a natural teacher of literature. One of his students, William Richardson, in a life of Archibald Arthur who later occupied the Glasgow Chair of Moral Philosophy (and who had himself studied under Smith), records: 'Those who received instruction from Dr. Smith, will recollect, with much satisfaction, many of these incidental and digressive illustrations, and even discussions, not only in morality, but in criticism, which were delivered by him with animated and extemporaneous eloquence, as they were suggested in the course of question and answer' (Arthur, *Discourses on Theological and Literary Subjects*, 1803: 507–8).

Richardson's words, though in the first instance about Smith's 'examination' hour, are known to be true of his lecturing in general; and it is significant that in the account of the lectures on rhetoric which follows (515), 'taste' is the first topic to be mentioned, before 'composition'. Arthur himself followed Smith's method 'and treated of fine-writing, the principles of criticism, and the pleasures of the imagination ... intended by him to unfold and elucidate those processes of invention, that structure of language, and system of arrangement, which are the objects of genuine taste': double evidence, in effect, of Smith's attitude to the first subject he had chosen to teach. George Jardine, another student of Smith's who, as Professor of Logic and Rhetoric at Glasgow from 1787, continued to teach along the lines his master had laid down, likewise concentrated on 'the principles of taste and criticism'. Thomas Reid, writing about 1791 in the *Statistical Account of Scotland* (vol. 21, 1799, 735), described Jardine's current practice thus:

> after dealing briefly with the art of reasoning and its history, he dedicates the greater part of his time to an illustration of the various mental operations, as they are expressed by the several modifications of speech and writing; which leads him to deliver a system of lectures on general grammar, rhetoric, and belles lettres. This course, accompanied with suitable exercises and specimens, on the part of the students, is properly placed at the entrance to philosophy: no subjects are likely to be more interesting to young minds, at a time when their taste and feelings are beginning to open, and have naturally disposed them to the reading of such authors as are necessary to supply them with facts and materials for beginning and carrying on the important habits of reflection and investigation.

It is significant that accounts of the tradition in rhetorical teaching acknowledged as stemming from Adam Smith so often dwell on the 'taste and feelings' of the students.

The title 'Rhetoric and Belles Lettres', which presumably (though we do not know) was Smith's own choice to describe his course, seems to go back to Charles Rollin's appointment to the Chair of Rhetoric at the Collège Royal in Paris in 1688. Rollin's lectures were published in 1726–8 as *De la manière d'enseigner et d'étudier les Belles-lettres, par rapport à l'esprit et au coeur* – later changed to *Traité des études*. Apart from the suggestions of the subtitle, the book cannot be shown to have taught Smith anything in the field of criticism. He needed no-one else's instruction on *l'esprit et le coeur*.

His pleasure as a critic is in several ways that of a philosopher. He is stimulated by prose and poetry which clearly reveal the author, and his eye (and ear) are made attentive by the conception he has worked out of the relation between the writer and the man. Rhetoric had, at least since the first century BC, always been taught with copious illustrations from writers, and students had been trained by exercises in the close analysis of texts. For Smith there is no separation between the two instructions, in handling language and in the enjoyment of that handling by the masters of the crafts. His most characteristic method is the comparative, the pinpointing of an author's essential quality by putting his work alongside that of a practitioner in the same field or a kindred one: Demosthenes and Cicero, Clarendon and Burnet. This method, used systematically over a great range of examples, is his most distinctive contribution to the literary criticism of his age. In English criticism only Dryden in, for example, the *Essay of Dramatic Poesy* and the Preface to the *Fables*, had so far used comparison in an extensive and self-conscious way. Smith certainly knew the examples in the rhetorical treatises of Dionysius of Halicarnassus (Demosthenes with Thucydides, Plato with Demosthenes, Isaeus with Lysias etc.), and in Quintilian's *Institutio Oratoria* Book X; but perhaps his immediate model was the series of comparisons of ancient writers published by René Rapin in 1664–81.

This was the age of collections of *The Beauties of . . . Shakespeare, Milton, Pope, Poetry*, and so on. Many of Smith's lectures must have delighted their audience by sounding like some such judiciously-selected anthologies. He read extensively from the texts in class, often in his own translation, an art he took great pleasure in and found instructive in its own right (Stewart, I. 9): hence the variation in length in the reported lectures. The immense popularity of these lectures was the result of their offering the spectacle of Smith's suppleness in moving easily over the whole field of ancient and modern writing and of his inventiveness in making illuminating connections.

II

The general continuity of the lecture course from 1748 to 1763, details apart, is established by its structure and by the set of central principles which inform all twenty-nine reported lectures and which could not have been added or superimposed on the argument at some intermediate stage of its development. Basic to the whole is the division into 'an examination of the several ways of communicating our thoughts by speech' and 'an attention to the principles of those literary compositions which contribute to persuasion or entertainment'.

This may be set out in summary. The first section, linguistic, includes: (a) Language, communication, expression (Lectures 2–7, i. 85); (b) Style and character (Lectures 8–11). The second section, the species of composition, includes: (a) Descriptive (Lectures 12–16); (b) Narrative or historical (Lectures 17–20); (c) Poetry (Lecture 21); (d) Demonstrative oratory, i.e. panegyric (Lectures 22–3); (e) Didactic or scientific (Lecture 24); (f) Deliberative oratory (Lectures 25–7); (g) Judicial or forensic oratory (Lectures 28–30).

Two features of the course enable us to make a plausible guess at the contents of the introductory lecture – whose absence tends to prove that this set of notes was not prepared with a view to sale. At the heart of Smith's thinking, his doctrine, and his method of presentation (the three are always related) is the notion of the chain (see LRBL ii. 133 and cf. Astronomy II. 8–9) – articulated continuity, a sequence of relations leading to illumination. Leave no chasm or gap in the thread: 'the very notion of a gap makes us uneasy' (LRBL ii. 36). The orator is to throw his argument 'into a sort of a narration, filling up in the manner most suitable . . . ' (LRBL ii. 206, 197). The art of transition is a vital matter (LRBL i. 146). Smith is concerned with this on the strategic level just as contemporary writers on Milton and Thomson were on the imaginative. As a lecturer giving an exhibition of the very craft he is discussing, he insists that his listeners know where they have been and where they are going. Dugald Stewart notes in his *Life of Thomas Reid* that 'neither he nor his immediate predecessor ever published any general *prospectus* of their respective plans; nor any *heads* or *outlines* to assist their students in tracing the trains of thought which suggested their various transitions' (1802: 38–9). In Smith's case the frequent signposts would have made such a prospectus superfluous, and readers of the lectures are more likely to complain of being led by the hand than of bafflement. What all this amounts to is that the opening theme phrase 'Perspicuity of stile' must have been led up to clearly.

The other habit of Smith's gives a clue to how this may have been done. He often shows his impatience with intricate sub-divisions and classifications of his subject, such as had long made rhetoric a notoriously scholastic game. La Bruyère speaks of 'un beau sermon' made according to all the rules of the rhetoricians, with the *cognoscenti* in the preacher's audience following with admiration 'toutes énumérations où il se promène'. But though Smith thinks it all very silly and refers anyone so inclined to read about it in Quintilian, his teacherly conscience compels him to ensure that his students have heard of the old terms. Lecture 1 no doubt defined the scope of this course by saying what it was not going to include. At least since the anonymous *Rhetorica ad Herennium* early in the first century BC, the orator's art had been divided into invention, arrangement, expression, memory and delivery; Quintilian's words (*Institutio Oratoria* III. iii. 1, and *passim*) are *inventio, dispositio, elocutio, memoria,* and *pronuntiatio* or *actio*. Smith in effect sees only the second and third as important, the third (style) occupying Lectures 2–11, the second underlying virtually all that Lectures 12–30 discuss.

It is to be hoped that for the sake of clarity one other traditional division was at least mentioned. As early as *Lectures on Rhetoric and Belles Lettres* i. 12, 'the didactick stile' is compared with that of historians and orators, and the phrase and the comparison occur repeatedly throughout the lectures as if their meaning was already known. The central place occupied in Smith's whole conception of discourse by 'the didactick stile' becomes clear in the Lecture (24) devoted to it, where it emerges as not only a mode of expression but as a procedure of thought: the scientific (LRBL ii. 132–5), that concerned with the exposition of a system, the clarification of a multitude of phenomena by one known or proved principle. Perhaps this was too early in the course; but the analogy with music set out in Imitative Arts II. 29 (see below, section V) by which many notes are related both to a leading or key-note and to a succession of notes or 'song', and the observation that this is like 'what order and method are to discourse', would have proved helpful to the many who, then as later, found it harder to apprehend pattern in language than in sound or colour. Smith

makes things harder by equating (at LRBL i. 152) the ancient
(indeed Aristotelian) division of speeches into Demonstrative,
Deliberative, Judicial, with his own philosophical division into
narrative, didactic, rhetorical (LRBL i. 149). This, it must be
admitted, involves some straining. 'It is rather reverence for
antiquity than any great regard for the Beauty or usefulness of the
thing itself which makes me mention the Antient divisions of
Rhetorick' (LRBL i. 152); but in this case he could have been less
scrupulous, since Quintilian (III. iv) asks 'why three?' rather than
a score of others. He is echoing Cicero; and Jean-François
Marmontel, author of the literary articles in the *Encyclopédie*, vols.
3–7 and Supplement (collected in *Eléments de Littérature*, 1787) pours
scorn on the terms themselves: *Deliberative* speech, where the orator
exerts all his energy to proving to the meeting that there is nothing
at all to deliberate; *Demonstrative*, which demonstrates nothing but
flattery or hatred (and, he should have added, the orator's virtuosity
– not showing, but showing off); *Judicial*, aiming at demonstrating,
and leaving it all to the judges' deliberation. In any case Smith in
the end does not scrap the ancient division but simply adds the
Didactic to it (Lectures 22–30).

III

By chance our surviving lecture notes begin at what Smith thought
was of first importance: style and language. 'Nobis prima sit virtus
perspicuitas' said Quintilian (VIII. ii. 22, echoing Aristotle's
Rhetoric III. ii. 1), and defined the main ingredient in perspicuity
as *proprietas*, each thing called by its *own*, its properly belonging
name. The root meaning of 'perspicuity' is the quality of being seen
through, and the subject of Smith's lectures may be said to be what
it is that language allows to show through it, and how. For Smith
there is much more to this transparency than the handing-over of
facts or feelings, and the first paragraph introduces some of this.
Words are no mere convenience; they are natives of a community,
as citizens are – and (as LRBL i. 5–6 shows) of a particular part
of the community. The Abbé du Bos devoted I. xxxvii of *Réflexions
critiques sur la poésie et sur la peinture* (1719) to showing the kind of
force the words of our own language have on our minds. When an
English-reading Frenchman meets the word 'God', it is to the word
Dieu and all its associations that his emotions respond.

A more immediate motive for this paragraph can best be

indicated by a well-known story about the poet of *The Seasons*. After completing his Arts course at Edinburgh, James Thomson's first exercise in the Faculty of Divinity was the preparation of a sermon based upon a section of Psalm cxix. When he read it to his class on 27 October 1724 it was severely criticised by his professor, William Hamilton, for its grandiloquence of style, as quite unsuitable for any congregation. Thomson, discouraged, gave up his studies, went off to London, and spent his life writing poems whose highly Latinate diction has often been remarked on, as was that of his fellow-countrymen in his own century. The Scoticisms against which Scottish writers were put on their guard, as by Hume and Beattie, were partly of this kind, and have been attributed to the Latin base of Scots law as well as of Scottish education. Hutcheson was the first professor at Glasgow to lecture in English, and this, quite apart from his teaching, was seen as a help to the students in unlearning their linguistic tendencies. A. F. Tytler (*Kames* (1807) i. 163) emphasises the influence of another Scottish professor in the same direction, that of the Edinburgh mathematician Colin Maclaurin, his 'pure, correct and simple style inducing a taste for chasteness of expression . . . a disrelish of affected ornaments'. Scots youths were encouraged towards 'an ease and elegance of composition as a more engaging vehicle for subjects of taste, in the room of the dry scholastic style in which they had hitherto been treated'. They were 'attracted to the more pleasing topics of criticism and the belles lettres. The cultivation of style became an object of study', replacing the ancient school dialectics. This, if only Tytler had provided evidence and illustration, would parallel the linguistic programme of the Royal Society as outlined by Sprat in its *History* in 1667: 'this trick of *Metaphors*', 'those specious *Tropes* and *Figures*', to be replaced by positive expressions 'bringing all things as near the Mathematical plainness as they can'.

A much wider context for Smith's lectures is thus created, though we must not forget the immediate one suggested by *Lectures on Rhetoric and Belles Lettres* i. 103: 'We in this country are most of us very sensible that the perfection of language is very different from that we commonly speak in.' Periodically throughout the history of style there occur combats between the respective upholders of the plain and the elaborate: Plato versus the sophist Gorgias; Calvus charging Cicero with 'Asianic' writing as opposed to Attic purity. Smith's teaching comes at such a moment. While

Smith was a student, John Constable's *Reflections upon Accuracy of Style* enjoyed a vogue. Not published till 1734 (reprinted 1738), this attack on the highly figurative language of Jeremy Collier's *Essays* (1697) had been written in 1701; and in the meantime Collier's 'huddle of metaphors' and conceits had been sharply criticised in John Oldmixon's adaptation of the influential *La manière de bien penser dans les ouvrages d'esprit* (1687) by Dominique Bouhours – *The Arts of Logick and Rhetorick* (1728). Behind all of them lies another combat: the Chevalier de Méré's strictures on the verbal extravagances of Voiture in *De la justesse* (1671), which gave Constable his title. These oppositions are of many kinds, and all differ from the one Smith sets up between the lucidity of Swift and the 'pompousness' of Shaftesbury – the shaping motive of much of Lectures 7–11. This is perhaps the earliest appreciation of Swift as writer; political and quasi-moral objections prevented his critical recognition till late in the century. Smith's admiration rests on something central in his *Lectures on Rhetoric*: 'All his works show a complete knowledge of his Subject . . . One who has such a complete knowledge of what he treats will naturally arrange it in the most proper order' (LRBL i. 105–6). Shaftesbury is a dilettante and does not know enough. Above all he has not kept up with modern scientific advances; he makes up for superficiality and ignorance by ornament (LRBL i. 140–1, 144). That his letters 'have no marks of the circumstances the writer was in at the time he wrote. Nor any reflections peculiarly suited to the times and circumstances' is the most telling fault. The writing does not *belong* anywhere or to anyone.

It is his criticism of the reverence paid to the figures of speech (whether departures from normal use of word, *figurae verborum*; or unusual modes of presentation, *figurae sententiarum* – Cicero, *Orator* xxxix–xl; Quintilian IX. i–iii; *Rhetorica ad Herennium* Book IV) that leads Smith to his decisive formulations of beauty of language. 'When the sentiment of the speaker is expressed in a neat, clear, plain and clever manner, and the passion or affection he is possessed of and intends, *by sympathy*, to communicate to his hearer, is plainly and cleverly hit off, then and then only the expression has all the force and beauty that language can give it.' Figures of speech may or may not do the job (See LRBL i. 56, 73, 79). 'The expression ought to be suited to the mind of the author, for this is chiefly governed by the circumstances he is placed in.' Language

is organically related not merely to thought in the abstract; it bears
'the same stamp' as the speaker's nature. Ben Jonson, writing
about 1622 (*Timber or Discoveries*), observed: 'Language most
shewes a man: speake, that I may see thee. It springs out of the
most retired and inmost parts of us, and is the Image of the Parent
of it, the mind. No glasse renders a mans forme of likenesse so true
as his speech.'

The discussion of this relationship is introduced by a nice piece
of Smithian economy. The character-sketches of the plain and the
simple man not only illustrate two styles and lead on to Swift and
Temple (LRBL i. 85–95); they offer the student models of *ethologia*,
the form prescribed (according to Quintilian I. ix. 3) to pupils in
rhetoric as an exercise, and they prepare for the instruction in
character-drawing in Lecture 15 and the discussion of the Character as a genre – invented by Theophrastus, edited by Isaac
Casaubon in 1592, introduced in England by Joseph Hall in 1608,
and practised by La Bruyère, who is Smith's favourite because his
collection is a microcosm of society and of mankind. When Hugh
Blair, as he tells us, was lent the manuscript of Smith's lectures (he
no doubt remembered hearing this passage) when preparing his
own, it was from these *ethologiae* that he drew hints:

> On this head, of the General Characters of Style, particularly,
> the Plain and the Simple, and the characters of those English
> authors who are classed under them, in this, and the following
> Lecture, several ideas have been taken from a manuscript
> treatise on rhetoric, part of which was shown to me, many
> years ago, by the learned and ingenious author, Dr Adam
> Smith; and which, it is hoped, will be given by him to the
> Public. (Blair, *Lectures on Rhetoric and Belles Lettres*, 1983, i. 381).

The Theophrastan form influenced the historians; see the collection
entitled *Characters of the Seventeenth Century*, edited by D. Nichol
Smith (1920). It is significant that the first critic to publish a series
of studies of Shakespeare's characters, William Richardson, the
Glasgow Professor of Humanity from 1773, was a student of Adam
Smith's; his *A Philosophical Analysis and Illustration of Some of Shakespeare's
Remarkable Characters* appeared in 1774, and two more volumes
followed in 1784 and 1788.

IV

Boswell, another student who heard the Rhetoric lectures (in

1759), was struck by Smith's emphasis on the personal aspects of writers, and he twice recalled the remark about Milton's shoes (absent from the report; it should have come at LRBL ii. 107): 'I remember Dr. Adam Smith, in his rhetorical lectures at Glasgow, told us he was glad to know that Milton wore latchets in his shoes, instead of buckles' (*Journal of a Tour to the Hebrides* 9). 'I have a pleasure in hearing every story, tho' never so little of so distinguished a Man. I remember Smith took notice of this pleasure in his lectures upon Rhetoric, and said that he felt it when he read that Milton never wore buckles but strings in his shoes' (*Boswell Papers* i. 107). Such was the training of the future author of the greatest of all biographies of a man of letters. In no. I of the *Spectator* (1 March 1711) Addison 'observed, that a Reader seldom peruses a Book with Pleasure till he knows whether the Writer of it be a black or a fair Man, of a mild or cholerick Disposition, Married or a Batchelor, with other Particulars of a like nature, that conduce very much to the right Understanding of an Author'.

Beauty of style, then, is *propriety* in the exact sense of the word: language which embodies and exhibits to the reader that distinctive turn and quality of spirit in the author 'qui lui est *propre*', as Marivaux insisted in the *Spectateur français*, 8e feuille (8 September 1722). Our pleasure is, as Hutcheson noted in his *Inquiry into the Original of our Ideas of Beauty and Virtue* (1725: I. sec. IV. vii), in recognising a perfect correspondence or aptness in a curious mechanism for the execution of a design. It is characteristic of Smith that his aesthetics should thus centre on correspondence, relation, affinity. What he finds wrong with Shaftesbury's style is that he arbitrarily made it up: it has nothing to do with his own character (LRBL i. 137–8). When the principle is extended from persons to societies – 'all languages . . . are equally ductile and equally accommodated to all different tempers' – very wide and illuminating prospects open up. Good examples are Trajan's Rome as formative background for Tacitus (Lecture 20), the comparison of Athens and Rome as contexts for Demosthenes and Cicero (Lecture 26), and the association of the rise of prose with the growth of commerce and wealth (LRBL ii. 144 ff.). Indeed, the accounts of historical writing and of the three types of oratory are made the occasions for elaborate excursus on different kinds of social and political organisation, ancient and modern.

'*By sympathy*' (LRBL i. v. 56): this phrase in the formulation of the highest beauty language can attain is one of the very few which Scribe A underlines, and pains had clearly been taken by Smith to bring out the parallel between his ethical and rhetorical principles. Just as we act under the eye of an impartial spectator within ourselves, the creation of an imaginative self-projection into an outsider whose standards and responses we reconstruct by sympathy or ability to feel as he does, so our language is enabled to communicate our thoughts and 'affections' (i.e. inclinations) by our ability to predict its effect on our hearer. This is what is meant by seeing the *Lectures on Rhetoric* and *The Theory of Moral Sentiments* as two halves of one system, and not merely at occasional points of contact. The connection of 'sympathy' as a rhetorical instrument with the vision of speech and personality as an organic unity need not be laboured. Again, it should be obvious how often Smith's concern is with the sharing of sentiments and attitudes rather than mere ideas or facts. The arts of persuasion are close to his heart for this reason. The opening of Lecture 11 is a key passage. The conveying to a hearer of 'the sentiment, passion or affection with which [his thought] affects him' – 'the perfection of stile' – is regulated by a 'Rule, which is equally applicable to conversation and behaviour as writing'; 'all the Rules of Criticism and morality when traced to their foundation, turn out to be some Principles of Common Sence which every one assents to'. One of the most frequent terms of critical praise in the *Lectures on Rhetoric* is 'interesting', bearing its original and normal eighteenth-century sense of *involving, engaging*, as at LRBL ii. 27 where, thanks to Livy's skill, 'we enter into all the concerns of the parties' and are as affected as if we had been there. The reason why history is enjoyed is that events which befall mankind 'interest us greatly by the Sympatheticall affections they raise in us' (LRBL ii. 16). The good historian shows the effects wrought on those who were actors or spectators of the events (LRBL ii.5; cf. ii. 62–3). Knowledge of the plot of a tragedy is an advantage since it leaves us 'free to attend to the Sentiments' (LRBL ii. 30). A variation on this is acutely described in dealing with the picture of Agamemnon's sacrifice of Iphigenia, by Timanthes. Indeed, the entire treatment of the art of description in Lectures 12–16 is profoundly instructive of Smith's main interests. Even minutiae such as the arrangement of words in a sentence (LRBL i. v. 42–v. 52b) repay an attention beyond the merely grammatical.

The species of writing are so intimately bound up with each other that Smith finds it difficult in Lectures 12–30 to demarcate them sharply. By instinct, as already noted, he is a historian in the sense that he sees narrative as the very type of human thought-procedure; but his interest in it is also that suggested by Hume's description of history's records as 'so many collections of experiments by which the moral philosopher fixes the principles of his science'. The first paper read to the Literary Society in the University, on 6 February 1752, was 'An essay on historical composition' by James Moor, the Professor of Greek (*Essays*, 1759). Moor's elaboration of the kinship of history and poetry, the unified pattern which both exhibit in events, throws interesting light on the position occupied by Lecture 21 in Smith's progression. Bolingbroke compared history and drama; and Voltaire wrote to the Marquis d'Argenson on 26 January 1740 (*Correspondence*, ed. T. Besterman, xxxv. 373): 'Il faut, dans une histoire, comme dans une pièce de théâtre, exposition, noeud, et dénouement.' There may be an echo of the ancient assimilation of history and poetry in 'the Poeticall method' of keeping up the connection between events, other than the causal (LRBL ii. 36); and history, like poetry, is said to 'amuse' (LRBL ii. 62), and to have originated with the poets. Leonard Welsted expounded this view fully in his *Dissertation Concerning the Perfection of the English Language* (1724). For Quintilian (X. i. 31) a history *is* a poem: 'Est enim proxima poetis et quodammodo carmen solutum.' There was indeed much collocation by the ancient rhetoricians of all these genres – history, poetry, rhetoric, philosophical exposition – as in Cicero's *Orator* (XX. 66–7). The Muses are said to have spoken in Xenophon's voice (*Orator* XIX. 62). They are all combined by Fénelon in the educational project he outlined to the French Academy, first in 1716. That panegyrical eloquence 'tient un peu de la poésie', as Voltaire maintained in the *Encyclopédie* article on Eloquence, is also Smith's view (LRBL ii. 111–2).

The Lecture on poetry (21), delivered extemporaneously, is both instructive and disappointing. The post-Coleridge student looks for more analysis of short poems; these are of little interest, naturally, to the philosopher. More important, why does not Smith, of all critics, tackle the problem of the pleasure afforded us by tragedy? This is specially strange since Hume, who had offered a highly ingenious answer in his essay on tragedy in 1757, expressed dissatisfaction with the treatment of sympathy in this context in *The Theory of Moral Sentiments* I. iii. i. 9 (Corr. Letter 36, 28 July 1759), and the second edition of *The Theory of Moral Sentiments* contained a footnote on the question. The insistence in the Lecture (LRBL ii. 82) on the tragic writer's heightening of the painful nature of his story in order to lead to a satisfying 'catastrophe' is an oblique solution of the problem and one frequently given: the difference between suffering on the stage and in real life resides in the artifice of the former. 'The delight of tragedy proceeds from our consciousness of fiction,' said Johnson in the Preface to Shakespeare (1765) – though Burke in 1757 took the opposite view, because 'we enter into the concerns of others'. Kames in *The Elements of Criticism* (1762: I. ii. i. sec. 7) discusses 'the emotions caused by Fiction'. The function of Lecture 21 is to prepare for the arts of persuasion used by the orator, playing down or exaggerating as the need demands, by describing the similar arts of the good storyteller. Tragedy and Comedy both *arrange* events so as to culminate in true conclusiveness. Note that Smith's imagination is as tuned to good *cadence* as is his ear.

That is why he delights in rhyme. Boswell reports that when Johnson was extolling rhyme over blank verse: 'I mentioned to him that Dr. Adam Smith, in his lectures upon composition, when I studied under him in the College of Glasgow, had maintained the same opinion strenuously, and I repeated some of his arguments.' Johnson had no love for Smith, but – 'had I known that he loved rhyme as much as you tell me he does, I should have HUGGED him' (Boswell, *Life of Johnson*, ed. Hill-Powell (1934–50), i. 427–8). Dugald Stewart associates this bias with Smith's ascription of our pleasure in the Imitative Arts (e.g. Stewart I, 16, III. 2) to admiration of *difficulté surmontée* (Stewart III. 14–15). The phrase is by Antoine Houdar de La Motte in his controversy with Voltaire over *Oedipe* (1730). La Motte opposed both the Unities and Rhyme in drama: 'toutes ces puérilités n'ont d'autre mérite que celui de la difficulté surmontée'. Both Voltaire and Smith counter this argument by pointing to the observed triumph over observed obstacles, as a source of our surprised delight in all the arts, both plastic and literary. Stewart (III. 15) wonders whether Smith's 'love of system, added to his partiality for the French drama', may have led him to generalise too much in this. Rhyme is not explicitly mentioned in the *Lectures on Rhetoric and Belles Lettres* manuscript at ii. 74 ff., but it is implicit in *couplet* and in the reference to Pope (cf. TMS V. i. 7).

'The principles of dramatic composition had more particularly attracted his attention' (Stewart III. 15); and though the dogmas about unity of Time and Place had often been attacked since Corneille's *Discours* in 1660 – in Farquhar's *Discourse upon Comedy* (1702) and Kames's *Elements of Criticism* (1762: chap. xxiii) – it is pleasant to find Smith transferring the question to 'Unity of Interest' (LRBL ii. 81). This time he is on La Motte's side. In the first of the *Discours sur la Tragédie* (1730) this is made the supreme law of dramatic art: but, as Smith remarks, the phrase is suscepti-ble of many interpretations, and it is a little surprising to find him not following La Motte's thesis that concentration of the audience's *sympathy* on a group of characters – always present, always acting, animating and vivifying the action of the piece – is what constitutes 'unité d'intérêt', as they are 'tous dignes que j'entre dans leurs passions'. 'That every part of the Story should tend to some one end, whatever that be' is of course also a typically Smithian formulation.

Beside the remark on Comedy (LRBL ii. 82) we must place the full account of the comic at i. 107 – v. 116. Smith's interest in the laughter-provoking (we must remember that that is simply what the eighteenth-century words ridicule and ridiculous mean) was no doubt kindled early by Hutcheson, whose criticism of Hobbes' view – 'the passion of laughter is nothing but sudden glory arising from some sudden conception of some eminency in ourselves' (*Leviathan* vi) – first appeared in the *Dublin Journal* 10–12 (June 1725), collected as *Reflections on Laughter* (1750). Smith's approach is proper to someone preoccupied with comparison: unexpected incongruities arising from the aggrandisement of the little (as in mock-heroic) or diminution of the grand. In *Lectures on Rhetoric and Belles Lettres* i. 112 he seems to allude to Leibnitz: 'All raillery includes a little contempt, and it is not just to try to make contemptible what does not deserve it' (Remarks on Shaftesbury's *Characteristicks*, 1711; printed in Masson's *Histoire critique de la République des Lettres*, 1715). He does not accept therefore Shaftes-bury's notion of laughter as a 'test of truth'. For Smith on wit and humour, compare the review of Johnson's *Dictionary* (EPS 240–1). Johnson would not have 'hugged' Smith for his words on tragi-comedy (LRBL ii. 83–4). This 'mixed' kind, described in *Spectator*

40 as monstrous, was several times vigorously defended by Johnson for its truth to life. See, for example, *Rambler* 156 (14 September 1751), as well as the *Preface* to Shakespeare in 1765.

To one tradition of rhetorical instruction Smith is faithful, in the readiness with which he quotes poetic examples side by side with prose. In *Lectures on Rhetoric and Belles Lettres* i. 9 he refers to Samuel Clarke's preface to his edition of the *Iliad* (1729) in praise of Homer's perspicuity – such, says Clarke, that no prose writer has ever equalled him in this, his 'perpetua et singularis virtus'. Clarke also makes an interesting distinction between the poet's *ars* and his *oratio*; so, in our day, Ezra Pound has insisted that poetry must have the qualities of good prose.

Like that later polymath, Coleridge, Adam Smith nursed till his last days the hope of producing a *magnum opus* of immense scope. 'I have likewise two other great works upon the anvil; the one is a sort of Philosophical History of all the different branches of Literature, of Philosophy, Poetry and Eloquence' (the other being his Jurisprudence); 'The materials of both are in a great measure collected, and some Part of both is put into tolerable good order.' So he wrote to the Duc de La Rochefoucauld on 1 November 1785 (Corr. Letter 248). This was no doubt why in 1755, in a paper read to Cochrane's Political Economy Club, he gave 'a pretty long enumeration . . . of certain leading principles, both political and literary, to which he was anxious to establish his exclusive right; in order to prevent the possibility of some rival claims' (Stewart IV. 25). Unfortunately Stewart does not tell us which 'literary' principles were listed. Smith describes the opinions as having formed the subjects of his lectures since he first taught Mr Craigie's class 'down to this day, without any considerable variation'.

One envies the eighteenth century the freedom and width of vision made possible to them by their not circumscribing the word 'literature' and narrowing the scope of its study as we have since done. Our two scribes enable us to glimpse that first work which would have become the foundation of the tantalizing 'Philosophical History' of all literature.

V

On 9 July 1764 Boswell wrote from Berlin to Isabella de Zuylen (Zélide): 'Mr. Smith whose moral sentiments you admire so much, wrote to me sometime ago, "your great fault is acting upon system", what a curious reproof to a young man from a grave philosopher.' The letter opens: 'You know I am a man of form, a man who says to himself, Thus will I act, and acts accordingly' (*Letters*, ed. C. B. Tinker, 1924, 46). In the absence of Adam Smith's letter (strange, considering what mountains of paper Boswell preserved), we cannot tell with what irony he wrote to his former student: but the incident draws attention to the two uses in the eighteenth century of the word and the concept 'system'. While Smith was giving these Lectures, two of the most powerful critiques of the idea appeared. In the wittiest and subtlest of all such attacks, *Tristram Shandy* (1759–67), Sterne presents a hapless philosopher-father's attempts to make his son's upbringing conform to theory, the Shandean system: the form of the novel itself criticises the notion of rigid form. And in 1759 Voltaire produced, in *Candide*, a demolition of the optimistic scheme of the universe, a series of disastrous frustrations of the illusion that all is for the best in the best of all possible worlds. Marivaux is fond of pillorying 'les faiseurs de systèmes' (for example, in *Lettres au Mercure*, May 1718), who are what 'le vulgaire' call 'philosophers'; and Shaftesbury had already in 1711 (*Characteristics*: Misc. III. ii) defined a formal philosopher as a 'system-writer'. 'System-monger' comes in about the same time. On 27 September 1748 we find Lord Chesterfield advising his son to 'read and hear, for your amusement, ingenious systems, nice questions, subtilely agitated with all the refinements that warm imaginations suggest', and less sardonically he complains: 'The preposterous notions of a systematical man who does not know the word tire the patience of a man who does.' Compare also Stewart's (V. 15) 'too systematical' of Smith; and the 'man of system' apt 'to be very wise in his own conceit', in *The Theory of Moral Sentiments* VI. ii. 2. 17.

'System' in the good sense is exemplified by Johnson's defence of *The Wealth of Nations* against Sir John Pringle's charge that Smith was not equipped to write such a work since he had never taken part in trade: 'there is nothing which requires more to be illustrated by philosophy than trade does' (Boswell, *Life of Johnson*, ed. Hill-Powell, ii. 430). Another example, used by James Wodrow in a letter to the Earl of Buchan (Glasgow Univ. Lib., Murray MS 506, 169) is the comparison of Smith's accounting for the principal phenomena in the moral world from the one general principle of sympathy, with 'that of gravity in the natural world'. Still another is set out by Smith in a letter (Corr. Letter 30, dated 4 April 1759) to Lord Shelburne on the course of study his son Lord Fitzmaurice should pursue in his future years at Glasgow, after completing his philosophical studies. He should, says Smith, attend the lectures of the Professor of Civil Law, as the best preparation for the study of English law even though civil law has no authority in the English Courts:

> The civil law is digested into a more regular system than the English Law has yet been, and tho' the Principles of the former are in many respects different from those of the latter, yet there are many principles common to both, and one who has studied the civil law at least knows what a system of law is, what parts it consist of, and how these ought to be arranged: so that when he afterwards comes to study the law of any other country which is not so well digested, he carries at least the Idea of a System in his head and knows to what part of it he ought to refer everything that he reads.

Compare this with the motive underlying the system of meanings laid out in the review of Johnson's *Dictionary* (EPS 232–41).

That something more than mere tidiness and intellectual coherence is involved for Smith is illustrated by a passage in 'Of the Nature of that Imitation which takes place in what are called the Imitative Arts' (II. 30, cf. section 2, above):

> A well-composed concerto of instrumental Music, by the number and variety of the instruments, by the variety of the parts which are performed by them, and the perfect concord or correspondence of all these different parts; by the exact harmony or coincidence of all the different sounds which are heard at the same time, and by that happy variety of measure which regulates the succession of those which are heard at different times, presents an object so agreeable, so great, so various, and so interesting, that alone, and without suggesting any other object, either by imitation or otherwise, it can occupy, and as it were fill up, completely the whole capacity of the mind, so as to leave no part of its attention vacant for thinking of any thing else. In the contemplation of that immense variety of agreeable and melodious sounds, arranged and digested, both in their coincidence and in their succession, into so complete and regular a system, the mind in reality enjoys not only a very great sensual, but a very high intellectual,

pleasure, not unlike that which it derives from the contemplation of a great system in any other science.

In other words, to watch the explanation of a great diversity and multiplicity of phenomena from a single general principle is to be confronted with beauty: 'the beauty of a systematical arrangement of different observations connected by a few common principles' (WN V. i. f. 25; cf. EPS, 13ff.). We remember that Smith's dominant interests while a student at Glasgow under Professor Robert Simson (Stewart I. 7) were mathematics and natural philosophy: this is where he learned 'the idea of a system' as set out in 'The History of Astronomy' IV. 19.

The issue is most clearly stated in the Lecture (24) on scientific and philosophical exposition, the 'didacticall' method (LRBL ii. 132–4). One may either explain phenomena piecemeal, using a new principle for each as it is encountered, as in the 'System of Husbandry' presented in Virgil's *Georgics* following Aristotle's procedure; 'or in the manner of Sir Isaac Newton we may lay down certain principles known or proved in the beginning, from whence we account for the several Phenomena, connecting all together by the same chain'. This *enchaînement* (the favourite term among French thinkers of the time) is in every branch of study – ethics, physics, criticism – 'vastly more ingenious and for that reason more engaging than the other. It gives us a pleasure to see the phaenomena which we reckoned the most unaccountable all deduced from some principle (commonly a well-known one) and all united in one chain, far superior to what we feel from the unconnected method' (cf. TMS II. ii. 2. 14). The task Smith set himself in the *Lectures on Rhetoric* was to substitute a 'Newtonian' (or Cartesian, cf. LRBL ii. 134), a philosophical and 'engaging' explanation of beauty in writing, for the old rigmarole about figures of speech and of thought, 'topics' of argument, subdivisions of discourse, characters of style and the rest. In this sense his Lectures constitute an anti-rhetoric; and though they could not by themselves rescue the word 'rhetoric', or for that matter the phrases *belles lettres* and *polite literature*, from the bad press from which they suffered, they exerted a profound and revolutionary influence (which has still not been properly investigated) on Hugh Blair, Kames, William Richardson, George Campbell, and those whom they in turn taught.

'There is no art whatever that hath so close a connection with all the faculties and powers of the mind as eloquence, or the art of speaking.' So George Campbell introduces *The Philosophy of Rhetoric* in 1776. To come closer to describing Smith's central informing principle, the formulations of two French writers whose work he knew well may help. 'Le style est l'homme même.' This famous and generally misunderstood remark was made by the naturalist Buffon on his admission to the French Academy in 1753, in what came to be called his *Discours sur le style*. He is contrasting the inert facts of unanimated knowledge with what language does to them. 'Ces choses sont hors de l'homme' – they are non-human. But utter them, and *how* you utter them, is 'very man', 'man himself'. From a different angle Marivaux, in *Le Spectateur français* of 8 September 1722 (huitième feuille), attacks the notion that you must write in the manner of this or that ancient or modern author, and aims 'prouver qu'écrire naturellement, qu'être naturel n'est pas écrire dans le goût de tel Ancien ni de tel Moderne, n'est pas se mouler sur personne quant à la forme de ses idées, mais au contraire, se ressembler fidèlement à soi-même . . . rester dans la singularité d'esprit qui nous est échue . . .'. Be like yourself: it was a lesson, Smith believed, the much-admired Shaftesbury had never learned.

Note

This article is drawn from J. C. Bryce's introduction to *Lectures on Rhetoric and Belles Lettres* (Oxford, 1983), sections 2, 4 and 5. To suit the purposes of the present volume, the material in sections 2 and 4 has been transposed. The passages are reprinted with the kind permission of Oxford University Press.

References and authorities

Adam Smith's life and thought
John Rae, *Life of Adam Smith* (London, 1895). Reprinted with 'Guide to Rae's *Life of Adam Smith*' by J. Viner (New York, 1965).
William R. Scott, *Adam Smith as Student and Professor* (Glasgow, 1937; reprinted 1965).
R. H. Campbell and A. S. Skinner, *Adam Smith* (London, 1982).
A. S. Skinner, *A System of Social Science: Papers Relating to Adam Smith* (Oxford, 1979).
T. D. Campbell, *Adam Smith's Science of Morals* (London, 1971).
The rhetoric
W. S. Howell, *Eighteenth-Century British Logic and Rhetoric* (Princeton, 1971). The Section on Smith, first published in 1969, was reprinted in *Essays on Adam Smith*, ed. Andrew S. Skinner and Thomas Wilson (Oxford, 1975).
V. M. Bevilacqua, 'Adam Smith's *Lectures on Rhetoric and Belles Lettres*', *Studies in Scottish Literature*, 3 (1965), 41–60. See also *Modern Language Review*, 63 (1968).

J. M. Lothian, ed., *Adam Smith: Lectures on Rhetoric and Belles Lettres* (London and Edinburgh. 1963).

R. Salvucci, 'La retorica come della communicazione' (on A. S.)., *Sociologia della communicazione*, I, 1982. See also R. Salvucci, *Sviluppi della problematica del linguaggio nel XVIII secolo: Condillac, Rousseau, Smith* (1982).

A. S. Skinner, 'Adam Smith: Rhetoric and the Communication of Ideas' in *Methodological Controversy in Economics: Historical Essays*, A. W. Coats, ed. (London, 1983).

Languages

Articles on 'Considerations' by C. J. Berry and S. K. Land in *Journal of the History of Ideas*, respectively 35 (1974), 130–8 and 38 (1977), 677–90.

2

Adam Smith: grammatical economist

FRANS PLANK

I

The Theory of Moral Sentiments says relatively little about language. It seemed to Adam Smith that the rules of justice, being precise, accurate, and indispensable, could usefully be compared to the rules of grammar, while the rules of the other virtues (such as chastity or veracity), on account of their looseness, vagueness, and indeterminacy, were more like 'the rules which critics lay down for the attainment of what is sublime and elegant in composition' (TMS III. vi. 11, VII. iv. 1). And, speaking of veracity, in a passage added in the sixth edition, Smith speculated that it was perhaps 'the desire of being believed, the desire of persuading, of leading and directing other people' upon which is founded the faculty of speech, speech being 'the great instrument of ambition' (TMS VII. iv. 25). Tangential though such comments may seem to the concerns of Adam Smith, the moral philosopher, the very aspects of language touched on so lightly in his first *chef-d'oeuvre* had once occupied much of his time. From 1748 to 1751 he had first distinguished himself among the Edinburgh *literati* as a public lecturer on that loose, vague, and indeterminate subject, rhetoric and belles-lettres. In 1751 his inaugural address as Professor of Logic and Rhetoric at the University of Glasgow was devoted to the origin of ideas, and throughout his thirteen years at Glasgow University, soon transferred to the Chair of Moral Philosophy, he continued to lecture on rhetoric and belles-lettres. His first publication, appearing in the *Edinburgh Review* of 1755, took issue with Dr Samuel Johnson on the insufficiently grammatical arrangement of the diverse meanings and uses of the items in his otherwise useful

Dictionary.[1] While Adam Smith did not care to have his rhetoric course preserved for posterity (on the contrary, he instructed his literary executors to burn the manuscript, but thanks to the notes students had taken in the session of 1762–3, which resurfaced in 1961, we know approximately what it was like), he set a high value on one part of it, namely the third lecture, treating 'Of the origin and progress of language'. He worked up this lecture into an article entitled 'Considerations concerning the first formation of Languages, and the different genius of original and compounded Languages' and published in *The Philological Miscellany* of 1761, a collection of translations mostly from the *Mémoires* of the Académie des Inscriptions et Belles Lettres of Paris, of which Smith was once supposed, perhaps wrongly, to have been the editor (cf. Bryce's Introduction to the Glasgow Edition, p. 26). Presumably because this *Miscellany* was not very accessible, Smith had this cherished essay of his reprinted as an appendix of the third (1767) and subsequent editions of *The Theory of Moral Sentiments*. He might with more justification have foisted this piece on the readers of his *Inquiry into the Nature and Causes of the Wealth of Nations*, who would perhaps more easily have recognised certain common conceptual themes. But this would have entailed a delay of about a decade as this second magnum opus, although likewise deriving from lectures Smith had given at Glasgow and Edinburgh, was rather long in the making – and the popularity of the topic of linguistic evolution was rising.

Notwithstanding the not very felicitous choice of a host, the parasitic existence of Smith's *Dissertation on the Origin of Languages*, as it was called on the title page of *The Theory of Moral Sentiments*, was remarkably successful. There were few contemporary writers on language, especially in Scotland, who would not acknowledge their indebtedness to Smith's dissertation (or his lectures on which it was based), irrespective of sometimes wide disagreements. Its impact abroad is reflected by the appearance of at least four different French translations, of which three were published independently of *The Theory of Moral Sentiments* (cf. Noordegraaf 1977). When ideological opponents of Smith, such as the brothers Schlegel, the prime movers of Romanticism, aired views after the turn of the century on the development and classification of languages that bore some resemblance to Smith's, this was soon noticed (for example, by Manget 1809), and they were eventually taken to task for having failed to acknowledge their predecessor (for example, by Pott 1876 and, more recently, by Coseriu 1968; cf. Plank 1987a).[2]

My aim in this chapter is to appraise the significance of Smith's dissertation as a contribution to language typology. That the celebrated moral philosopher and political economist did pioneering work also in this rather more peripheral department of learning has not gone unnoticed, and has lately become the conventional wisdom of historians of linguistics, owing in particular to Eugenio Coseriu (1968) who, much like August Friedrich Pott (1876) a century earlier, saluted Adam Smith as the actual founder of typology, or at least as the anticipator of the typological scheme(s) which Friedrich and August Wilhelm Schlegel used to be credited with. It also transpired, however, that Adam Smith, the language typologist, had incurred intellectual debts too. And his chief creditors were easy to identify because Smith himself had acknowledged, not in his dissertation but in a letter to George Baird, that it was Gabriel Girard's *Les vrais principes de la langue française* (1747), meanwhile also widely recognised as an early typological classic, 'which first set me a thinking upon these subjects', and that the grammatical articles in Diderot and d'Alembert's *Encyclopédie* 'have given me a good deal of entertainment' (Rae 1895, p. 160). There is an unfortunate tendency among historians of linguistics to regard early typology as amounting to no more than a rough classification of languages into ones with much and ones with little or no inflexional morphology, with perhaps concomitant variations in the rigidity of word order. This preconception about what could, at the most, be apprehended about the systematic diversity of languages in the eighteenth century was responsible for a certain inattention to matters of detail; and in the case of Smith's considerations about grammatical structures, their origins and transformations, their real typological significance does lie in subtle details, as I hope to show in my reading. It had, at any rate, long been appreciated that languages could be grossly divided into inflecting and non-inflecting (or rudimentarily inflecting) ones, and it certainly was not Smith's intention merely to promulgate this sweeping generalisation, adopted even in such general works of the past century as Francis Bacon's *De dignitate et augmentis scientiarum* (1623) or John Locke's *Some Thoughts Concerning Education* (1693). His idea was to outline structural classes which would represent, and be explicable as, successive stages of linguistic, cognitive and social evolution.

From the original setting of the *Considerations Concerning the First Formation of Languages* one might infer that Smith's interest in language diversity and its *raisons d'être* must have been derivative of his primary concern with rhetoric and stylistics. In fact, however, it is only the short final section of the *Considerations* (paragraphs 42–5), evaluating ancient and modern languages, which is of such provenance. The most substantial first part (paragraphs 1–32) is an exercise in 'conjectural' or 'theoretical' history (as Dugald Stewart characterised this method of probing into the very distant past, already in vogue in contemporary France, in the wake especially of Locke and Montesquieu), developing a scenario of the early formation of languages with particular reference to parts of speech (or word classes) and inflexional morphology, that indispensable core of grammar where, as in justice, precision and accuracy reign. The second part (paragraphs 33–41) deals with actual history and highlights the role of the mixture of languages and peoples in changes of grammatical structure. These two historical issues, conjectural and actual, arguably were the subjects upon which Adam Smith was set thinking by the Abbé Gabriel Girard, with a little further prompting from Jean-Jacques Rousseau, whose discourse *Sur l'origine et les fondements de l'inégalité parmi les hommes* of 1755, instantly taken notice of by Smith (see his Letter to the *Edinburgh Review* of 1755), had made a memorable, though not entirely unequivocal case for 'le premier langage de l'homme' being 'le cri de la Nature'. Rousseau in turn had drawn inspiration on this matter from Etienne Bonnot de Condillac's *Essai sur l'origine des connoissances humaines* (1746) as well as from John Locke's *Essay Concerning Human Understanding* (1690), and at least the earlier of these two essays obviously was not news to Smith. Nicolas Beauzée's appearance in the *Encyclopédie* came too late (1765) to entertain and instruct Smith; César Chesneau du Marsais, his predecessor as chief linguistic contributor to the *Encyclopédie*, was less concerned with the Smithian theme of linguistic evolution than with key grammatical categories, but such knowledge could also be useful.[3]

Adam Smith was not an empirical comparatist of the calibre of his Edinburgh contemporary, James Burnett (Lord Monboddo), to mention only one of the philosophers who were beginning to see the natural history of man and his institutions, including language, as an 'experimental' rather than as a purely theoretical and conjectural enterprise. To be sure, Smith, too, had sought to acquaint himself with peoples living in the different states through which mankind was, in his view, bound to pass (hunting, pasturage, farming, commerce). In his *Theory of Moral Sentiments* and especially his *Lectures on Jurisprudence* he would refer, if often only *en passant*, to North American Indians (in particular the Iroquois and the West Indian Sugar Islanders), to Hottentots and negro inhabitants of the coast of Guinea and Africa in general, to the Chinese, Japanese, Koreans, Javanese and East Indians, to Caucasians and Armenians, to Scythians, Tartars, Turkomans and Arabs, to Jews and Muscovites, and to Greeks, Romans, Teutons and their descendants. As to languages, mention is made in the *Considerations* of Ancient and Modern Greek, Etruscan, Latin, Gothic, the older Germanic tongues of the Lombards, Franks, and Saxons, French, Italian, (Old) Armenian, Hebrew, the languages of some savage nations Smith had read of (presumably in Charlevoix's *Histoire et description générale de la Nouvelle France* (1744), Lafitau's *Mœurs des sauvages amériquains* (1724), and Kolb[en]'s *The Present State of the Cape of Good Hope* (1731) – acknowledged sources in his *Lectures on Jurisprudence*), and above all, English. Smith was certainly less knowledgeable about the grammars of most of these languages than he was about the modes of subsistence of their speakers. But for him this was not something to worry about unduly:[4] at least to begin with, he ostensibly did not care for any of these languages actually attested in history at all, occupying himself instead with 'original' languages and even 'primitive jargons', whose existence was in the realms of conjectural history.

Smith's interest is not so much in the very first origins of what might legitimately be called human speech – the question that had been taxing the ingenuity of Condillac and Rousseau – as in the principled elaboration of the primitive jargons by those already endowed with these languages of sorts.[5] Crucial for this process are, first of all, the mental operations which the language-formers are capable of performing, and which are essentially the same as those still performed, if more expertly, by present-day man: (a) comparison, leading to discrimination or generalisation in response to differences or similarities in nature, and (b) abstraction, enabling mental representations to arrive at 'metaphysical analyses' of monolithic realities of nature.[6] There are, secondly, momentous conditions on the formation, or (as one might put it) 'articulation', of language which derive from psychological propensities and physiological limitations of sign-users of all ages: inclining towards (c) diagrammatisation (called 'love of analogy' by Smith), they seek to mirror the syntagmatic and paradigmatic relationships between the *denotata*, as represented in the mind, in the form of the denotations; and, being subject to (d) limitations of memory, they are prevented from storing an infinite number of expressions in their attempts to cope with the infinity of potential *denotata*. Aesthetic propensities, too, exert an influence on the elaboration of language: possessed of 'a certain spirit of system' and 'a certain love of art and contrivance' (which, as was explained in *The Theory of Moral Sentiments* IV. i. 11, make man value the means more than the end, but all the same tend to promote the public welfare), language-formers are given to embellishing their sign systems with (e) 'similarities of sound', 'returns of the same syllables', i.e. rhyme.[7] These mental operations and cognitive and aesthetic conditions are intended to account for the way the pathetically modest categorial outfit of primitive jargons, little more than *cris de la Nature*, is expanding with increasing expressive demands, and in particular for the appearance of inflexional morphology prior to separate words with purely grammatical functions. A last general psychological assumption, intended to account for later, more revolutionary grammatical developments, is (f) that the untutored learning of a foreign language by adults is incomparably more difficult, hence more disruptive, than children's acquisition of their first language.

Language, or rather jargon, formation begins when particular events, existing in nature, are denoted by linguistic expressions. This primordial mode of denotation is holistic: complete events are denoted by atomic expressions without any internal structure (except a phonetic one). All particular events differing from one another, however minimally, call for distinct expression, and thus accumulates a lexicon of event denotations. These are called 'impersonal verbs' by Smith, but unlike their namesakes and descendants in later languages (such as Latin *pluit* 'it rains') they are applicable initially to particular events only, rather than to classes of similar events. By abstraction, events are then cognitively divided into their metaphysical elements, namely substances and attributes, and with linguistic expression following suit, these are denoted respectively by nouns substantive and personal verbs. In principle, the separation of substances from attributes, with nouns substantive thus 'ascertaining and determining the signification' of, as it were, unsaturated personal verbs, is a step that may be repeated. In his *Considerations* Smith only illustrates the externalisation of substances which are destined to be combined with personal verbs as their grammatical subjects; but, given initial complete event denotations such as 'the-hunter-kill-the-wolf-with-the-stone-in-the-forest', it is virtually inevitable that objects and more circumstantial specifications will also be separated from the increasingly less comprehensive verbal core by the metaphysical analysts. In Smith's letter to George Baird of 7 February 1763 it is in fact suggested that subjects are only the first substances to be divided from attributes, and that objects would come next, yielding double unsaturated, or bivalent or transitive, personal verbs.

As an exclusively lexical denotation system is thus being transformed into a grammatical, i.e. combinatorial one, the obvious gain is that fewer distinct basic expressions are needed: instead of having to coin and memorise a novel denotation for any new event even when it shares the substance(s) or the attribute with another event, the new smaller-sized basic building blocks, namely nouns substantive and personal verbs, can now be intercombined freely. Much labour of the memory is facilitated and abridged by the application of proper, i.e. grammatical, expressive machinery – to adapt a phrase from *The Wealth of Nations* (I. i. 8). A coincidental advantage of the advent of the combinatorial mode is that the similarities between events sharing one or the other of their elements are now reflected diagrammatically by the partial formal identities of their composite denotations.

Smith is strangely non-committal concerning the relative historical priority of substance and event expressions. His exposition begins with nouns substantive (resembling Girard's, who also had the verb trailing the nominal parts of speech), but by the logic of his theoretical assumptions it is clearly the impersonal verb which must have come first in evolution.[8] For Smith this issue is, at any rate, less important than the subsequent elaboration of the stock of denotations of particular events and particular substances, proceeding in parallel.

Once the original proper names of particular substances have been transformed, by comparison–generalisation, into common

nouns substantive denoting multitudes of substances of the same
kind[9] – at which point 'primitive jargons' become 'original
languages' – there ensues the expressive necessity to distinguish
substances from others of the same kind, now sharing the same
general denotation; this is accomplished by the recognition of
qualities peculiar to them. Once events have been metaphysically
analysed into their constituent parts (see above), substances are
also distinguished as to their syntagmatic relations (such as, in
modern parlance, agent, patient, recipient, instrument, or subject,
object, adverbial) relative to attributes or other substances. A third
sort of difference, suggested by comparison–discrimination, consists in the quantities in which substances occur. In accordance
with the increasing difficulty they present for the generalising and
abstracting mind, quality distinctions are made before relational
ones, which in turn precede quantity distinctions. The appearance
of some quality distinctions (such as those of animacy, sex, size, or
colour) before others, of some relational distinctions (such as local
ones) before others, and of same quantity distinctions (such as
those between individuals, pairs, and larger groups) before others,
likewise reflects their relative cognitive difficulties.

In order to be able to express all such distinctions made in the
mind, a speech community could create a multitude of distinct
expressions of the class of nouns substantive, each denoting holisti-
cally a particular substance or kind of substance together with the
respective quality, relation, and quantity. This, however, would
soon overburden the speakers' memories, and would also run
counter to their fondness for diagrammatisation. On both grounds
a grammatical, combinatory solution would again, as in the case
of the breaking-up of event denotations into substance and attribute denotations, be preferable to a lexical one. By means of
distributing the expressive labour between basic lexical units and
grammatical elements with a distinguishing function, novel composite expressions could be produced for the different qualities,
relations, and quantities of one and the same substance as well as
for the same qualities, relations, and quantities of different substances, which would partially resemble one another in form
corresponding to the partial identities between their *denotata*. Smith
now envisages two variants of the grammatical solution: one
consists in the innovation of new classes of basic expressions for the
newly distinguished classes of *denotata*, namely, of nouns adjective for

qualities, prepositions for relations, and quantifiers (including numerals) for quantities, syntactically recombinable to yield complex substance expressions; the other introduces morphological complexity, consisting in the formal variation of the inherited nouns substantive themselves. Initially the morphological variant will be more congenial to language-formers, not yet at the height of their comparing and especially abstracting powers.

Smith's contention that it requires less comparative and abstractive effort to express distinctions by formal variations of nouns substantive than by separate words predisposes him to ascribe peculiar formal properties to these morphological variations or modifications. Qualities, relations and quantities inseparably co-exist with substances in nature; their metaphysical separation is only accomplished by abstraction. It is, thus, most 'natural', as well as most diagrammatic, to express quality, relational and quantity distinctions by inflexions of nouns substantive for gender (or also diminution/augmentation), case and number, since such formal variations too are, morphologically speaking, inseparable from the substance denotations they serve to vary: the meaningful parts 'thoroughly mixed and blended' after all constitute single words rather than syntactic constructions. Historically, these inflexional variations are supposed to have actually grown out of the originally invariable nouns substantive. Without especially emphasising this point, Smith implies that language-formers vary parts, in particular terminations, of the original form of words, thereby creating paradigmatic contrasts and imbuing the variable parts with meaning or, more precisely, semantically distinctive force. (For example, by altering the two final sounds of an originally invariable noun substantive such as *lupus* ('wolf'), one could produce a pair of words, *lupus* and, say, *lupa*, containing an invariable core, *lup-*, and variable terminations, *-us* and *-a*, and this paradigmatic contrast could be used to express distinctions such as the qualitative one between wolves of male and female sex.) Given a stock of nouns substantive differing randomly in their phonetic make-up, the variations of their terminations thus semanticised will initially also differ a great deal from one word to the other, and will continue to do so as long as truly general notions of qualities, relations and quantities, invariably recurring with all different kinds of substances, have not been attained. (For example, given two nouns substantive such as *lupus* ('he-wolf') and *arbor* ('tree'),[10]

it is to be expected that, once their terminations are varied to
express relational contrasts, the sets of their inflexions will be
different, consisting, say, of *-us/-ī/-ō/-um/-ō/-e* with *lup-* and of *-Ø/-is/
-ī/-em/-e/-Ø* with *arbor-*.) When nouns substantive need to be qualified for more than one category at the same time, the necessary
changes could be made in different places, provided the original
words are sufficiently long. Smith, however, tacitly assumes that
all distinctions will be expressed cumulatively in the termination.
(For example, a single final sound *-ō*, contrasting with *-ae*, as well
as with *-us/-ī/-um/-e*, as well as with *-īs*, could thus be made to
differentiate gender (masculine), case (dative), and number (singular) in association with *lup-* ('wolf').) Consequently, as qualities,
relations and quantities proliferate, the variations of the terminations of nouns substantive needed to express them will multiply. If
there are as few as three genders (which is the maximum Smith
had encountered), ten cases (as supposedly in Old Armenian),[11]
and three numbers (as in Greek, Gothic and Hebrew), a word
would need as many as ninety variants to distinguish them all
cumulatively by contrasts in its termination. The non-uniformity
of these terminal inflexions across different words further increases
the formal variations that need to be memorised at this stage.

Owing to the haphazard manner of their creation, inflexional
systems of this kind are liable to grow unwieldy, unless they are
regularised at least to some extent. What causes most offence in
Smith's view is the near-random variety of the set of inflexions
associated with words of the same class, nouns substantive. In
consequence of the love of analogy, the human disposition that is
so fundamental to grammar, these sets of inflexions are made more
uniform, presumably (and this is my interpretation) by the trans-
ference of one inflexional set to words which had previously been
inflected differently or not inflected at all. This transition from
chaos to order, from inflexions peculiar to individual words, hence
to be memorised individually, to inflexions applicable to larger
groups of words, hence predictable by more or less general rules,
is effected 'insensibly, and by slow degrees' and 'without any
intention or foresight in those who first set the example, and who
never meant to establish any general rule' (paragraph 16). As if led
by an invisible hand, the language-improvers thus promote ends
which were not part of their original intention (to adapt another
phrase which Smith was so fond of as to use it in both *The Theory*

of Moral Sentiments IV. i. 10 and *The Wealth of Nations* IV. ii. 9, and indeed already in an essay on the history of astronomy, written prior to 1758).

If the formers of original languages, despite such gradual improvements in point of regularity, eventually switch from the morphological to the syntactic mode of composite denotation and introduce special parts of speech to take care of tasks previously fulfilled by inflexion, it is because their powers of comparison and abstraction have matured and because syntax is more economical than even regularised inflexion. Considering that sex and animacy are only two of a huge number of qualities potentially qualifying kinds of substances, the creation of a special word class, noun adjective, is virtually inevitable for economical reasons alone. Certain kinds of qualities, in particular sex/animacy, representing the 'most extensive species of qualification', may nevertheless continue to be distinguished inflexionally.[12] If nouns adjective then accompany nouns substantive in syntactic construction, speakers, out of 'love of similarity of sound' and 'delight in the returns of the same syllables', make them agree in the inflexional variations exhibited by the substance denotations; and, owing to this unmistakable indication of their connectedness, they need not place substantives and adjectives next to one another. The inflexional variation of adjectives introduced in the process of cutting down on substantival inflexion may again become considerable: in order to be able to agree with nouns substantive in three genders, five cases, and two numbers (as in Ancient Greek), nouns adjective, provided they all inflect alike, ideally need as many as forty-five variant forms. Of relations it is the least abstract and general ones, especially those to do with spatial qualifications, which first find expression in a word class of their own, namely as prepositions. The more abstract and general ones, such as those denoted by *to, from, by, for, with,* and especially *of* (which denotes relatedness as such) in English, tend to resist this innovation and continue to be expressed by case inflexions, or also by rigid constituent order, at the original stage.[13] Quantity, the most abstract and general category of all, continues longest in the inflexional mode, minimally in the form of a two-way opposition between singular and plural, notwithstanding the availability of separate quantity words in a class of their own.[14]

The elaboration of attributes, expressed by verbal phrases,

proceeds along similar lines, and is treated more cursorily in the
Considerations. There is, firstly, an analogous development from the
particular to the general. When the complete events of old, as the
perfect simplicity and unity which events have in nature was still
conceived as such in the mind and reflected in language (or rather
jargon), are metaphysically analysed into substances and attributes, and their denotations artificially split and divided accordingly, attribute expressions are initially particular rather than
general terms, in so far as they are only attributable to particular
substances and, eventually, particular kinds of substances. For
example, once the substances are externalised from complete
events such as 'the-lion-come' and 'the-wolf-come', categorisations
of these particular (kinds of) substances will continue to inhere in
attribute denotations, whose meanings could thus be rendered as
'terrible-animal-come' or, already more generally, 'terrible-
substance-come'. With increasing generalisation such substance-
related categorisations become virtually empty, degenerating to
mere reminders that the impersonal verb is, as we called it above,
unsaturated and requires a noun substantive 'to ascertain and
determine its signification'. Observing that those impersonal, not
metaphysically divided verbs which have managed to survive in
languages such as Latin are all third person singular forms, Smith
conjectures that this must also have been the form of verbs when
they first turned personal. There is actually no reason, by Smith's
own principles, why the impersonal verbs of the holistic stage
should have been in any person-number form at all. However, if
third person and singular are understood as the unmarked, nega-
tively defined categories of person ('neither speaker nor addressee')
and number ('absence of number specification'), it is plausible to
assume that general valency indicators on already personalised
verbs will take the form of precisely these categories and that
surviving impersonal verbs, too, will adopt such markers indicating
the absence of a speaker-addressee and number-specified subject.
(Note that by the logic of Smith's principles, personal verbs should
be associated with further markers of this kind once substances in
relations other than that of subject are externalised as well.)

Like nouns substantive, personal verbs, secondly, need to be
further diversified as comparison and abstraction increase the fund
of their *denotata*. Abstract though the idea of three speech-act roles
is, it will sooner or later occur to language-formers that attributes

can hold of the speaker, the addressee, or a non-participant in the speech act, or of any combinations of these. It will likewise be recognised that attributes may be ascribed to substances involved in the event in opposite capacities, for example as agent or as patient; that events may be localised in time as anterior to, simultaneous with, or posterior to the speech act; and that attributions may be affirmed or denied or put forward as a request, wish, or mere possibility. Originally separate personal verbs are coined, and individually memorised, to take care of all such distinctions; but the lexical mode of denotation is eventually superseded by the inflexional one, where, more economically as well as diagrammatically, the terminations of personal verbs are varied to express distinctions of person (or, more precisely, role) and number of the substance and of voice, tense and mood of the attribution.[15] Even though Smith is less explicit here, verbal inflexions may be expected to have the same formal properties as their nominal counterparts, i.e. to be thoroughly mixed and blended with the invariable part of verbs, to differ a great deal from one verb to the other, and to cumulate the several inflexional categories. And this haphazardly created system of verbal inflexions will also be regulated by successive generations of language-improvers, insensibly striving, and (as if led by an invisible hand) succeeding, to reduce the conjugational variety to some order. Owing to continuing limitations especially of their abstracting powers, these improvers, however, will not be quick to seize on the least 'natural' syntactic mode of combination, to which end they would have to avail themselves of entirely new classes of words specifically to denote person and number (i.e. personal pronouns) and voice, tense, and mood (i.e. auxiliaries).

Shunning the inductive search for interdependencies in grammatical systems, a method already favoured by a few more empirically minded linguistic comparatists, Smith emphasised speculative reasoning in his portrayal of the original genius, and accordingly qualified most of his statements by phrases such as 'probably', 'it is natural to suppose' or 'it is easy to conceive how'. In view of his explanatory pretensions this approach was virtually forced upon him. Since the crucial structural traits of the original genius were only explicable in terms of the circumstances of the first, or at any rate the early, formation of languages, and since he did not expect that such formations almost *ab ovo* might actually be anywhere observable, an excursion to the realms of conjectural history was inevitable. These realms, nevertheless, were not entirely imaginary. Smith believed that there were indeed actual-historical languages which were not removed from their formative periods far enough to have been deprived entirely of their original genius. 'Ancient' languages in this sense were Ancient Greek, Old Armenian, Hebrew, and probably the languages of savage nations about which Smith had read (but was not so well informed as to be able to tell with any confidence). In a way, Smith was merely posing as a conjectural historian, modelling the original genius, or at least its later stages, on the genius of Ancient Greek, the ancient language within his purview where all in all he found the richest inflexional system. His aim as an actual historian, then, was to confirm the seniority of the ancient over the modern languages, a seemingly self-evident supposition which had, nevertheless, been seriously questioned, notably by the Abbé Girard's insistence on the immutability of genius (see below), and also by all those who took the dearth or even absence of inflexions from words in syntactic construction, as perhaps best exemplified by Chinese among modern languages, for conclusive proof of originality.[16] To make his point, Smith needed to argue that the structural mechanisms of the ancient languages could be traced further back in time than those of modern languages. His considerations about the first formation of languages were one part of this argument. The second part was to show how the structure of modern languages could develop from that of those ancient ones which had, perhaps for surprisingly long, managed to guard their original genius. As it turned out, what was being contrasted to the genius of original languages was not in fact the genius of modern, but that of 'compounded' languages.

Before we turn to compounding, it is instructive to consider a question on which Smith was somewhat evasive: what would have been the outcome if the reformation of original languages along Smithian lines had continued undisturbed? The variety of in-flexional classes, already in the process of being (insensibly) regularised, would eventually have been reduced to a single declension for all nouns substantive and nouns adjective, and to a single conjugation for all personal verbs. Cumulatively expressed inflexional categories would eventually have been divided up between separate variable parts of words, with one portion of the termination of nouns substantive, for example, denoting number and another denoting case; if there were two numbers and six cases, eight forms would suffice to make all distinctions (since the singular suffix could now be combined with the nominative, accusative, genitive, etc. case suffixes, and likewise the plural suffix), as opposed to the twelve forms needed as long as number expression was not disentangled from case expression. The tight links between the invariable part of words and their inflexions would have been loosened and eventually severed in the wake of improving abstraction, so that ultimately the original morphological constituents of words, i.e. the inflexions, would be transformed into syntactic constituents of nominal and verbal phrases, i.e. into words of their own – namely quality, in particular gender words, relation words (prepositions), quantity words (quantifiers, numerals), person-number words (personal pronouns), voice, tense, and mood words (auxiliaries). From the point of view especially of formal economy, this result would have been eminently desirable; and yet Smith chose not to extend his evolutionary scenario from conjectural antiquity into the not-so-distant actual-historical past or even the present in this principled manner. What he would have found rather implausible, I believe, was the idea of separate function words originating from inflexions grown syntactically autonomous. Nothing in the form of prepositions, quantifiers, numerals, personal pronouns, or auxiliaries in languages such as English or French pointed to such a bound morphological origin; and these function words, moreover, all preceded their principal words, whereas inflexions had been word-final. What appeared much likelier was that these function words had always been genuine words, if of a fairly general meaning, hence of late origin. The tense and voice auxiliaries, for example, seemed to be, and to have been coined as, general verbs of possession (*have*) and existence (*be*) in English. Therefore, inflexions must surely have had a different fate than that of being converted into function words. Presumably they had simply disappeared. But this material loss was not something the invisible hand, instrumental in the optimisation of poorly-organised inflexional systems, could be held responsible for. Such discontinuities required more extraordinary circumstances, like those attending 'the mixture of several languages with one another, occasioned by the mixture of different nations'.

No matter how extraordinary their effects, language mixtures in

fact were nothing unusual.[17] According to Smith, Latin is compounded of Ancient Greek and Etruscan, Modern Greek of Ancient
Greek and apparently Turkish, Italian of Latin and the Germanic
dialect of the Lombards, French of Latin and the Frankish variety
of Germanic, and English – the most compounded language of all
– of Norman French and Saxon. These ubiquitous and possibly
repeated mixtures are the catastrophes in the natural history of
languages, responsible for the most conspicuous demarcations of
an otherwise continuous temporalised chain of structural variations. It is only on such occasions that linguistic structures are
fundamentally remodelled, because 'the intricacy of declensions
and conjugations', while not beyond the reach of children 'insensibly' and slowly acquiring their original mother tongues, is an
insurmountable obstacle in the learning of a foreign language
under the less favourable circumstances of conquests or migrations
of nations. The tendency here is for the inflexions not to be learned
at all by the new non-native speakers, and the languages resulting
from such imperfect learning will accordingly be simpler 'in
rudiments and principles' than those previously spoken by native
speakers. The expressive tasks of inflexions are now, with increasingly fewer exceptions (such as perhaps two nominal numbers),
performed by function words, uniformly accompanying all principal words of a given class, or also, even more economically, by 'the
place of the words', 'the order and construction of the sentence'.
The opposition of personal and impersonal verbs is bound to
disappear, as is agreement between nouns substantive and nouns
adjective, simply as a concomitant of the loss of the relevant
inflexions. The relationship between genealogical and inflexional
complexity, to put it in a nutshell, is this: 'the more simple any
language is in its composition, the more complex it must be in its
declensions and conjugations; and, on the contrary, the more
simple it is in its declensions and conjugations, the more complex
it must be in its composition' (paragraph 36).[18]

By insisting on the necessity of mixture for changes of genius,
Smith was in principle free to include ancient as well as modern
languages in either structural class. While he did not specifically
mention any modern language that was structurally original
(because uncompounded),[19] Latin, ancient as well as allegedly
compounded of Greek and Etruscan, provided most of the inflexional exemplification. If mixture as such was to be the genealogical

watershed, ancient Latin would have had to be classed with modern French and Italian, themselves mixtures of Latin with Germanic ingredients, while Ancient Greek, presumed uncompounded, would have been in the opposite class. Here Smith seemed to be at odds with virtually all eighteenth-century comparatists (including Girard), whose structural classifications recognised more similarities between the two principal ancient tongues of Europe than between Latin and modern Romance. And it would indeed have been difficult for Smith to deny that the difference between Ancient Greek and Latin was but slight on his own structural criteria. What he was guilty of was to have exaggerated the impact of mixture as such (which, on my interpretation, he had to do in order to solve the problem of the material loss of inflexions). The structural distance between the original and the compounded genius undeniably increased when mixtures recurred, Smith's extremes being Ancient Greek and, its descendant by multiple compounding, contemporary English. But this increase was steady throughout. There was in particular no great leap forward when Greek lost its compositional virginity and brought forth Latin in intercourse with Etruscan, by comparison with the advances which the offspring of this union, impure from its conception, made subsequently, coupling promiscuously. Smith's structural contrast basically was between languages with inflexional and with function-word expression of accessory categories, and the transitions between the attested extremes were evidently more or less continuous, showing no single sharp boundary at the first historical passage from uncompoundedness to compoundedness. The dividing line Smith wished to draw between the original and the compounded genius, thus, was structurally more artificial than he was prepared to admit.

In the evaluative part of the *Considerations* the focus indeed was on structural contrasts as exemplified by the ancient and modern literary languages of Europe rather than on the purely geniological distinction. Smith's aesthetic evaluations concurred with conventional Classicist wisdom but were less arbitrary, in so far as they were tied to those structural features which had been derived from general principles of language formation and transformation, evolutionary or revolutionary. Modern, multiply-compounded languages, while superior in simplicity of rudiments and principles, are inferior to ancient, closer-to-original (i.e. uncompounded or less compounded) languages in three respects: they are more 'prolix' because they need more words to express the same *denotata* (compare concise Latin *amavissem* with verbose English *I should have loved*); they are 'less agreeable to the ear', owing to the lack of variety of terminations; and, devoid of inflexional markers of connectedness, they are more severely constrained in the syntactic arrangement of words. As to prolixity, it should be noted that its single measure was the number of words, the unit which still used to take pride of place (in Smith's case not only for purposes of evaluation), rather than the number of sound segments, syllables,[20] or smallest meaningful units (such as invariable word-cores and terminations). On the second point, agreeableness to the ear or 'sweetness', Smith could seem inconsistent, in so far as his praise of variety of terminations squares oddly with his previous motive for the creation of inflexional agreement, namely 'the love of similarity of sound'. His idea apparently was that the danger of phonetic monotony was greater if a language was entirely innocent of inflexions, hence would have to use the same function words uniformly with all principal words.[21] As to constraint, Smith evidently saw no great inherent value in the rigid adherence of word order to the 'ordo naturalis' of subject–verb–object, reflecting the cognitive sequence cause–action–effect, which had struck many a *lumière* in France as the single most beneficial excellency of his native tongue. His preference here was for 'latitude'. As long as perspicuity was guaranteed by inflexions, one could give free play to one's passions and 'invert' or 'transpose' words freely even in prose, according to the rule (as it was put in the fifth lecture on rhetoric and belles-lettres): 'Let that which affects us most be placed first, that which affects us in the next degree next, and so on to the end' (i. v. 52b).[22]

III

What was it that the typological *discours* that had unfolded spasmodically since around 1600 AD owed to the intervention of Adam Smith? In particular, how did his *Considerations* relate to their first stimulus, the Abbé Gabriel Girard's *Les vrais principes de la langue françoise: ou La parole réduite en méthode, conformément aux loix de l'usage*, which had just appeared, in 1747, as Smith began his first series of public lectures on rhetoric and belles-lettres at Edinburgh?

Girard's *Les vrais principes*, essentially a contrastive grammar of

French and Latin, set out the parts of speech in a sequence that was supposed, as was the custom, to correspond to their historical evolution. The origin and progress of language, however, was not really his subject; what he was concerned with primarily was to show that French differed rather radically from Latin and that these two languages should be seen as representatives of two fundamentally different types (or *génies*). French, like Italian and Spanish, exemplifies the 'génie analogue'. Here the linear order of the major clause constituents mirrors the natural sequence of ideas, with the agent (subject) coming first, followed by the action (verb), followed by whatever is acted on or aimed at or otherwise involved in the action (objects, adverbials). Concomitants of this natural order, fairly resistant to inversions, are the absence of nominal case marking, hence also of case agreement between nouns and adjectives, and the presence of a definite article as a separate part of speech. Further, to compensate for the lack of cases, analogous languages employ prepositions to identify the relations especially of circumstantial specifications. They also use function words (adverbs, perhaps aided by the definite article) rather than inflexion for the gradation of adjectives. Latin, like Russian and Church Slavonic, represents the 'génie transpositive'. Here constituent order is flexible and arbitrary, unrestrained by the natural order of ideas and instead following the speaker's momentary imagination. Case marking is present, and is also exploited in adjective agreement. Prepositions play a less prominent role. Adjective grading is inflexional. And there is no definite article. There is yet a third class recognised by Girard, called 'mixte' or 'amphilogique' and exemplified by Ancient Greek and Teutonic. It shares the definite article with the analogous class, and cases (and presumably further inflexional categories) and the imaginative free constituent order with the transpositive class. (A further mixed class would be logically possible, but is tacitly assumed unattested: it would be characterised by a natural rigid constituent order and the absence of cases, herein resembling the analogous class, and by the lack of a definite article, sharing this trait with the transpositive class.)

Girard was not at a loss for explanations of the major systematic interdependencies which he had induced from the range of languages with which he (*Secrétaire interprète du Roy* for Slavonic) had some familiarity. The two, by no means novel, principles which he

invoked to explain the correlation between the rigidity or flexibility
of constituent order, the absence or presence of case inflexion, and
the more or less extensive use of prepositions, were ambiguity
avoidance (*la clarté*) and economy: the lack of any distinctive
relational marking could cause confusion, but the simultaneous use
of more than one kind of marking would needlessly overburden the
speaker or writer, who will therefore opt either for rigid natural
order, plus, where necessary, prepositions, or for case inflexion,
perhaps also supplemented by some prepositions, but not for both.
The analogous or transpositive/mixed expression of adjective grading by special function words or by inflexions remained
unaccounted for by Girard, but could have been explained as
following the genius-specific mode of expression of the most
conspicuous, i.e. the relational categories of accidence. Why rigid
order and the absence of cases should imply a definite article was
a mystery, unless one put faith in Girard's whimsical conjecture
that the original formers of transpositive languages, eager to
distinguish and name, immediately invented nouns and omitted to
avail themselves ever after of 'those words which announce and
particularise without naming', which properly were the first part
of speech they should have invented, as did the framers of
analogous and mixed languages.

Girard showed little interest in mechanisms of grammatical
change as occurring in fully-formed languages. He was of course
not blind to the possibility of mixtures, but their effect to him
seemed essentially limited to the borrowing of words. The interdependent traits which constituted his three *génies* in particular were,
in his view, as immutable as species still were for the vast majority
of natural historians. This enabled the linguistic patriot, unconven-
tionally but not entirely idiosyncratically, to deny that French was
a daughter of Latin, with which it shared no more than the
grammatical universals and a portion of its vocabulary – for how
could all these inflexions have been lost, the word order been firmly
fixed, and a definite article as well as some prepositions been
innovated?

The structural similarity between Smith's original and compounded genii and Girard's transpositive and analogous *génies*
respectively is unmistakable. In a way Smith's systematic interdependencies were more comprehensive because they included the
inflexional or function-word expression of accessory categories of

verbs as well as of nouns, the verbal sphere having been neglected by Girard.[23] As to inflexional categories in the nominal sphere, Smith included non-relational ones such as gender and number, but disregarded adjective grading, which, however, could have been added without difficulty as a further accessory category whose expression was governed by Smith's general principles. Smith came down more resolutely than Girard in favour of inflexions rather than linear ordering as the fundamental trait determining the genius. For Smith, the freedom of word order seemed a rather trivial *implicatum* of the availability of segmental (inflexional or function-word) relational markers, and he did not much care, either, how subject, verb, and object were arranged once their order had become fixed, owing to the demise of inflexions. Considering that the all-decisive choice in Smith's system was between the inflexional or function-word expression of the accessory categories of principal words, it could seem surprising that he disregarded the definite article, the one part of speech whose presence or absence had been found typologically significant by Girard. The reason for this omission of Smith's presumably was not that he doubted the empirical validity of Girard's definite-article implication, but that he lacked evidence for a change from inflexional to function-word expression of definiteness in accordance with his developmental principles; in Ancient Greek, for instance, there had already been definite articles, whereas in Latin, its descendant by compounding with Etruscan, this part of speech was unaccountably missing. While there was, thus, no equivalent of Girard's *génie mixte* in Smith's geniology, it could accommodate a distinction, relevant perhaps only for the remote past, between pre-inflexional as well as pre-syntactic languages, equipped only with impersonal verbs, and not-yet-inflexional but rudimentarily syntactic languages, dividing event denotations into personal verbs and nouns substantive.

If impersonal verbs, in Smith's sense, were taken as the point of departure, subsequent linguistic developments had perforce to be analytic. That they actually had been in this direction was at the time a fairly common assumption.[24] From the Abbé Jean-Baptiste du Bos (*Réflexions critiques sur la poésie et sur la peinture* (1719), mentioned in Smith's *Theory of Moral Sentiments* as well as in his *Lectures on Rhetoric and Belles Lettres*) to Denis Diderot (*Lettre sur les sourds et muets* (1751)), many a writer had praised the comprehensiveness of the inflected words of the classical languages, largely lost in their modern descendants. What Smith, however, seized on as the hallmark of primeval jargons and languages was a particular species of such pre-analytic words, encompassing entire events and thus being tantamount to whole sentences. In this he echoed Rousseau's opinion about the first language formers: 'ignorant la Division du Discours en ses parties constitutives, ils donnérent d'abord à chaque mot le sens d'une proposition entiére' (1755).[25] What Smith added was the designation of these sentence-words as 'impersonal verbs', which he borrowed from the grammar of classical languages where he believed that same such all-encompassing words had actually survived. This, too, was not without precedent closer to home: in *An Enquiry into the Life and Writings of Homer* (1735), Thomas Blackwell, Professor of Greek and Principal of Marischal College at Aberdeen, had also called 'the *primitive Parts* of the Languages reputed *Original*' 'rough, undeclined, impersonal Monosyllables' (pp. 58–9). If Smith's familiarity with exotic tongues had been more thorough, he might have discovered that the impersonal verbs of Greek and Latin were not the only non-conjectural witnesses to the verisimilitude of his theory. It seemed to be in a speculative vein what Maupertuis, for example, remarked on this matter: 'Un sauvage dont la langue n'est point encore formée, pourroit confondre et exprimer tout à la fois le pronom, le verbe, le nombre, le substantif, et l'adjectif; et dire en un seul mot: *J'ai tué un gros ours*' (*Dissertation sur les différens moyens dont les hommes se sont servis pour exprimer leurs idées*, 1756). However, experts in American Indian languages had for some time been reporting that the sentences especially in Huron and Iroquois indeed appeared to consist of nothing but verbs which incorporated all accessory specifications as well as subjects and objects, so that there was scarcely a need for word-external syntax.[26] It was to take some time yet before the full significance of 'polysynthetic' or 'incorporating' languages was grasped by comparatists. Among these, both James Burnett (see especially the first volume of his *Origin and Progress of Language*, 1773) and Peter S. Du Ponceau (see especially his final account of 1838) were much indebted to Smith for preparing this recognition theoretically by making the point that verbs could be semantically (and, as it then turned out, also morphologically) more inclusive than those of English or even Latin and Ancient Greek.[27]

As to the two genii of indubitably actual-historical standing,

Smith's evolutionary perspective was more conducive than Girard's tenet of geniological immutability to perceiving the difference between them as gradual rather than categorical with respect to inflexion. The traditional position that languages were either inflecting or uninflecting had been overly general: taken literally, the systemic implication was that either all or none of the *words* of a class of words potentially susceptible to inflexion (i.e. nouns, adjectives, verbs) would have to be inflected, and that either all or none of the *classes* of potentially inflectable words would have to be inflected. In a way, Smith was more of a traditionalist than Girard, who exempted the accessory categories of verbs from the obligation to conform to nominal and adjectival standards. On Smith's principles, nominal and verbal inflexions had to be expected to flourish or to wilt in unison – which in fact was not always what they really did, with verbal inflexions often being richer and more robust than nominal ones, as had already dawned on an earlier *grammarien-philosophe*, Tommaso Campanella (1638). Where Smith instead saw gradual differences between older and younger original languages, and also between original and even multiply-compounded languages, was in their more plentiful or more meagre supply of inflexional categories and categorial differentiations. Since, in accordance with their increasing abstractness and generality, quality inflexions (gender) will appear first, followed by relational inflexions (case), followed in turn by quantity inflexions (number), there should be original languages with gender alone, with gender and case, and with all three. Synchronically, number would, thus, imply case, and case would imply gender. This law of permissible inflexional variation, however, would only seem to hold for phases of inflexional expansion, because, as function words are gradually taking over, gender is apparently destined to go first, followed by case, with number as the longest-lasting inflexional survivor, which reverses the synchronic implications.[28] And there should be similar, equally phase-specific, implications between the realisations of individual categories – for example between the more and the less abstract relations, i.e. the subject/object/attribute and the local/adverbial cases, or between the more and the less general numbers, i.e. the plural and the singular/dual. Smith further suggested interdependencies between the inflexions of different parts of speech: there was to be no dual number with personal verbs unless there was also one with nouns substantive, and there were to be no inflexions of nouns adjectives which were not also found on nouns substantive – as predicted by the analogical mechanism of creating agreement by rhyme.

Girard's main explanatory notions had been the need to avoid (especially relational) ambiguities and that of doing so economically. On this Smith no doubt concurred; but for him economy, dictated by the basic principle of the limited human memory, served to explain not only why word order need not be rigid if there are case inflexions, but also, and more importantly, why the lexical mode of denotation was continually replaced by the combinatorial mode as the expressive demands were growing, and why inflexions, always coming in several declensions and conjugations, were abandoned for function words, ensuring uniform or 'universal' declension and conjugation. Formal economy in fact had already had a long tradition as a force counterbalancing the communicative requirement that the expressive resources be copious. It used to be invoked to explain why, instead of new words being coined, those already existing had their meanings extended metaphorically.[29] In Locke's *Essay Concerning Human Understanding*, the second most important end of language was said to be that of conveying ideas 'with as much ease and quickness as is possible', which was prevented if there were no distinct names for complex ideas and these therefore had to be made known 'by an enumeration of the simple ones that compose them' (1690, III, x). In his discourse on inequality (1755) Rousseau noted that, unless particular terms had been supplemented or replaced by general terms, the dictionaries of the original language-formers would have grown inconveniently copious. And this idea was applied also to number inflexion in such a minor work as Dr Blacklock's: 'To assist the memory, and shorten discourse, general terms have been invented, which may naturally contain all the individuals of a kind; or, by a small alteration in the same word, express them singly' (1756, p. 8). In his *Encyclopédie* article on 'Conjugaison' (1753) du Marsais remarked that, if languages had been devised by philosophers, they would contain no more than a single conjugation for all verbs alike, and that there indeed were languages which distinguished such verbal categories, 'avec netteté', by 'particules'. Economy as a force more or less fundamentally shaping the structure of languages was

thus in the air in the mid eighteenth century; but it could well have
been Smith, in his *Considerations* and earlier lectures, who first
brought it to bear on such specific a phenomenon as the variety of
inflexion classes. Very soon after, Joseph Priestley, in *A Course of
Lectures on the Theory of Language, and Universal Grammar* which he
gave at Warrington Academy and which he made available in print
for the use of his pupils (1762), justified the superiority of prepositions (or postpositions) and auxiliaries over inflexions in exactly
the same economical terms, without, however, listing Smith's
Considerations among his sources.[30] And in the anonymous article
'Language' in the first edition of the *Encyclopædia Britannica* (1771,
vol. II), probably manufactured by the editor, William Smellie,
himself, inflexion classes were recognised as a contingent characteristic of the transpositive genius; but, motivated by the need to keep
grammars within the bounds of what can be handled with facility
by humans, this abundance of forms was claimed to be typically
reduced, even at the expense of accuracy, by making 'the same
word serve a double, treble, or even quadruple office', i.e. by
neutralising or syncretising inflexional distinctions (as for example
in Latin *puellae*, which may be genitive, dative, or ablative singular
or nominative or vocative plural). Thus the gospel of Adam Smith,
the grammatical economist, began to be spread.

Smith placed perhaps a little too much trust in the explanatory
value of the mental operation of abstraction. Recall that his
contention was that inflexions are less abstract than, hence
developmentally prior to, function words. This rationale, however,
tends to exaggerate the difference between morphological (word-
level) and syntactic (phrase-level) constructions. According to
Smith, separate function words could only be innovated for the
expression of accessory categories if these categories as such were
mentally abstracted, i.e. metaphysically divided from the *denotata*
of the principal words. But the alternative expression of such
categories, namely variation of the termination of principal words,
also presupposes this same metaphysical division, or else there would
have been no reason to vary the terminations in the first place. The
difference, thus, is a mere formal one, pertaining to the ways the
expressions of primary *denotata* and of accessory categories are
separated and combined linguistically.[31] The alternative, which
seemed more 'natural' because less 'metaphysical' to Smith,

involves less separation only in so far as meaningful parts are combined in tighter morphological rather than in looser syntactic constructions, i.e. in words rather than phrases.

Despite this internal weakness, Smith's reliance on the interplay of metaphysical division and formal separation lead him to postulate a most interesting novel interdependency between these three traits of inflexional systems: (i) inflexions are intimately joined to stems, (ii) owing to synonymy of inflexions there are coexisting inflexion classes (i.e. declensions and conjugations), and (iii) inflexions express several categories cumulatively. (A further correlate was soon to be added, in 'Language' in the *Encyclopædia Britannica*: (iv) owing to homonymy of inflexions paradigmatic distinctions may be neutralised.) Smith's perception of these properties was no doubt inspired by the classical languages, and on the strength of his principles he took their co-occurrence for granted. The anonymous author of 'Language' in the *Encyclopædia Britannica* was more cautious, and saw these co-occurrences as 'moral certainties' rather than 'physical necessities'. Even if this should be only an empirical contingency, these three or four properties in fact do tend to co-vary. If Smith's acquaintance with Turkish, one of the languages he mentioned in passing, had been closer, he would have noticed that the declensions and conjugations there are more or less uniform, that there is virtually no inflexional cumulation (as well as virtually no inflexional neutralisation), and that inflexions are far less thoroughly mixed and blended with stems. In short, the inflexions of languages such as Turkish would have been seen to resemble postposed function words – except that they were still part of morphological rather than syntactic constructions, if less close-knit ones. The only parameter that would have had to be recognised as admitting of gradual variation was (i), relating to the tightness of morphological fusion, and Smith would have been the first to realise, from theory rather than observation, the systemic contrast between what came to be known as flective and agglutinative morphology.[32]

What all of Smith's general principles were designed for was the explication of structural genii as developmental stages. In contradistinction to Girard, Smith thus had a theory of linguistic change, or at any rate of the evolutionary (growth by semanticisation, regularisation) and revolutionary (loss) changes in inflexions. Smith's inflexional history was linear and irreversible. Inflexions appeared out of principal words, were perhaps transferred to other words of the same class, and disappeared again in the wake of language mixtures. (There were no objections, then, to acknowledging Latin as a grammatical, rather than only as a lexical, ancestor of French.) Once the original genius was lost, it could not be revived: with the advent of economically superior function words, there could have been no point in principal words beginning again to grow inflexions, and for history thus to repeat itself. What Smith's diachronic theory had nothing to say about, however, were the function words. Relative latecomers owing to the generality of their meaning, they seemed otherwise immutable. There were no reasons, in Smith's scenario, to expect them to have lost semantic or formal substance in the process of being appropriated, from the fund of principal words, for specific grammatical functions, or even to be potentially capable of losing further substance and indeed their syntactic autonomy and thereby to become veritable inflexions, and eventually to wear out and disappear – at which point the cycle of grammaticisation, coalescence and erosion would begin anew. Developments of this kind, providing an alternative source of inflexions, would have been counter to Smithian principles. And yet speculations that this was precisely what had happened, as inflexional languages were first formed as well as later, when compounded languages such as French recreated some verbal inflexions, were already on record – for example in Condillac's influential *Essai sur l'origine des connoissances humaines* (1746, II, i, ix).[33] A heated debate would soon begin to rage over this issue.[34]

But Adam Smith had had enough of this and left grammatical economy to others. His view of *homo oeconomicus* was not going to be entirely dissimilar from his portrait of *homo grammaticus*, but his system of economics now demanded his exclusive attention, and perhaps promised to provide even better entertainment.[35] A certain, well, indifference had after all often come over him when discoursing on the subject of grammar – which no doubt was why, during his professorship at Glasgow, he used to cut short the second of his annual lectures on rhetoric and belles-lettres, much to the relief of the scribblers: 'but this as well as many other grammaticall parts we must altogether pass over as taedious and unentertaining'.

Notes

This paper is dedicated to the memory of Thomas Frank, esteemed fellow student of the linguistic thought of the Enlightenment and amiable 'Ambassador from the Dominions of Learning to those of Conversation' (to borrow a phrase of David Hume's).

Earlier versions were read at the Edinburgh Institute for Advanced Studies in the Humanities on 10 September 1986, reporting on research done with the Institute Project on the Scottish Enlightenment (where Tom was a co-Fellow), and in the Department of Linguistics of the University of Edinburgh on 22 October 1987.

1. Of the two words Smith used as examples, one, 'but', had already been dealt with in Locke's *Essay Concerning Human Understanding* (III. vii. 5), and the other, 'humour', also resembled an example of Locke's, 'liquor' (III. ic. 16).

2. See Plank (1987b) for a case study on the possible propagation of Smith's linguistic ideas. It would be interesting to know whether any of Smith's linguistic assumptions had been included in the 'pretty long enumeration . . . of certain leading principles, both political and literary, to which he was anxious to establish his exclusive right; in order to prevent the possibility of some rival claims which he thought he had reason to apprehend' (Stewart, 1795, p. lxxx), which he had drawn up in 1755 and the manuscript of which is lost.

3. There is a direct reference in the *Considerations* (paragraph 30) also to Sanctius's *Minerva* (1587/1733), concerning impersonal verbs. I wonder whether Smith was perhaps given further entertainment by the grammatical articles in Ephraim Chambers' *Cyclopædia* (1728 or later editions), by James Harris's *Hermes* (1751), Anselm Bayly's *Introduction to Languages* (1758), by Classical Philologists, or by the grammar of Port-Royal (1660, often re-edited).

4. However, Manget (1809, p. xv), his French translator, commentator and editor, already thought that he should have.

5. Incidentally, Smith did not occupy himself with the question of linguistic monogenesis or polygenesis. His developmental scheme would have been more compatible with the latter.

6. A number of studies have been devoted specifically to the exposition of Smith's principles, of which at least the following should be mentioned here: Berry (1974), Land (1977; 1986, pp. 133–59), Windross (1980) and Christie (1987). None of these, however, fully appreciates Smith's subtlety as a comparative grammarian.

7. In contrast to natural rhyme, verse is considered conventional in *The Theory of Moral Sentiments* (IV. i. 6–7).

8. The letter to George Baird of 7 February 1763 is unequivocal on this point: 'Verbs . . . being, in my apprehension, the original parts of speech, first invented to express in one word a compleat event' (*Correspondence*, p. 88).

9. The idea that particular terms become general, rather than the other way round, was a traditional one (also held by Locke, among others) but was not entirely uncontroversial. Evidence in its favour is supposedly the natural disposition of mankind, and especially of

little children and a clown (i.e. idiot) Smith knew, 'to give to one object the name of any other' (*Considerations*, paragraph 1). Thus, by antonomasia, we call a philosopher a 'Newton', or the clown would have called any river, had he but been carried to another, a 'river', which term in his use was the proper name of the river which ran by his own door.

10. I have replaced Smith's own example *Hercules* by *lupus*, which shares fewer inflexions with *arbor*.

11. Bryce, in the Glasgow Edition of the *Considerations* (pp. 211–12), has found no source for Smith's attribution of ten cases to Armenian. I have. Chambers' *Cyclopædia* (4th edition, 1741) as well as du Marsais in the French *Encyclopédie* (vol. II, 1751) referred s.v. *Case/Cas* to F., or P., Galanus as their authority for the claim that Armenian had as many as ten cases. Father Clemente Galano's *Grammaticae et logicae institutiones linguae literalis armenicae Armenis traditae* of 1645 was for a long time the best-known source of information for this language, and his ten-case theory was a persistent one, even though there were rival claims conceding Armenian no more than six cases.

12. Presumably it is its lack of 'extensiveness' which has prevented such a prominent qualitative category as colour, supposedly perhaps the least metaphysical one, from ever being expressed inflexionally.

13. Words denoting qualities and relations 'in abstract' (such as 'greenness' or 'superiority'), derived from words denoting them 'in concrete' ('green', 'superior'), are yet later developments.

14. On the model of nouns adjective, relation and quantity words, once innovated, might be expected to be supplied with inflexions enabling them to agree with nouns substantive. This is a point disregarded by Smith, though.

15. Smith mentions that event denotations can be affirmations or denials, but does not dwell on the mode of expression of these fundamental categories, which might perhaps have been related to mood. Unlike verbal person, emanating from verbs themselves, verbal number is supposed to be transferred from nouns substantive by agreement.

16. An interesting source, perhaps unknown to Smith, was John Webb's 'essay endeavouring a probability that the language of the empire of China is the primitive language spoken through the whole world before the confusion of Babel' (1669/1678). Uninflected words are of course also characteristic of Smith's earliest stage, where they are not, however, joined in genuinely syntactic constructions, as they reputedly are in Chinese.

17. And they were also a popular topic of linguistic writings ever since the story of Babel. In *The Philological Miscellany* (1761), for example, Smith's *Considerations* were followed by (anonymous) 'General Remarks on the Origin and Mixture of antient Nations, and on the Manner of studying their History', excerpted from essays of Mons. Freret. And, like Smith, James 'Hermes' Harris would in fact call mixed languages 'compounded' (1751, p. 408) – a term which is used ambiguously in the *Considerations*, greatly confusing commentators such as Coseriu and Land.

18. It is here that Smith makes the enormously influential comparison

(see Plank, 1989) between languages and mechanical engines, also allegedly continuously simplified by successive generations of improvers (a thesis belied by James Watt's complication of the Newcomen engine). Smith favoured this mechanistic imagery for systems of all kinds.

19. The Slavonic languages, where the Abbé Girard's special extra-ecclesiastical expertise was, might have fitted this bill.

20. Manget (1809, p. 104) counted no more syllables in 'I should have loved' than in *amavissem*, viz. four.

21. Employing this criterion a little differently, the author of 'Language' in the *Encyclopædia Britannica* (1771) on the contrary found a greater variety of sounds in uninflecting than in inflecting languages.

22. The only other, subsidiary, word-order rule worthy of attention was that 'your Sentence or Phrase never drag a Tail' (*ibid.*).

23. Girard was in fact deliberating whether to include the optional or obligatory accompaniment of finite verbs with subject personal pronouns (as in Latin and French respectively) in his geniological system.

24. Support for it came from current beliefs about similar developments of writing systems. In the *Considerations* (paragraph 30), Smith in fact drew on this supposed parallel, pointing out that economy was the driving force in the replacement of characters representing whole words by characters representing phonetic parts of words. William Warburton's ideas about hieroglyphs, as aired in his *Divine Legation of Moses* (1738–41), carried great authority in this matter.

25. For a verse rendering of this theory one may compare the blind Dr Thomas Blacklock's (mistitled) *Essay on Universal Etymology* (1756, p. 5), panegyrising 'The advantages of Grammar':

> As when, subjected still to Discord's sway,
> All Nature dark, deform'd, and blended lay;
> Till twins of Heav'n, fair Light and Order, came;
> And that illum'd, and this adorn'd the frame:
> Thus from these *atoms*, to our wond'ring eyes,
> Discourse, a fair-proportion'd pile, shall rise.

Blacklock felt particularly indebted to Harris's *Hermes* (1751), but may well have been in the audience when Smith first lectured on rhetoric and belles-lettres at Edinburgh.

26. On such grounds Gabriel Sagard (1632) had concluded that there was no point in writing a grammar of Huron; a dictionary, primarily of verbal phrases, was all that could be supplied for such a deficient language. Lafitau (1724, vol. II, p. 488) already came closer to penetrating the design of these idioms: 'Les langues huronnes et iroquoises n'ont proprement que des verbes qui en composent tout le fonds, de sorte que tout se conjugue et que rien ne se décline; mais dans ces verbes, il se trouve un artifice admirable.' Lafitau was among Smith's sources in his *Lectures on Jurisprudence*, but was evidently not exploited to the full.

27. Whether Wilhelm von Humboldt's co-discovery of the incorporating type was as independent of the Smithian tradition as some historians (e.g. Rousseau, 1984) would have it, is a question that would merit closer attention.

28. For this phase there would be analogous implications between different classes of function words: numerals/quantifiers imply prepositions, which in turn imply adjectives.

29. Jones (1982, p. 141) points to the currency of such ideas in his outline of the background of David Hume's linguistic thinking.

30. In several anonymous additions to Priestley's lectures, included in their republication (1824), the striking similarities to Smith's principles are noted.

31. Cf. Land (1977, p. 686) for this criticism.

32. From the way paradigms were presented in descriptive or pedagogical grammars of agglutinative languages, one could long have inferred the systematic difference between this morphological type and Latin- or Greek-style inflexion. But no-one had, so far as I can tell. In the heyday of morphological typology, the nineteenth century, the interdependent parameters (ii)–(iv) were given far less attention than they had received from Smith and the encyclopædic Anonymous.

33. Condillac accordingly assumed that originally there had only been a single, uniform conjugation for all verbs, supplied by inflexions deriving from formerly autonomous words. The cause for the multiplication of inflexion classes in this scenario, the reverse of Smith's, were mixtures of languages.

34. The list of protagonists was to include John Horne Tooke, Friedrich Schlegel, Franz Bopp and a latecomer, Otto Jespersen. See Plank (1989) for a historical survey of the Secretion (Smith, Schlegel, Jespersen *et al.*) *vs.* Coalescence (Horne Tooke, Bopp *et al.*) controversy.

35. Apart from languages and economies, mechanical engines and the universe were Smith's other favourite systems *où tout se tient*. Living organisms or the earth were the favourites of others. Perhaps Skinner (1974, p. 45) exaggerates the influence of the Physiocrats, and in particular Quesnai, upon systemic thinking when he states that they were among the first to proposition that 'in nature everything is intertwined'.

References

Anonymous (1761) On the Origin and Mixture of Antient Nations, and on the Manner of Studying their History. In *The Philological Miscellany; Consisting of Select Essays from the Memoirs of the Academy of Belles Lettres at Paris and other Foreign Academies*, vol. I, 480–510, [London:] T. Beckett & P. A. Dehondt.

Anonymous (1771) Language. In *Encyclopædia Britannica; or, a Dictionary of Arts and Sciences, Compiled upon a New Plan* ..., by a Society of Gentlemen in Scotland, vol. II, 863–80, Edinburgh: A. Bell & C. Macfarquhar.

[Arnauld, A. & C. Lancelot] (1660) *Grammaire générale et raisonnée* ..., Paris: Pierre le Petit.

Bacon, F. (1623) *Opera Francisci Baronis de Verulamio, vice-comitis Sancti Albani, tomus primus. Qui continet de augmentis scientiarum Libros IX*, London: J. Haviland.

Bayly, A. (1758) *An Introduction to Languages, Literary and Philosophical;*

especially to the English, Latin, Greek, and Hebrew . . ., London: J. Rivington *et al.*

Berry, C. J. (1974) Adam Smith's *Considerations* on Language, *Journal of the History of Ideas* 35, 130–8.

Blacklock, T. (1756) *An Essay on Universal Etymology: or, The Analysis of a Sentence. Containing an Account of the Parts of Speech, as Common to All Languages*, Edinburgh: Sands *et al.*

Blackwell, T. (1735) *An Enquiry into the Life and Writings of Homer*, London.

[Burnett, J.] (1773) *Of the Origin and Progress of Language*, vol. I, Edinburgh: A. Kincaid & W. Creech, London: T. Cadell.

Campanella, T. (1638) *Philosophiæ rationalis partes quinque. Videlicet: Grammatica, dialectica, rhetorica, poetica, historiographia, iuxta propria principia. Suorum operum tomus I*, Paris: Ioannes du Bray.

Chambers, E. (1728) *Cyclopædia: or, an Universal Dictionary of Arts and Sciences* . . ., London: J. & J. Knapton *et al.* (4th edn., 2 vols., London: D. Midwinter *et al.*, 1741.)

Charlevoix, P. F. X. de (1744) *Histoire et description générale de la Nouvelle France, avec le Journal historique d'un voyage fait par ordre du Roi dans l'Amérique Septentrionnale*, 3 vols., Paris: Didot.

Christie, J. R. R. (1987) Adam Smith's Metaphysics of Language. In A. E. Benjamin, G. N. Cantor and J. R. R. Christie (eds.) *The Figural and the Literal: Problems of Language in the History of Science and Philosophy, 1630–1800*, 202–29, Manchester: Manchester University Press.

Condillac, E. B. de (1746) *Essai sur l'origine des connoissances humaines. Ouvrage où l'on réduit à un seul principe tout ce qui concerne l'entendement humaine* . . ., Amsterdam: P. Mortier.

Coseriu, E. (1968) Adam Smith und die Anfänge der Sprachtypologie. In H. E. Brekle and L. Lipka (eds.) *Wortbildung, Syntax und Morphologie. Festschrift Hans Marchand*, 46–54, The Hague: Mouton.

Diderot, D. (1751) *Lettre sur les sourds et muets, à l'usage de ceux qui entendent & parlent. Adressée à M***, [Paris].

Du Bos, J. B. (1719) *Réflexions critiques sur la poésie et sur la peinture*, 2 vols., Paris: J. Mariette.

Du Marsais, C. C. (1751) Cas. In *Encyclopédie, ou Dictionnaire raisonné des sciences, des arts et des métiers*, par une Société de Gens de Lettres, vol. II, 734–6, Paris: Briasson *et al.*

Du Marsais, C. C. (1753) Conjugaison. In *Encyclopédie* . . ., vol. III, 879–83, Paris: Briasson *et al.*

Du Ponceau, P.-E. (1838) *Mémoire sur le système grammatical des langues de quelques nations indiennes de l'Amérique du nord* . . ., Paris: A. Pihan.

Galano, C. (1645) *Grammaticae et logicae institutiones linguae literalis armenicae Armenis traditae* . . ., Romae: Typographia S. Congreg. de Propag. fide.

Girard, G. (1747) *Les vrais principes de la langue françoise, ou La parole réduite en méthode, conformément aux loix de l'usage. En seize discours*, Paris: Le Breton (2 vols.), Amsterdam: J. Wetstein (1 vol.).

Harris, J. (1751) *Hermes: or, a Philosophical Inquiry Concerning Language and Universal Grammar*, London: H. Woodfall.

Jones, P. (1982) *Hume's Sentiments: Their Ciceronian and French Context*, Edinburgh: University Press.

Kolben, P. (1731) *The Present State of the Cape of Good-Hope: or, a Particular Account of the Several Nations of the Hottentots . . . Written Originally in High German . . .*, London: W. Innys.

Lafitau, J. F. (1724) *Mœurs des sauvages ameriquains, comparées aux mœurs des premiers temps*, 2 vols., Paris: Saugrain l'aîné.

Land, S. K. (1977) Adam Smith's 'Considerations Concerning the First Formation of Languages', *Journal of the History of Ideas* 38, 677–90.

Land, S. K. (1986) *The Philosophy of Language in Britain: Major Theories from Hobbes to Thomas Reid*, New York: AMS Press.

Locke, J. (1690) *An Essay Concerning Human Understanding. In Four Books*, London: T. Bassett.

Locke, J. (1693) *Some Thoughts Concerning Education*. Reprinted in *The Educational Writings of John Locke*, ed. by J. L. Axtell, 111–338, Cambridge: Cambridge University Press, 1968.

Manget, J., ed. (1809) *Essai sur La première formation des langues, et sur la différence du génie des langues originales et des langues composées; traduit de l'anglais d'Adam Smith. Avec des notes. Suivi du premier livre des Recherches sur la langue et la philosophie des Indiens, extrait et traduit de l'allemand de F. Schlegel*, Genève: Manget & Cherbuliez.

Maupertuis, P. L. M. de (1756) Dissertation sur les différens moyens dont les hommes se sont servis pour exprimer leurs idées. In *Mémoires de l'Académie Royale des Sciences de Berlin pour l'année 1754*. (Also in *Oeuvres de Maupertuis*, vol. III, 437–68, Lyon: Bruyset, 1756.)

Noordegraaf, J. (1977) A Few Remarks on Adam Smith's Dissertation (1761), *Historiographia Linguistica* 4, 59–67.

Plank, F. (1987a) The Smith–Schlegel Connection in Linguistic Typology: Forgotten Fact or Fiction? *Zeitschrift für Phonetik, Sprachwissenschaft und Kommunikationsforschung* 40, 198–216.

Plank, F. (1987b) What Friedrich Schlegel could have learned from Alexander ('Sanscrit') Hamilton besides Sanskrit, *Lingua e Stile* 22, 367–84.

Plank, F. (1989) Language and Earth as Recycling Machines. Paper read at the conference on 'Relations between the Sciences of Language and of the Earth', Bad Homburg, 2–5 October 1989; to appear in the proceedings, ed. by B. Naumann and F. Plank, Amsterdam: Benjamins, 1991.

Pott, A. F. (1876) *Wilhelm von Humboldt und die Sprachwissenschaft*, Berlin: Calvary.

Priestley, J. (1762) *A Course of Lectures on the Theory of Language, and Universal Grammar*, Warrington: W. Eyres. (Republished in *The Theological and Miscellaneous Works of Joseph Priestley, LL.D. F.R.S. &c.*, edited, with Notes, by J. T. Rutt, vol. XXIII, 119–252, London: G. Smallfield, 1824.)

Rae, J. (1895) *Life of Adam Smith*, London: Macmillan.

Rousseau, J. (1984) Wilhelm von Humboldt et les langues à incorporation: Genèse d'un concept (1801–1824). In S. Auroux and F. Queixalos (eds.) *Pour une histoire de la linguistique amérindienne en France*, 79–105, Paris: A.E.A. (Amerindia, numéro spécial 6).

Rousseau, J. J. (1755) *Discours sur l'origine et les fondemens de l'inégalité parmi les hommes*, Amsterdam: M. M. Rey.

Sagard, G. (1632) *Le grand voyage du pays des Hurons, situé en l'Amérique vers la mer douce, és derniers confins de la Nouvelle France, dite Canada . . . Avec un dictionaire de la langue huronne . . .*, Paris: D. Moreau.

Sanctius, F. (1587) *Minerva, seu de causis linguae Latinae*, Salmanticae: I. & A. Renaut. (5th edn., Amstelaedami: apud Janssonio-Waesbergios, 1733.)

Skinner, A. (1974) Introduction. In *Adam Smith, The Wealth of Nations, Books I–III*, 11–97, Harmondsworth: Penguin.

Smith, A. (1755) Review of *A Dictionary of the English Language*, by Samuel Johnson, *Edinburgh Review* 1. (Again in *Essays on Philosophical Subjects (and Miscellaneous Pieces)*, ed. by W. P. D. Wightman, 232–41, Oxford: Clarendon Press, 1980, Glasgow Edition III.)

Smith, A. (1755) A Letter to the Authors of the Edinburgh Review, *Edinburgh Review* 2. (Again in *Essays on Philosophical Subjects . . .*, ed. by W. P. D. Wightman, 250–4, Oxford: Clarendon Press, 1980, Glasgow Edition III.)

Smith, A. (1759) *The Theory of Moral Sentiments*, London: A. Millar, Edinburgh: A. Kincaid & J. Bell. (3rd edn., *To which is added A Dissertation on the Origin of Languages*, London & Edinburgh, 1767.) (Glasgow Edition I, ed. by D. D. Raphael and A. L. Macfie, Oxford: Clarendon Press, 1976.)

Smith, A. (1761) Considerations Concerning the First Formation of Languages, and the Different Genius of Original and Compounded Languages. In *The Philological Miscellany . . .*, vol. I, 440–79. (Republished in the 3rd and subsequent editions of *The Theory of Moral Sentiments*, 1767ff.) (Glasgow Edition IV, ed. by J. C. Bryce, 201–26. Oxford: Clarendon Press, 1983.)

Smith, A. (1762–3) *Lectures on Rhetoric and Belles Lettres*, Delivered in the University of Glasgow . . . (Glasgow Edition IV, ed. by J. C. Bryce, 1–200. Oxford: Clarendon Press, 1983.)

Smith, A. (1762–3/1766) *Lectures on Jurisprudence*. (Glasgow Edition V, ed. by R. L. Meek, D. D. Raphael and P. G. Stein, Oxford: Clarendon Press, 1978.)

Smith, A. (1776) *An Inquiry into the Nature and Causes of the Wealth of Nations*, 2 vols., London: W. Strahan & T. Cadell. (Glasgow Edition II, ed. by R. H. Campbell, A. S. Skinner and W. B. Todd. Oxford: Clarendon Press, 1976.)

Smith, A. (1795) The Principles which Lead and Direct Philosophical Enquiries; Illustrated by the History of Astronomy. In [J. Black and J. Hutton (eds.)] *Essays on Philosphical Subjects. By the late Adam Smith . . .*, 1–93, London: T. Cadell & W. Davies, Edinburgh: W. Creech. (Glasgow Edition III, ed. by W. P. D. Wightman, Oxford: Clarendon Press, 1980.)

Smith, A. (1977) *The Correspondence of Adam Smith*, ed. by E. C. Mossner and I. S. Ross, Oxford: Clarendon Press (Glasgow Edition VI).

Stewart, D. (1795) Account of the Life and Writings of Adam Smith, LL.D. In *Transactions of the Royal Society of Edinburgh*. (Also in [J. Black and J. Hutton (eds.)] *Essays on Philosophical Subjects. By the late Adam Smith . . .*, ix–xcv, London: T. Cadell & W. Davies, Edinburgh: W. Creech, 1795.)

Warburton, W. (1738–41) *The Divine Legation of Moses Demonstrated on the Principles of a Religious Deist . . .*, 2 vols., London: F. Gyles.

Webb, J. (1669) *An Historical Essay, Endeavouring a Probability that the Language of the Empire of China is the Primitive Language*, London: N. Brook. (2nd edn., with expanded title, London: O. Blagrave, 1678.)

Windross, M. (1980) Adam Smith on Language, *Linguistica Antverpiensia* 14, 277–88.

3

The aesthetics of Adam Smith

PETER JONES

In a well known passage from his *Account of the Life and Writings of Adam Smith, LL.D*, delivered to the Royal Society of Edinburgh in 1793, Dugald Stewart wrote:

> His acquaintance with the polite literature both of ancient and modern times was extensive; and amidst his various other occupations, he had never neglected to cultivate a taste for the fine arts; – less, it is probable, with a view to the peculiar enjoyments they convey, (though he was by no means without sensibility to their beauties), than on account of their connection with the general principles of the human mind; to an examination of which they afford the most pleasing of all avenues. To those who speculate on this very delicate subject, a comparison of the modes of taste that prevail among different nations, affords a valuable collection of facts; and Mr. Smith, who was always disposed to ascribe to custom and fashion their full share in regulating the opinions of mankind with respect to beauty, may naturally be supposed to have availed himself of every opportunity which a foreign country afforded him of illustrating his former theories. (EPS, p. 305)

As on all such occasions, it is important to identify something of the contexts in which Smith both formulated and subsequently expressed his views: what had he read, seen and heard, and at what stages in his thinking? What issues particularly interested him, when and why? To whose views was he particularly responding? To answer such questions, appeal must be made to his biography, his texts, and his library. Two points may be made at once. Like most of his contemporaries, Smith did not burden his published texts with acknowledgements of his sources and debts; sometimes these can only be guessed. Further, most of his remarks on the arts are incidental to some other discussion; he did not publish a comprehensive theory of aesthetics (or 'criticism' as it was typically called), and his only sustained essay, on imitation, which we shall discuss below, cannot be precisely dated although it is probably a late piece.

That Smith was widely read, even by the standards of the day, is evident from the student notes of his *Lectures on Rhetoric and Belles Lettres*, delivered first in 1748, and thereafter for several years. He had, of course, already spent some nine years of study at Glasgow and Oxford. During this period, however, we do not know what access he had to the non-verbal arts – what pictures or sculptures he had seen, or what music he had heard. After becoming Professor at Glasgow in 1751, Smith had entry not only to the University Library and collections, but also increasing opportunity to see and hear works in private ownership. He advised Foulis on what paintings and sculptures might be copied by students, or be made more generally available in the form of prints. In the city he was an active member of the Literary Society (founded in 1752), enjoyed the dining and singing at the Anderston Saturday dinners,[1] and enlarged his social acquaintance still further by travelling through to Edinburgh, where, in 1754, he took a major part in founding the Select Society. The idea for this society was mooted by the painter Allan Ramsay – who left the following year for Rome – and Smith was active from the beginning, becoming one of the managers of its sub-committee, 'The Edinburgh Society for encouraging arts, sciences, manufactures, and agriculture in Scotland'. Both Hume and Smith served on the Committee for Belles-Lettres and Criticism, and in 1755 the Society announced a prize for the 'best essay on taste'. The prize was won by Alexander Gerard, and his revised essay was published in 1759. In the meantime, however, Ramsay had already published his 'Dialogue on Taste' in 1755, and Hume brought out his own essay 'Of the Standard of Taste' in 1757.[2] Internal evidence from *The Theory of Moral Sentiments*, suggests that Smith was indeed familiar with these discussions.

At precisely the same time, Smith was involved in another Edinburgh venture. A new literary magazine, the *Edinburgh Review*, appeared in 1755 and ran for only two issues; but Smith contributed a review of Samuel Johnson's *Dictionary*, and an even more remarkable Letter, which sets out, in the course of praising the *Encyclopédie*, an agenda for learning in Scotland; he also summarises and quotes extensively from Rousseau's *Discourse on Inequality*.[3]

The principal means by which anyone in the mid eighteenth century could enlarge their knowledge of the arts was by travel. Smith's travels with the young Duke of Buccleuch between 1764 and 1766 were neither extensive nor adventurous for the times and covered less ground that Hume had done in the 1740s; after eighteen months in Toulouse, they travelled for two months in the South of France, and another two in Geneva; thereafter they spent ten months in Paris, where they frequented a number of fashionable *salons*. Smith greatly admired the French dramatists and, although the Earl of Buchan said he had no ear for music, he was very fond of opera.[4] Many of the reflections in Smith's 'Essay on the Imitative Arts' are based on French examples and texts. It should be remembered that in 1775 Smith joined the Literary Club of Johnson, Burke and Reynolds, which also boasted as members Gibbon and Garrick. Here again were sources for Smith's own reflections on aesthetic issues.

An aid to our grasp of Smith's knowledge and interests lies in the list James Bonar was able to compile of his library.[5] Bonar's identification of perhaps two-thirds of Smith's fine collection revealed that almost a third of the total were in French, and a fifth on literature and art; there are almost no books of theology or prose fiction. Smith owned most of the standard ancient and modern works which discussed what we now call aesthetics, and to judge from publication dates his books on music were perhaps acquired when writing his essay on Imitation.

It will be convenient to begin with an overview of Smith's position. Like Hume, Smith seems to have been strongly influenced by the Abbé Dubos, but he adds little to what Hume had already said about the rise and progress of the arts.[6] Poetry is the first form of discourse, although primitive music and dancing may predate it as, in some sense, pleasurable social activities; the fine arts – or 'the arts of luxury' – develop much later, on the basis of the leisure, wealth and political stability of reasonably self-sufficient communities. Three aesthetic issues particularly exercised Smith's contemporaries: the nature of beauty, of taste and of critical judgement.

He himself says very little on the first two topics and almost nothing on the third. Instead, he wrote at considerable length on kinds of effective communication, in his lectures on rhetoric, and on what he calls the 'imitative arts', that is, on the ways in which works of art represent their 'subjects' and convey their meaning to audiences. Although both Hume and Smith derive their views from Dubos, Hume stresses the ineradicable role of context in making critical judgements of art, and Smith underlines the implication of that point by stressing that our overriding concern is with the meaning of such works.[7] It is largely for this reason that he insists on the 'very high intellectual pleasure' which accompanies our sensual pleasure in the arts (EPS, p. 305). As with Hume, however, Smith grounds his views primarily on literature, and there is some discontinuity between his thoughts on what they both call the 'narrative' arts and the 'merely decorative'; his views on painting, for example, ignore the special character of the medium, and directly contradict those of his painter friends, such as Ramsay and Reynolds, or of earlier artists such as Jonathan Richardson.[8] Although he comes to recognise the unique character of music, precisely because it is not obviously representational, he fails to extend his conclusions to other media.

Smith never articulated a detailed epistemological theory, of course, although many of Hume's views seem to be presupposed in the account of sympathy, and he certainly discusses the origins and development of language at some length. Like all authors, he makes incidental remarks without further backing; for example, he subscribes to the incongruity view of laughter, thinks that the 'uneasy emotions' of tragedy give us a 'pleasing anxiety' and that we return to tragedies because we enjoy seeing new actors (LRBL, pp. 43, 88, 97).

We can now turn to the texts in greater detail. We do not know how closely Smith's 1762 Glasgow *Lectures on Rhetoric and Belles Lettres*, of which we have only students' notes, resembled the first set he gave in Edinburgh in 1748.[9] No doubt his extensive reading enabled him to enrich his examples, and some changes may have followed his work on *The Theory of Moral Sentiments*, published in 1759. A major theme of the lectures is effective communication and thus the notions of intelligibility and understanding loom large. The fundamental assumptions are that human beings use language intentionally and with specific purposes in mind, the overriding one of which is to convey their ideas and feelings to a listener. Since poetry is held to be the first form of such discourse these views underpin Smith's remarks on all the arts.

Smith characterises an ideal which, he concedes, is 'no more than common sense', although it bears little resemblance to what we 'generally hear': 'the perfection of style consists in Expressing in the most concise, proper and precise manner the thought of the author, and that in the manner which best conveys the sentiment, passion or affection with which it affects or he pretends it does affect him and which he designs to communicate to his reader' (LRBL, pp. 42, 55). Language is the clothing of thought and linguistic expressions have no intrinsic worth of their own; their beauty flows solely from the propriety of the expression to the sentiment expressed (LRBL, pp. 26, 35). He lists three criteria of a good writer: a complete knowledge of his subjects, a proper arrangement of all the parts, and a properly expressive description of his ideas (LRBL, p. 42). In Smith's judgement, Swift satisfied all these criteria although very few readers understand his real worth, because most have been seduced by his precision into thinking that they themselves could have formulated and expressed similar ideas with equal felicity (LRBL, p. 41).

In order to clarify differences between narrative, didactic and rhetorical discourse, Smith separates two sorts of fact, external and internal, and two modes of describing them, directly and indirectly. Internal facts are what passes in the mind, and the indirect method of describing any fact involves describing its effects on an observer, rather than its constituent parts (LRBL, pp. 62, 67). He points out that although Pliny, Balzac and the Earl of Buckingham all verbally described their villas, no commentators agree upon the plan and arrangements of them; indeed, 'any one who sees Buckingham house will find it very different from the idea he had formed from the description' (LRBL, p. 74). No verbal account will suffice in the absence of drawn plans or illustrations – this was a standard point which Dubos, among others, had made about Vitruvius. 'We form a much better idea of these works from the effects they have on the beholder than by any description of their several parts' (*ib.*). Thus 'we form a more distinct notion of the size and proportions' of St. Peter's from Addison's account of its effects, than if he had 'given us the most exact dimensions without a plan' (*ib.*). Smith is in fact talking about effective ways of conveying different kinds of information, although he fails to mention that specialists can learn to give and interpret information inaccessible to the uninitiated. To convey how we feel, particularity is needed, although in cases of the deepest grief no words are adequate; in such cases, the best method is barely to relate the circumstances of those concerned and their state of mind before the tragedy occurred (LRBL, pp. 87, 94). Smith quotes a favourite classical example, namely, the painting of the Sacrifice of Iphigenia, in which the face of the grieving Agememnon is veiled. He frequently comments on the clarifying force of gesture, and he admires opera partly because one can experience the maximum combination of clues to meaning, particularly expressive meaning.

Smith accepts the ancient view that facts to be narrated must be interesting and important. These must be the actions of men such as have contributed to great revolutions and changes in States and Governments; it is only for the human species that we can feel sympathy, that is, 'feel for them in some respect as if we ourselves were in the same condition'. What chiefly interests us are 'Design and Contrivance' and not 'the changes or accidents that have happened to inanimate or irrational beings' (LRBL, p. 90). The fundamental difference between history, the main purpose of which is instruction, and an epic or romance, whose primary purpose is to entertain, lies in the fictionality of the story. For the purposes of instruction, 'the facts must be real, otherwise they will not assist us in our future conduct, by pointing out the means to avoid or produce any event. Feigned events . . . can not . . . assist us in a plan of future conduct' (LRBL, p. 91). There is no evidence that Smith modified this extreme view, although to some extent it mirrors the muddle that his contemporaries (such as Hume) felt over imaginative but testable scientific hypotheses, on the one hand, and mere metaphysical fictions on the other. Smith acknowledged that 'even the vague hypotheses of Des Cartes . . . contributed to give some coherence to the appearances of nature' (EPS, p. 43 – 'The History of Astronomy'). It may not be irrelevant that his extensive library contained almost no works of fiction – he seems to suggest, with irritation, that we typically count the pages in a novel 'to get to the event' that is supposed to concern us (LRBL, p. 97). His apparent rejection of fiction, however, requires us to look at his remarks on historical narrative.

Following Cicero, Smith notes that our interest in causes is typically proportionate to the dramatic impact of the events. We are more interested in the causes of thunder than of gravity (LRBL, p. 93), and we take little notice of internal events in spite of the fact that the progress of our passions and ideas are the most interesting causes to relate. Such causes, he says in echo of Hume.[10] do not affect the event but do influence the minds of the chief actors 'so as to alter their conduct from what it would otherwise have been' (LRBL, p. 93). Smith's apparent inconsistency here is resolvable by reference to his distinction between internal and external causes; the latter alone are said to 'directly' produce the event. We should notice that Smith links very closely the indirect method of description, which is concerned with the effects of events on people's minds, and the internal causes of events, which are the mental processes of the participants (see LRBL, p. 96). Smith holds that, among historians at least, non-participants typically speculate on the mental processes behind someone else's actions; the actors themselves rarely do so. Only later does Smith explore the sceptical issues here which his friend Hume frequently discussed throughout his *History*.[11] Hume's point was that spectators typically over-emphasise the roles and efficacy of rational thought and reflection, whereas in fact human beings are motivated primarily by their passions and habits. The search for intelligibility, which is itself an act of the understanding, inclines us to project on to events the influence of the understanding. Later, Smith argues that no strict proof can be provided of the causes of human actions, so fluctuating are men's characters, so complex the circumstances in which they act (LRBL, p. 171). One problem facing the historian is that many events 'would appear altogether unintelligible unless those which produced them were also understood' (LRBL, p. 98). There are at least two related difficulties: 'the distinctness of events and the connection of causes with events' (LRBL, p. 99). Historians must decide how to link the events they select for narration. Livy, for example, blatantly ignores causal connections and resorts to 'the poetical method' of association; Tacitus simply leaves gaps, which 'makes us uneasy for what should have happened'. But the historian who is to remain impartial in 'narrating facts as they are' cannot legitimately resort to rhetorical or didactic devices (LRBL, p. 101). Smith is alert to the fact that fashions in history have changed. 'There are now several sects in Religion and political disputes which are greatly dependent on the truth of certain facts' and this explains why 'historical truths are now in much greater request than they ever were in the ancient times' (LRBL, p. 102). Smith asserts that the 'dissertations which are everywhere inter-woven into Modern histories' make them much less interesting than ancient works; moreover, the ubiquitous demand for evidence immediately implies that the matter is dubious (*ib.*). Smith holds the surprising view that, in general, the drawbacks outweigh the advantages of raising such doubts in historical narratives.

Having adopted the classical view that 'the poets were the first historians', because the first writing is always concerned with the marvellous (LRBL, p. 104), Smith turns more directly to the nature of poetry. It is precisely because the purpose of poetry is to amuse, that poetical licence is allowed to writers; their manner 'plainly' shows 'that it is not their design to be believed' (LRBL, p. 118). All story-tellers need to improve their tale, and the overriding principle is Unity of Interest. This means that 'every part of the Story should tend to some one end' (LRBL, p. 120). Arguments given in support of unity of time are largely specious, since they appeal to deception (LRBL, p. 121). But Smith agrees with most of his contemporaries, particularly among the French, that 'in reality we are never thus deceived. We know that we are in the play-house, that the persons before us are actors, and that the thing represented either happened before or perhaps never happened at all. The pleasure we have in a dramatical performance no more arises from deception than that which we have in looking at a Picture' (LRBL, p. 122). Rather, when the unity of time is ignored, we feel uneasiness 'in being kept in the dark' about what happened (*ib.*). There is every reason to think that Smith would have agreed with an additional point made by Dubos in this context, that painters and poets affect us only in so far as we desire it ourselves.

In contrast to poems, paintings, as Dubos and Jonathan Richardson insisted, can only represent a situation at one moment of time (LRBL, p. 123). And since, as Poussin said, we like tranquil works best because we can enter into their spirit more easily, 'we are more pleased with those that represent a state not far different from that we are generally in when we view the Picture' – in the Raphael Cartoons, for example, Peter receiving the keys rather than Paul preaching at Athens (LRBL, p. 126 – the examples are lifted from Dubos). The point, which Smith later expands in his reflections on music (see EPS, pp. 197–8), is that the representation of violent movement induces some analogous state of mind in the spectator or listener; contemplation is thus precluded by definition, even in the non-performing arts, because of the excessive motion of the mind. The modern view that television presentation cannot engage in reflective analysis itself, and inhibits it in the viewer, is a distant relative of Smith's remark.

Smith held standard views on the development of poetry and prose in primitive societies. The most barbarous nations, 'after the labours of the day are over', enjoy dancing and music, and 'poetry is a necessary attendant on music'. Opulence and commerce are necessary, but not sufficient, conditions of improvement in the arts (LRBL, p. 137). His point is that rich city-dwellers who have no need to work, 'have nothing to do, but employ themselves in what most suits their taste, and seek out pleasure in all its shapes'. Under such conditions, prose is self-consciously refined and cultivated as the language of business, and its merits come to be appreciated beside longer established poetry.

Most of the remarks on aesthetic issues in *The Theory of Moral Sentiments* derive from Hume, although Smith seeks to augment them. He agrees that 'utility is one of the principal sources of beauty', but argues that it is usually a derivative or subordinate source, rather than a fundamental one. Moreover, in the field of morality, as elsewhere, the aesthetic dimension can be accorded illicit priority. Owners of property, for example, frequently value the 'fitness' of their possessions over the ends they serve; thus a watchmaker may dispense with a watch that loses two minutes a day although he himself has no interest in the time of day (TMS IV. i. 5). Smith observes that we are typically 'charmed with the beauty' of the arrangements and economy of great palaces which secures the ease of their owners, but 'if we consider the real satisfaction which all these things are capable of affording, by itself and separated from the beauty of that arrangement which is fitted to promote it, it will always appear in the highest degree contemptible and trifling. But we rarely view it in this abstract and philosophical light' (TMS IV. i. 9). Smith reiterates the human failing: 'From a certain spirit of system . . . from a certain love of art and contrivance, we sometimes seem to value the means more than the end' (TMS IV. i. 11). Our approval of virtue, although enhanced by perception of the beauty resulting from its utility, is originally grounded in a sense of its propriety or rightness; that is why our approbation of virtue is not a sentiment 'of the same kind' as that with which we 'approve of a convenient and well-contrived building' (TMS I. i. 4. 4; IV. ii. 4).

A topic that much exercised Smith's Edinburgh friends in the 1750s was that of taste. Allan Ramsay and Hume, Alexander Gerard and others, all wrote at length on the issue, usually citing the extensive French discussions over the previous century. Since Smith uses the very same examples – as his friend Reynolds was to do later – it must be presumed that he was familiar with these discussions. Smith argues that two related principles, fashion and custom, 'extend their dominion over our judgments concerning beauty of every kind'; 'Dress and furniture are allowed by all the world to be entirely under the dominion of custom and fashion. The influence of those principles, however, is by no means confined to so narrow a sphere, but extends itself to whatever is in any respect the object of taste, to music, to poetry, to architecture' (TMS V. i. 3–4). Smith, inadvertently perhaps, links this observation with two concepts that came to play a considerable role in later theories of the arts, style and tradition:

> A well-contrived building may endure many centuries: a beautiful air may be delivered down by a sort of tradition, through many successive generations: a well-written poem may last as long as the world; and all of them continue for ages together, to give the vogue to that particular style, to that particular taste or manner, according to which each of them was composed. (TMS V. i. 4)

Few men, Smith asserts, have the 'opportunity' or 'experience and acquaintance with the different modes which have obtained in remote ages and nations' . . . 'to judge with impartiality between them'; accordingly, few men allow that 'custom or fashion have much influence upon their judgments concerning what is beautiful, or otherwise, in the productions of any of those arts; but imagine, that all the rules, which they think ought to be observed in each of them, are founded upon reason and nature, not upon habit or prejudice' (*ib.*). Smith then uses Ramsay's own example of the fashions for the five orders of pillars and associated decorations. Smith, like Hume, holds that a presumption always lies in favour of what custom has established; in architecture, change merely for the sake of change 'is absurd' (TMS V. i. 5). And he adopts a Humean story of habit:

> When two objects have frequently been seen together, the imagination acquires a habit of passing easily from the one to the other. If the first appear, we lay our account that the second is to follow. Of their own accord they put us in mind of one another, and the attention glides easily along them. Though, independent of custom, there should be no real beauty in their union, yet when custom has thus connected them together, we feel an impropriety in their separation. (TMS V. i. 2)

Smith recognises that 'an eminent artist will bring about a considerable change in the established modes' and introduce 'a new fashion of writing, music, or architecture', but he does not expand upon how this happens (TMS V. i. 7). He insists, nevertheless, that however dominant a fashion becomes, it is entirely contingent which styles become accepted as fitting and appropriate. Of the architectural orders, for example, he remarks: 'It seems . . . a little difficult to be conceived that these forms, though, no doubt, extremely agreeable, should be the only forms which can suit those proportions, or that there should not be five hundred others which, antecedent to established custom, would have fitted them equally well' (TMS V. i. 5).

He holds that custom and fashion also influence our judgements about the beauty of natural objects: 'every class of things has its own peculiar conformation, which is approved of, and has a beauty of its own, distinct from that of every other species' (TMS V. i. 8). He agrees with Buffier that perhaps the beauty of every object 'consists in that form and colour, which is most usual among things of that particular sort to which it belongs'.[12] Smith then outlines a view which is clearly the source of Dugald Stewart's own account of universals half a century later, and foreshadows Wittgenstein's notion of family resemblances:

> When a number of drawings are made after one pattern, though they may all miss it in some respects, yet they will all resemble it more than they resemble one another; the general character of the pattern will run through them all. . . . In the same manner, in each species of creatures, what is most beautiful bears the strongest characters of the general fabric

of the species, and has the strongest resemblance to the greater part of the individuals with which it is classed. (TMS V. i. 8) For Buffier, 'the most customary form, therefore, is in each species of things' the most beautiful. Thus 'a certain practice and experience in contemplating each species of objects is requisite, before we can judge of its beauty, or know wherein the middle and most usual form consists. The nicest judgment concerning the beauty of the human species, will not help us to judge of that of flowers, or horses, or any other species of things' (*ib.*). Smith is insistent that 'in different climates, and where different customs and ways of living take place, as the generality of any species receives a different conformation from those circumstances, so different ideas of its beauty prevail' (*ib.*). Smith cannot agree, however, that 'our sense even of external beauty is founded altogether on custom'; 'the utility of any form, its fitness for the useful purposes for which it was intended, evidently recommends it, and renders it agreeable to us, independent of custom' (TMS V. i. 9). In his later essay, it should be noted, he closely follows remarks of Hume in stating that there is an 'intrinsic beauty' in a man or a horse, independent of any resemblance or, presumably, utility (EPS, p. 177).

An earlier remark in Smith's discussion should be noted. He suggests that whereas the rules of justice may be compared to those of grammar, the rules of the other virtues may be compared to 'the rules which critics lay down for the attainment of what is sublime and elegant in composition'. These 'are loose, vague, and indeterminate, and present us rather with a general idea of the perfection we ought to aim at, than afford us any certain and infallible directions for acquiring it' (TMS III. vi. 11). He reiterates these comparisons later, when objecting to casuists who 'direct by precise rules what it belongs to feeling and sentiment only to judge' (TMS VII. iv. 33; cf. VII. iv. 2). Such remarks, like those in the opening sections, where Smith commends 'the acute and delicate discernment of the man of taste, who distinguishes the minute, and scarce perceptible differences of beauty and deformity' (TMS I. i. 4.3), are clear echoes of the contemporary debates about taste.

The few observations on aesthetic matters in the *Wealth of Nations* need not detain us, although we might note his contrast between the low rewards of poets and 'fine' artists, notwithstanding the knowledge and experience required for excellence, and the 'exorbitant rewards' of actors, singers and dancers whose work, as 'unproductive labourers' 'perishes in the instant of its production' (WN I. x. b. 25; c. 23; II. iii. 2). He is careful to add that such performers do have value, namely pleasure of a high intellectual kind.

Smith's essay 'Of the Nature of that Imitation which takes place in what are called the Imitative Arts' cannot be precisely dated. It may have originated from his sojourn in France, but it is known that he was working on it in the 1780s. Like almost all of his contemporaries, Smith used 'imitation' broadly, to cover any kind of what we might call 'representation', whether natural or symbolic. He explicitly linked the notions of imitation, representation, resemblance, correspondence, and expression, sometimes using them interchangeably; such apparently casual oscillation between one notion and another generates needless muddles as the discussion proceeds. Fundamentally he is interested in how meaning, both expressive and cognitive, is conveyed and recognised in the different mediums of the various arts: 'to make a thing of one kind resemble another thing of a very different kind, is the very circumstance which, in all the Imitative Arts, constitutes the merits of imitation' (EPS, p. 191).

Following Hume, Smith observes that in contrast to identity, resemblance is always and only in certain respects, and that in aesthetic contexts the criteria of relevant resemblances vary. As decorative features of a room, for example, only the niches, pedestals or picture frames may or need share broad resemblances (EPS, pp. 177–8). By contrast, 'each picture, in order to be seen distinctly, and understood thoroughly, must be viewed from a particular station, and examined by itself as a separate and unconnected object'. Smith holds that in painting a two-dimensional surface 'of one kind, is made to resemble . . . all the three dimensions of a solid substance', and that 'the pleasure arising from the imitation seems to be greater in proportion as' the 'disparity between the imitating and object imitated' . . . 'is great' (EPS, pp. 179–80). That is why painted statuary fails to please, and the deceptive appearance of artificial fruits and flowers soon bores us. 'The works of the great masters in Statuary and Painting . . . never produce their effect by deception' (EPS, p. 184). Disparity must also be linked with medium: 'in appreciating a piece of Tapestry or Needle-work, we never compare the imitation of either with that of a good picture. . . . We take into consideration, not only the disparity between the imitating and the imitated object, but the awkwardness of the instruments of imitation' (EPS, p. 182). Moreover, in the case of tapestry, the great expense, which restricts it to the purse of the very rich and their palaces, enhances its magnificence for many and compensates 'the imperfection of its imitation' (EPS, p. 182). Smith, like Hume before him and Veblen afterwards, is not surprised that awe and admiration attend the rich and rare (cf. WN I. xi. c. 31), and he even uses an example from Hume; if we once suspect that someone is wearing false jewels, both the ornament and its wearer are diminished in our judgement (EPS, p. 183). But Smith did not think that 'the arts which address themselves . . . to the rich and the great' (EPS, p. 183) necessarily lacked merit in themselves; only that spectators seduced by the grandeur of the context cannot properly appreciate them. He observes that because topiary is no longer the preserve of the rich, and anyone can shape his trees and shrubs as he wishes, snobbery prevents people discerning that the results 'are not without some degree of beauty; . . . they give the air of neatness and correct culture . . . to the whole garden' (EPS, p. 184). Smith held, as Dugald Stewart noted (EPS, p. 305), that some of our pleasure in the imitative arts derived from the skills exercised in the medium, but admiration for difficulty surmounted did not extend to the content of works; meaning should always be clear, however recalcitrant the medium in which it is expressed might be.

Like some of his French sources, Hume had argued for transparency of meaning in works of art, and communication in general. In line with such a view, Smith holds that even unskilled spectators derive pleasure from, and achieve modest understanding of, at least the best works; he omits to acknowledge the necessary assumption that everyone has to learn their repertoire of responses in a familiar tradition and culture, although his observations on different cultures entitle him to the admission.

> The nobler works of Statuary and Painting . . . carry, as it were, their own explication along with them, and demonstrate, even to the eye, the way and manner in which they are produced. The eye, even of an unskilful spectator, immediately discerns, in some measure, how it is that a certain modification of figure in Statuary, and of brighter and darker colours in Painting, can represent, with so much truth and vivacity, the actions, passions, and behaviour of men, as well as a great

variety of other objects. The pleasing wonder of ignorance is
accompanied with the still more pleasing satisfaction of
science. (EPS, p. 185)

The notion that understanding enhances our pleasure was a
central tenet of Jonathan Richardson's influential writings, and
had recently been emphasised by Ramsay and Gerard. It is more
likely, however, that Smith was following Dubos, who had urged
that painters ought to choose subjects that are easy to understand.
It is surely the case, however, that an uninformed spectator is more
likely to discern *that* something has been done in a representational
painting, rather than *how* it has been done. Smith contrasts our
responses to a looking-mirror and to a painting. The former 'does
not at all demonstrate to the eye how this effect is brought about';
whereas, 'every good statue and picture ... carries, in some
measure, its own explication along with it' (EPS, p. 185). Such a
claim gains plausibility only if it is taken to mean that works are
deemed to be successful in part because they eventually yield up
their character, meaning and value to careful and informed scrutiny. In his earlier lectures on rhetoric, however, Smith had
suggested that 'the fine arts, matters of taste and imagination, ...
require little labour' on the part of the spectator (LRBL, p. 57).
And in the same chapter, when commending as good style 'conversation and behaviour [in which] all seems natural and easy'
(LRBL, p. 55) the onus is placed exclusively on the speaker or
artist to engage, inform, entertain and persuade the audience,
rather than on a spectator who must himself contribute positively
to the transaction; the latter judges whether perspicuity has been
achieved, but carries no special responsibility of effort or attention.
Elsewhere, on the other hand, Smith follows his friend Hume in
underlining the importance of any spectator correctly identifying
the original context and intention of the speaker, and comparing it
with his own context of response. For Smith, the moral worth of
actions depends on the worth of the agent's motives, whereas the
worth of art depends crucially on its effects; in both cases there is
a critical task for the spectator to perform but, as we have seen
already (TMS I. i. 4.4; IV. ii. 4), his sentiment is 'not of the same
kind' in each case.

Smith reflects on the mutual advantages of juxtaposing arts in
different media. He finds that sculpture and painting do not
enhance each other's effects; on the contrary, in a room containing

works of both mediums, and of equal merit, 'the statues draw off our eye from the pictures'. The reason is that a statue may be approached from a variety of viewpoints, from each of which it 'presents a different object' (EPS, p. 186); the richness of the resulting experiences contrasts with that deriving from the usually limited viewpoints of paintings. Smith in fact conflates two issues, namely, the overall harmony of different works in a setting (EPS, p. 177), where the judgement focuses on the whole effect, and the influence of one work on another when each is considered singly. Smith knew well that his French contemporaries, under the considerable influence of Claude Perrault's commentary on Vitruvius (which Smith owned), placed some weight on the achievement of *distribution*, that is, the overall harmony of spaces and their contents, and the balance of diverse fixed and moveable furnishings in an architectural setting – paintings, sculpture, furniture, fabrics, doors, mantles, ceilings, wall coverings, etc. It might be noted that Smith himself had seen almost none of the antique sculptures he claimed to admire (EPS, p. 179), because they were in places he had not visited; he would have known of them only by report, in respected commentators such as Dubos, or by small engravings and reduced copies.

Part II of the essay deals with music, and notwithstanding his *a priori* anthropological speculations we find there, in many ways, the most interesting of Smith's aesthetic ideas. He begins by repeating his view that music and dancing seem to be the most natural pleasures, found even among the 'savage nations'. Our first ancestors, Smith supposes, would gradually have replaced something like sol-faing with words 'which expressed some sense or meaning', although to fill the measures of their songs they might readily resort to unmeaning sounds (EPS, p. 188). As always, Smith's principal concern is with 'sense and meaning' and with what 'could be clearly and distinctly understood' (EPS, p. 188); the assumption behind his claims is that anyone dancing or singing, say, is engaged in intended and meaningful social acts. He holds that a pantomime dance might 'serve to give a distinct sense and meaning to Music many ages before the invention, or at least before the common use of Poetry' (EPS, p. 189). Here he contrasts the capacities of poetry and dance. Poetry can distinctly express what dance either cannot or can only obscurely represent (he uses the terms interchangeably), 'such as the reasonings and judgments of the understanding; the ideas, fancies, and suspicions of the imagination; the sentiments, emotions and passions of the heart. In the power of expressing a meaning with clearness and distinctness, Dancing is superior to Music, and Poetry to Dancing' (*ib.*).[13] Unlike vocal music, which naturally 'calls for the support of Poetry' (EPS, p. 190), 'Instrumental Music' can 'subsist apart', not least because its tone and movements can be 'so managed as to seem to resemble' those of conversation and passion; indeed, neither prose nor poetry can 'venture to imitate those almost endless repetitions of passion' which are familiar to us all and which music alone can capture (EPS, p. 191). Rather strangely, to our ears, but echoing Avison, Smith asserts that music can best imitate those sentiments and passions 'which unite and bind men together in society; the social, the decent, the virtuous, the awful and respectable'; the unsocial, indecent or vicious passions cannot easily be imitated by music (EPS, p. 192).

In direct contradiction to the views of his friend Sir Joshua Reynolds, and of French writers with whose works he was familiar, Smith assigns no aesthetic functions to the medium of paint or stone, nor to the varying textures and combinations they can exhibit. He holds that statuary and painting 'cannot be said to add any new beauties of their own to the beauties of Nature which they imitate', whereas music 'clothes them . . . with a new and an exquisite beauty of its own; it clothes them with melody and harmony, which, like a transparent mantle, far from concealing any beauty, serve only to give a brighter colour, a more enlivening lustre, and a more engaging grace to every beauty which they infold' (EPS, pp. 193–4).

Smith holds that music is capable of three sorts of imitation: a general one, in which it resembles discourse; a particular one, in which it expresses the sentiments and feelings with which a particular situation inspires a particular person; and a third, when 'the person who sings may join to this double imitation of the singer the additional imitation of the actor' (EPS, p. 194). But he acknowledges a problem, since the 'unmeaning' sounds of instrumental music cannot 'express clearly and so as to be understood by every hearer' (EPS, p. 195). Instrumental music does not, as has been claimed, 'imitate motion': 'it only either imitates the particular sounds which accompany certain motions, or it produces sounds of which the time and measure bear some correspondence to the variations, to the pauses and interruptions, to the successive accelerations and retardations of the motion which it means to imitate' (EPS, p. 196). But 'without the accompaniment of some other art, to explain and interpret its meaning, it would be almost always unintelligible' (*ib.*). James Beattie, like Kames before him, had argued that music should not be treated as an imitative art, and that expression was the essential notion to stress. And Smith himself certainly moves towards a distinction between the transitive and intransitive sense of expression; that is, between the view that music elicits response because it expresses emotion and implants that emotion, albeit in a reduced and possibly transformed state, in the listener, and the view that the expressive character of music is in the music.

Smith insists that imitation sufficient only 'to suggest' the imitated object is required, but like most of his contemporaries he fails to grasp the conventions attaching to representation and its interpretation: 'It would be a strange picture which required an inscription at the foot to tell us, not only what particular person it meant to represent, but whether it meant to represent a man or a horse, or whether it meant to be a picture at all, and to represent any thing' (EPS, p. 196). He adds that whereas a 'picture would not be much mended by' an inscription, a work of instrumental music might be enabled to 'produce all the effects of the finest and most perfect imitation' (*ib.*).

Smith adopts a view common to his time, that certain sounds and rhythms are naturally expressive: 'acute sounds are naturally gay, sprightly, and enlivening; grave sounds solemn, awful, and melancholy. There seems to be some natural connection between acuteness in tune and quickness in time of succession, as well as between gravity and slowness' (EPS, p. 197). He holds that music, provided the listener's mind 'is so far vacant as not to be disturbed by any disorderly passion . . . can . . . produce every possible modification of each of those moods or dispositions' (*ib.*). The pleasure derivable from instrumental music seems to depend on its expressive character, that is, imitation in the second sense of particularity mentioned by Smith above:

> In a concert of instrumental Music the attention is engaged, with pleasure and delight, to listen to a combination of the most agreeable and melodious sounds. . . . The mind being thus successively occupied by a train of objects, of which the

nature, succession, and connection correspond, sometimes to
the gay, sometimes to the tranquil, and sometimes to the
melancholy mood or disposition, is itself successively led into
each of those moods or dispositions; and is thus brought into
a sort of harmony or concord with the Music which so
agreeably engages its attention.' (EPS, pp. 197–8)

Music expresses, by resemblance, and arouses, by association; it
implants its moods by virtue of our mental capacity to attend to
the sequence and character of its sounds. 'Music can, by a sort of
incantation, sooth and charm us into some degree of that particular
mood or disposition which accords with its own character and
temper' (EPS, p. 197). Smith seems here to have adopted the
notion of an analogue proposed by P. G. de Chabanon, whose work
he owned. Smith is keen to separate these effects of instrumental
music from 'imitation proper', since it is neither by means of a story
nor by means of sympathy (as Sir William Jones held) that it
succeeds. Rather, music

becomes itself a gay, a sedate, or a melancholy object; and the
mind naturally assumes the mood or disposition which at the
time corresponds to the object which engages its attention.
Whatever we feel from instrumental Music is an original, and
not a sympathetic feeling: it is our own gaiety, sedateness, or
melancholy; not the reflected disposition of another person.
(EPS, p. 198)

Instrumental music, like gardens, 'though it can excite all those
different dispositions, cannot imitate any of them' (EPS, p. 198).
On these matters Smith is close to Rousseau, whom he quotes
explicitly, although he insists that any particular representation
requires the additional assistance of scenery or poetry – then,
indeed, music can dispose 'the mind to the same sort of mood and
temper which it would feel from the presence of that object, or from
sympathy with the person who was placed in that situation' (EPS,
p. 200): success, however, 'is an art which requires all the judgment, knowledge, and invention of the most consummate master'
(EPS, p. 201).

Smith holds that our pleasure in opera is of a more 'sensual'
nature than that in 'common comedy or tragedy'; because 'the
latter produce their effect principally by means of the imagination',
their effect in the closet 'is not much inferior to what it is upon the
stage' (EPS, p. 202). Although Smith enthusiastically defends

opera, he mentions only French works by Lully, Marais and Destouches (because he is following Dubos at this point?), along with Handel and Pergolese. Smith expands on the notion of understanding:

> Time and measure are to instrumental Music what order and method are to discourse. . . . without this order and method we could remember very little of what had gone before, and we could foresee still less of what was to come after; and the whole enjoyment of Music would be equal to little more than the effect of the particular sounds which rung in our ears at every particular instant. (EPS, p. 204)[14]

Smith emphasises the role of intellect in our attention to music, and the pleasures we derive from it; to discern what is happening, as Gerard had insisted, we must develop the capacities both to remember and compare. The best instrumental music, for example, 'can occupy, and as it were fill up, completely the whole capacity of the mind, so as to leave no part of its attention vacant for thinking of any thing else'; 'the mind in reality enjoys not only a very great sensual, but a very high intellectual pleasure, not unlike that which it derives from the contemplation of a great system in any other science' (EPS, p. 205).

Smith next amplifies his points about the different roles of the intellect in music. He insists that: 'music seldom means to tell any particular story, or to imitate any particular event, or in general to suggest any particular object, distinct from that combination of sounds of which itself is composed. Its meaning, therefore, may be said to be complete in itself, and to require no interpreters to explain it' (EPS, p. 205). It is essential to contrast the notions of 'subject' and 'expression' in music and in painting. In instrumental music the subject 'is a part of the composition'; in a poem or a picture it is 'always something which is not either in the poem or in the picture, or something quite distinct from that combination, either of words on the one hand, or of colours on the other, of which they are respectively composed' (EPS, p. 205). The 'expression' of instrumental music is its effect 'upon the mind'; but

> the effect of the expression of Painting arises always from the thought of something which, though distinctly and clearly suggested by the drawing and colouring of the picture, is altogether different from that drawing and colouring. . . . The melody and harmony of instrumental Music, on the contrary,

do not distinctly and clearly suggest any thing that is different
from that melody and harmony. (*Ib.*)

Musical melody and harmony 'in fact signify and suggest nothing'
(EPS, p. 206). Smith is here following Charles Avison's important
essay of 1752 which he owned, although he upbraids the Newcastle
organist for conflating contingent and logical points.[15] For whereas
'expression in painting is not the necessary effect either of good
drawing or of good colouring, or of both together', 'that effect upon
the mind which is called expression in Music, is the immediate and
necessary effect of good melody' (EPS, p. 206). Smith concludes by
saying that 'imitation is by no means essential to' instrumental
music, 'and the principal effects which it is capable of producing
arises from powers altogether different from those of imitation'
(EPS, p. 207).

The final, and presumably incomplete, section of the essay
addresses 'the imitative powers of Dancing', which are said to be
'at least equal, perhaps superior, to those of any other art',
although 'it can produce very agreeable effects, without imitating
any thing' (EPS, p. 207). 'The allegorical meaning which it
originally intended to express' is rarely if ever thought of by those
who nowadays dance the minuet. 'All the subjects' of statuary and
historical painting 'are within the compass' of the dancer's 'imitative powers', because dancing 'is not confined to the situation of a
single instant; but, like Epic Poetry, it can represent all the events
of a long story, and exhibit a long train and succession of connected
and interesting situations' (EPS, p. 208). In modern times the
effects reportedly achieved by the Roman pantomime dances, for
example, have been lost. Another difference characterises modern
music. Our ancestors seem to have danced to vocal, rather than
purely instrumental music, and since vocal music is 'essentially
imitative, their dances became so too' (*ib.*). When country dances
are accompanied by singers, in his own day, Smith notes that the
best dancers 'become more or less pantomimes, and by their
gestures and motions express, as well as they can, the meaning and
story of the song' (EPS, p. 209).

In an independent passage annexed to the Essay, Smith claims
that we distinguish between dancing and other movements by
assuming the intentions to dance of anyone who moves in the
manner observed; he does not add that such inferences are legitimised by reference to the practices of a given culture (EPS, p. 210).

Similar considerations explain our capacity to distinguish singing from talking, or other activities (EPS, p. 212). 'We expect and require' that responsible people 'in every . . . ordinary action' 'should attend only to the proper purpose of the action' (EPS, p. 212). This strong condition of effective and intelligible communication, as well as of responsible citizenship, is nevertheless a capacity that has to be learned in any community; agents and spectators alike will vary in the skill with which they exercise such capacities.

Smith observes that musical treatises understandably devote their attention almost exclusively to the notion of 'tune' rather than 'time', because of the subtleties and difficulty of the subject. He himself thinks it unlikely that 'the first rude efforts of uncivilized nations towards singing' could have been accompanied by attention to 'the niceties of tune'; so he doubts the great antiquity of those national songs which allegedly 'have been delivered down from age to age by a sort of oral tradition, without having been ever noted, or distinctly recorded for many successive generations' (EPS, p. 212). The Ossian episode did not help the cause of understanding oral traditions, and Smith observes that since, in his own lifetime, 'the method of singing what we reckon our old Scotch songs, has undergone great alterations', 'it may have undergone still greater before'.

In conclusion it should be mentioned that Smith's remarks on the arts had little if any influence on later writers. His emphasis on the intellectual aspects of our responses, as distinct from the sensual, is important but one-sided, and the anchorage of his views in literature had inevitable consequences for his often disappointing remarks on the non-verbal arts. He agreed, of course, that we derive great pleasure from the arts, but he failed to build on his ideas about the distinctive expressive character of music.

Notes

1. Rae (1895), p. 98.
2. (Allan Ramsay, Yr.), 'A Dialogue on Taste', *The Investigator*, CCCXXII, 1755; David Hume, 'Of the Standard of Taste', *Four Dissertations*, 1757; Alexander Gerard, *An Essay on Taste*, 1759.
3. Smith's review and letter are in EPS, pp. 232–56.
4. *The Bee*, June 1791, iii.
5. Bonar (1932). Among the classical authors who wrote on aesthetics, Smith owned works by Plato, Aristotle, Horace, Cicero, Longinus, Pliny and Plutarch; he had Quintilian's *Declamationes*, but not the *Institutio*. Of his near contemporaries, he owned works by Shaftesbury,

Hutcheson, James Harris and Hume; Ramsay's essay, Kames
(edition of 1762), Burke (1782), and Reynolds's *Discourses* (1778);
Blair's *Rhetoric* (1783), and Campbell's *Rhetoric* (1776). Of greater
significance, in the light of the French sources of his ideas, he owned
some works by Batteaux (1764 edition), Boileau (1729) and
Bouhours (1693); also Crousaz's *Traité du Beau*, some of de Piles,
Félibien, d'Alembert, Diderot, Rousseau, Perrault (his Vitruvius),
and of course the immensely influential *Réflexions* by Dubos, in the
1755 edition. He had English translations of Alberti on sculpture
and Italian editions of Bellori (1672), Palladio (1570), Vasari (1674)
and Vitruvius (1759). To judge from their dates of publication,
many of his books on music must have been acquired whilst he was
preparing his essay on imitation. Alongside Alexander Malcolm
(1721), Rameau (1737), Avison (1752) and John Brown (1763), we
find Burney (1789), Chabanon (1779), Chastellux (1765), Lacépède
(1785), John Maxwell (1781) and Thomas Robertson (1781).

6. For a detailed study of Hume's aesthetic views, together with an
   account of their sources, especially his fundamental debt to the Abbé
   J-B. Dubos, see Jones (1982).
7. For further comment, see Jones (1989).
8. See especially Jonathan Richardson, *An Essay on the Theory of Painting*,
   London, 1715; and *Two Discourses*, London, 1719.
9. It must be remembered that the students' notes (there are at least
   two distinct hands), however accurate, were not seen by Smith;
   quotations from them cannot be assumed to be Smith's *ipsissima
   verba*. For further observations on the nature and context of the
   lectures, see the chapter in this volume by J. C. Bryce.
10. Particularly Hume's discussion of 'Of Liberty and Necessity',
    Section VIII of *An Enquiry Concerning Human Understanding*.
11. For discussion of this point see Jones (1990).
12. Claude Buffier, *Traité des premières vérités et de la source de nos jugements*.
13. Cf. John Brown, *A Dissertation on the Rise, Union, and Power, the
    Progressions, Separations, and Corruptions, of Poetry and Music*, 1763.
14. This point had been underlined by Alexander Gerard, *An Essay on
    Taste* (1759), Part I, Sect. V, and there is reason to think that Smith
    might have been following Gerard's order of discussion at this point.
15. Charles Avison, *An Essay on Musical Expression*, London, 1752.

References

Bonar, J. (1932) *A Catalogue of the Library of Adam Smith*, London.

Jones, P. (1982) *Hume's Sentiments: Their Ciceronian and French Context*,
Edinburgh.

Jones, P. (1989) *The 'Science of Man' in the Scottish Enlightenment*,
Edinburgh.

Jones, P. (1990) 'On Reading Hume's History of Liberty', in Capaldi,
N., Livingston, D. W. (eds.), *Liberty in Hume's History of England*,
Kluwer.

Rae, J. (1895) *Life of Adam Smith*, London.

4

'The History of Astronomy':
a twentieth-century view

H. CHRISTOPHER LONGUET-HIGGINS

'The Principles which Lead and Direct Philosophical Enquiries; Illustrated by the History of Astronomy' first appeared in 1795, five years after Adam Smith's death, in a substantial volume edited by his friends Joseph Black and James Hutton, entitled *Essays on Philosophical Subjects*. There were two brief companion pieces, in which the Principles are illustrated by 'The History of the Ancient Physics' and 'The History of the Ancient Logics and Metaphysics', but these will not concern us. In his scholarly introduction to the Glasgow edition of the *Essays*, W. D. Wightman remarks that 'to none of these essays would a modern scholar turn for enlightenment on the history of the sciences' (EPS, p. 5) but this judgement leaves open the question whether Smith's 'Principles' overlap significantly with modern ideas about the methods of science or the structure of scientific revolutions. Professors Raphael and Skinner, in their general introduction to the volume, claim that the subjectivity of the 'Principles' might commend them more strongly to modern philosophers of science than to Smith's contemporaries; but before coming to his own conclusions the twentieth-century scientist will want to be sure that this patron saint of the Scottish Enlightenment understood the finer points of Newtonian astronomy no less clearly than the sources of national wealth or moral insight. Amazingly, it seems that he did.

'The History of Astronomy' is an oddly structured work. There is an introduction and four Sections, but only the last – happily by far the longest – is directly concerned with astronomy. The first three Sections are entitled: (I) Of the Effect of Unexpectedness, or

of Surprise; (II) Of Wonder, or of the Effects of Novelty, and (III)
Of the Origin of Philosophy. What in heaven's name, one may ask,
do the first two of these topics have to do with astronomy or its
history? To approach this question one has to set aside conventional ideas about the scientific method and enter, in imagination,
the mind of a highly gifted and articulate youth who is struggling
to understand why he finds one set of ideas so much more attractive
than another. Many years later, in a letter to David Hume, whom
he expected to be his literary executor, Smith was to express his
own reservations about the outcome of this particular enterprise:
'Whether [The History of Astronomy] might not be published as
a fragment of an intended juvenile work, I leave entirely to your
judgement; tho I begin to suspect that there is more refinement
than solidity in some parts of it' (quoted EPS, p. 6) The Essay
opens with the startling sentence: 'Wonder, Surprise, and Admiration, are words which, though often confounded, denote, in our
language, sentiments that are indeed allied, but that are in some
respects different also, and distinct from one another' (EPS, p. 33).
We wonder 'at all the rarer phaenomena of nature', we are
surprised at the unexpected and we admire 'the beauty of a plain
or the greatness of a mountain'. The young Smith feels free to
reprove the poets for their use of these words: 'Milton, upon the
appearance of Death to Satan, says, that

> The Fiend what this might be admir'd
> Admir'd, not fear'd.

> But if this criticism be just, the proper expression
> should have been wonder'd.' (EPS, p. 33)

[As Wightman points out, Milton actually wrote 'Th'undaunted
Fiend . . .'.] 'It is the design of this essay *to consider particularly the
nature and causes of each of these sentiments*, whose influence is of far
wider extent than we should be apt upon a careless view to
imagine. I shall begin with Surprise, [my italics] (EPS, p. 34).

Section I, entitled 'Of the effect of Unexpectedness, or of
Surprise', enunciates a number of psychological claims that readers
are presumably intended to assess on the basis of their own
experience. Whereas the emotion excited by what is foreseen 'glides
gradually and easily into the heart', the unexpected may provoke
'the most violent and convulsive emotions, such as sometimes cause

immediate death'. We break bad news as gently as possible, but sudden joy may precipitate an even greater emotional shock, and more upsetting still is a succession of extremes. But repetition dulls the pain of misfortune, and custom 'deadens the vivacity of both pain and pleasure'. (Such sentiments flow more naturally from the pen of a lovesick youth than a historian and philosopher of science.)

It is not until the next Section – 'Of Wonder, or of the effects of Novelty' – that Smith permits himself any explicit reference to natural philosophy. The mind takes pleasure, he notes, in discovering resemblances between different objects. We classify plants and animals into Genera and Species, and the botanist makes even finer distinctions than the casual observer. But when something quite new and singular is presented, it is our failure to classify it, and the emotion that this excites, 'which constitute the sentiment properly called *Wonder*, and which occasion that staring, and sometimes that rolling of the eyes, that suspension of the breath, and that swelling of the heart, which we may all observe, both in ourselves and others, when wondering at some new object, and which are the natural symptoms of uncertain and undetermined thought' [Smith's italics] (EPS, p. 39). To intrude on Smith's rhetoric for a moment: wonder appears as the frustration of a person's natural desire to classify things and happenings; its nearest equivalent in a modern vocabulary is probably 'puzzlement', rather than mere 'curiosity'.

The naturalist (to continue with Smith's exposition) can only rid himself of the Wonder excited by a strange fossil by 'enlarging the precincts' of some species or creating a new species 'on purpose to receive it'. Similar problems arise when a particular happening violates an expected train of events: we experience both Surprise and Wonder. The attraction of a piece of iron by a loadstone causes us to

> gaze and hesitate, and feel a want of connection betwixt two events which follow one another in so unusual a train. But when, with Des Cartes, we imagine certain invisible effluvia to circulate round one of them,[1] and by their repeated impulses to impel the other, both to move towards it, and to follow its motion, we fill up the interval betwixt them, we join them together by a sort of bridge, and thus take off that hesitation and difficulty which the imagination felt in passing from the one to the other. (EPS, p. 42)

An over-eager historian of science might infer that Smith (or Descartes, perhaps) had anticipated the modern idea that electromagnetic interactions involve the emission of a photon by one particle and its absorption by another. But the real interest of the passage lies in Smith's implication that action at a distance is counterintuitive in a way in which proximate action is not – a problem that Newton was bold enough to ignore in formulating his Theory of Universal Gravitation. 'The imagination feels a real difficulty in passing along two events which follow one another in an uncommon order' (EPS, p. 43). A person 'transported alive to some other planet, where nature was governed by laws quite different from those which take place here . . . would soon feel the same confusion and giddiness begin to come upon him, which would at last end in the same manner, in lunacy and distraction' (EPS, p. 43).

We must not suppose, however, that what seems incoherent and disjointed to one will seem equally so to another; in the workhouses of even the commonest artisans such as dyers, brewers and distillers, 'we observe a number of appearances, which present themselves in an order that seems to us very strange and wonderful'. Likewise 'the more practised thought of a philosopher, who has spent his whole life in the study of the connecting principles of nature, will often feel an interval betwixt two objects, which, to more careless observers, seem very strictly conjoined' (EPS, pp. 44–5). It is the role of Philosophy, Smith affirms, to represent the invisible chains which bind together the disjointed elements of experience,

> to introduce order into this chaos of jarring and discordant experiences, to allay this tumult of the imagination, and to restore it, when it surveys the great revolutions of the universe, to that tone of tranquility and composure, which is both most agreeable in itself, and most suitable to its nature . . . Let us examine, therefore, all the different systems of nature, which, in these western parts of the world . . . have successively been adopted by the learned and ingenious; and, *without regarding . . . their agreement or consistency with truth and reality*, let us . . . content ourselves with enquiring how far each of them was fitted to sooth the imagination, and to render the theatre of nature a more coherent, and therefore a more magnificent

spectacle, than otherwise it would have appeared to be. [My italics] (EPS, pp. 45–6)

Section II ends with the award of credits, for such achievements, to mathematics, medicine and the fine arts, and a booby prize to chemistry, whose connecting principles

> are such as the generality of mankind know nothing about, have rarely seen, and have never been acquainted with; and which to them, therefore, are incapable of smoothing the passage of the imagination betwixt any two disjointed objects. Salts, sulphurs, and mercuries, acids, and alkalis, are principles which can smooth things to those only who live about the furnace; but whose most common operations seem, to the bulk of mankind, as disjointed as any two events which the chemists would connect together by them. (EPS, pp. 46–7)

Be patient, Adam: the Atomic Theory has yet to be formulated!

Section III – 'Of the Origin of Philosophy' – adds little either to the earlier Sections or to the much more substantial 'History of Astronomy' that follows it, and for which it looks suspiciously like a first draft. Essentially two points emerge: that civilisation replaces fear with Wonder, this being a necessary precondition for the pursuit of Philosophy; and that the Mediterranean was the home of 'the first philosophers, of whose doctrine we have any distinct account'.

Having reached this watershed in the essay, it is appropriate to ask how far Smith has succeeded in clarifying 'the Principles which lead and direct Philosophical Enquiries', in preparation for their application to the history of astronomy. One thing is clear: the Principles are not intended as a guide to astronomical research or other forms of scientific enquiry; they are offered by Smith as a contribution to the philosophy of history – particularly the history of ideas. Where Marx might identify technology as the motive force behind the development of science, Smith opts for the human imagination, spurred on by the emotions of Surprise, Wonder and Admiration. But what is quite unclear at this juncture in the Essay is how Smith imagines he can ignore, in considering the various systems invented by astronomers, all questions of 'their agreement or consistency with truth and reality'. For an astronomer to do so would be to allow his emotions to usurp the role of his reason in the pursuit of truth, and as the essay proceeds to its climax – the work of the great Sir Isaac – Smith stops short of commending Newton's achievements on aesthetic grounds alone. But an appraisal that fails for the 'Principia' may hold for the 'History of Astronomy' itself; its conception may be most naturally explained not in rational, but in emotional terms.

We know that, while a schoolboy in Glasgow, Smith had been a brilliant student of mathematics and philosophy. When he entered Balliol College, Oxford in 1740 at the age of 17, Newtonian physics and astronomy was universally regarded as the finest existing achievement of the human intellect, and Smith must have shared the general admiration in which the theory was held. He must have marvelled, as anyone might, at the awesome power of the Newtonian system in explaining the Wonders of the heavens. Smith's unerring intellectual taste left him no option but to embrace this new account of the natural order, and to acknowledge its palpable superiority to the geocentric and other cosmologies that preceded it. To put the matter quite simply, Smith must have enjoyed, at an early age, the heady experience of intellectual excitement in both mathematics and philosophy. In such an exalted condition, there are two questions that someone in his position might have asked. First: what are the qualities that make Newton's theory so much better than its predecessors? Second: what are the inner dispositions that lead us to embrace one account of the world and reject another?

In deciding to pose the second of these questions rather than the first, Smith adopts the perspective of the artist rather than the scientist, of the mathematician rather than the physicist, and of the humanist rather than the naturalist – though all such dichotomies should be viewed with the utmost caution. It is fashionable to assume, in our own century, that mathematicians judge one another's work by mainly aesthetic criteria; if this were so, it would seem entirely reasonable to examine the history of mathematics in the light of our aesthetic sensibilities. In Smith's day the modern distinctions between mathematics and physics, or between physics and astronomy, hardly existed. So now that mathematics had conquered the heavens, surely the time was ripe for a history of astronomy informed by genuinely aesthetic principles?

One can imagine Smith, fortified by such arguments, dashing off the first few sections of 'Astronomy' and then pausing to reflect what Principles he has actually succeeded in unveiling, and how he is going to use them to illuminate the successive revolutions in astronomical thinking. But when he actually comes to write Section IV – 'The History of Astronomy' – he seems to find the principles something of an embarrassment, like a cast-off mistress. The first 'regular system of Astronomy' described by Smith is the system of concentric spheres, one for the Sun, one for the Moon and one for the stars, the planets being counted as 'wandering' stars. Of this sytem Smith writes: 'If it gained the belief of mankind by its plausibility, it attracted their wonder and admiration; sentiments that still more confirmed their belief, by the novelty and beauty of that view of nature which it presented to the imagination' (EPS, p. 56) It is difficult to reconcile this claim with Smith's earlier account of Wonder as a state of intellectual dissatisfaction – something much closer to puzzlement than to the aesthetic pleasure suggested here. Perhaps his spelling of 'wonder' with a small 'w' is a sign of his own unease on the point.

The next development Smith describes is the attempt, by Eudoxus and others, to account for the anomalous motions of the Sun, the Moon and the Five Planets by endowing each of these heavenly bodies with several spheres connected together. Originally introduced in order to minimise certain discrepancies between theory and observation, the system eventually got quite out of hand, and when in the sixteenth century Fracostoro 'endeavoured to revive this ancient Astronomy, . . . he found it necessary to multiply the number' of Celestial Spheres to seventy-two; neither were all these enough' (EPS, p. 59). The mind boggles – or as Smith puts it, more elegantly: 'This system had now become as intricate and complex as those appearances themselves, which it had been invented to render uniform and coherent. The imagination, therefore, found itself but little relieved from that embarrassment, into which those appearances had thrown it, by so perplexed an account of things' (EPS, p. 59). One could hardly disagree.

The next cosmological model to receive Smith's attention is the system of Eccentric Spheres and Epicycles, associated with the names of Apollonius, Hipparchus and Ptolemy. Central to the Ptolemaic system was the concept of the Equalizing Circle, which Smith deems specially worthy of mention:

> Nothing can more evidently show, how much the repose and tranquility of the imagination is the ultimate end of philosophy, than the invention of this Equalizing Circle. The motions

of the heavenly bodies had appeared inconstant and irregular, both in their velocities and their directions. [But by transporting themselves, in fancy, to the centres of these Circles] those philosophers took pleasure in surveying from thence, all those fantastical motions, arranged, according to that harmony and order, which it had been the end of all their researches to bestow upon them. Here, at last, they enjoyed that tranquillity and repose which they had pursued through all the mazes of this intricate hypothesis. (EPS, p. 61)

Smith's central thesis is at last emerging: that the Imagination is restless in its search for order and coherence, or as Wittgenstein maintained two centuries later, that philosophy is a cure for headaches. A modern essay on scientific creativity would probably introduce Surprise and Wonder (if at all) as secondary concepts – as our responses to disorder and incoherence; but in the opening sections of his essay Smith has committed himself to treating them as primary concepts, identifying disorder as that which excites Surprise, and incoherence – 'lack of connection' – as that which occasions Wonder.

In the pages that follow, Smith describes clearly and accurately the main stages through which astronomy passed on its way to the Newtonian revolution. Broadly speaking, the Ptolemaic system, with the earth fixed at its centre, held sway for more than a thousand years, until displaced by the Copernican theory in the late fifteenth century. The Copernican system places the Sun at its centre (as orginally proposed in the third century BC by Aristarchus of Samos – a fact of which Smith seems unaware) and assumes the Earth and the Five Planets to revolve around it at different distances. The Earth was supposed to rotate every day about its own axis, from west to east, as well as revolving annually around the Sun. The Copernican system offered immediate explanations for the apparent rotation of the Stars and the cycle of the seasons; by assuming, furthermore, that the orbits of Venus and Mercury lie inside the Earth's orbit, it explained simply why they, of all the Five Planets, were only visible at times near sunrise or sunset.

If this new hypothesis thus connected together all these appearances as happily as that of Ptolemy, there were others which it connected together much better . . . Neither did the beauty and simplicity of this system alone recommend it to the imagination; the novelty and unexpectedness of that view of nature, which it opened to the fancy, *excited more wonder and surprise* than the strangest of those appearances, which it had been invented to render natural and familiar, and these sentiments still more endeared it. For, though it is the end of Philosophy, *to allay that wonder*, which either the unusual or seemingly disjointed appearances of nature excite, yet she never triumphs so much, as when, in order to connect together a few, in themselves, perhaps, inconsiderable objects, she has, if I may say so, created another constitution of things, more natural indeed, and such as the imagination can more easily attend to, but more new, more contrary to common opinion and expectation, than any of those appearances themselves. [My italics] (EPS, pp. 73, 75)

One can imagine Smith's tutor at Balliol listening to his pupil reading this breathless paragraph, and interrupting, impatiently: 'Make up your mind, Sir, about these emotions of Wonder and Surprise: are you supposing them to lead and direct the Imagination *towards* a new system of thought or *away from* it?'.

One aspect of the Copernican theory that Smith mentions only as an afterthought is its prediction that Venus should appear as a crescent, waxing and waning like the Moon as it revolves round the Sun. In our own time, Einstein's General Theory of Relativity was to stand or fall by the equally startling prediction that light should bend as it passes near the Sun – a prediction whose confirmation during the eclipse of 1919 was regarded as a triumphant vindication of that theory. A present-day history of astronomy would highlight such events as turning-points in the subject, but it is not entirely clear how they would fit into Smith's philosophy of scientific history. One can only suppose that Smith would have counted the predictive failure of a theory as an occasion for Wonder or Surprise – as an indication that one should either modify the theory or abandon it in favour of another – but nowhere in the Essay is such a view explicitly stated.

Smith next introduces the reader to the astonishing 'Tycho Brahe, the great restorer of the science of the heavens, who had spent his life, and wasted his fortune upon the advancement of Astronomy' (EPS, p. 80). Tycho apparently never managed to believe that the Earth was really hurtling so rapidly through the heavens, and evolved a private theory of his own,

    in which the Earth continued to be, as in the old account, the immovable centre of the universe, round which the firmament revolved every day from east to west, and, by some secret virtue, carried the Sun, the Moon, and the Five Planets along with it, notwithstanding their immense distance, and notwithstanding that there was nothing betwixt it and them but the most fluid ether. (EPS, p. 81)

As Smith rightly observes, Tycho's theory created far more problems than it solved – though it located them at a relatively safe distance from the Earth – and thus failed 'to connect together . . . these incoherences'. He has some equally penetrating observations to make about the importance of Galileo's observations in consolidating the essentials of the Copernican theory and laying the foundations of Newtonian theory by demonstrating the 'composition of motion' – the invariance of mechanics under the Galilean transformation named after him.[2] Smith's discussion of these matters, in remarkably modern terms, is unencumbered by any reference to his Principles; but in his admirable account of Kepler's Laws of Planetary motion he does slip into asserting that 'an ellipse is, of all curved lines after a circle, the simplest and most easily conceived' (EPS, p. 89): this despite the scorn he heaps on the now-forgotten Bouillaud, for insisting that 'the Planets . . . always revolve in circles; for that being the most perfect figure, it is impossible they should revolve in any other' (EPS, p. 88). As the essay approaches the dawning of the Newtonian enlightenment, such wisps of sophistry gradually recede into the medieval obscurity from which they came.

Smith comments perceptively on the theoretical significance of Cassini's observations on the satellites of Jupiter and Saturn, made possible by Galileo's invention of the telescope. These observations 'seem to establish it as a law of the system, that, when one body revolved round another, it described equal areas in equal times; and that, when several revolved round the same body, the squares of their periodic times were as the cubes of their distances' (EPS, p. 90). In a geocentric theory these impressive generalisations would fail miserably – yet another nail in the Ptolemaic coffin.

Nothing now embarrassed the system of Copernicus, but the difficulty which the imagination felt in conceiving bodies so immensely ponderous as the Earth, and the other Planets, revolving round the Sun with such incredible rapidity . . . The imagination had been accustomed to conceive such objects as

tending rather to rest than motion . . . It was in vain that
Kepler . . . talked of some vital and immaterial virtue, which
was shed by the Sun into the surrounding spaces . . . The
imagination had no hold of this immaterial virtue . . . The
imagination, indeed, felt a gap, or interval, betwixt the
constant motion and the supposed inertness of the Planets,
and had in this, as in all other cases, some general idea or
apprehension that there must be a connecting chain of intermediate objects to link together these discordant qualities.
(EPS, p. 91)

To the rescue of the beleaguered imagination rode the philosopher
Des Cartes: 'According to that ingenious and fanciful philosopher,
the whole of infinite space was full of matter, for with him matter
and extension were the same, and consequently there could be no
void' (EPS, p. 92). Smith then embarks on a careful exposition of
Descartes' ideas, according to which the Planets are carried round
the Sun by a gigantic system of whirlpools, but ultimately concludes that the system is fatally flawed in failing to account for the
detailed regularities established by Cassini. Thereafter, 'the philosophy of Des Cartes, which could afford no reason, why such
particular laws should be observed, might continue to amuse the
learned in other sciences, but could no longer satisfy those that
were skilled in Astronomy' (EPS, p. 97).

It was Newton, as Smith says, who gave the first physical theory
of planetary motion, by combining his 'laws of impulse' with the
idea of a universal attraction between massive bodies, of which the
force of gravity is a direct manifestation.

> The superior genius and sagacity of Sir Isaac Newton, there-
> fore, made the most happy, and, we may now say, the greatest
> and most admirable improvement that was ever made in
> philosophy, when he discovered, that he could join together
> the movements of the Planets by so familiar a principle of
> connection, which completely removed all the difficulties the
> imagination had hitherto felt in attending to them. (EPS, p.
> 98).

The remainder of the essay is an expository *tour de force*. Smith
marches surefootedly through the minefield of misunderstanding
that commonly surrounds the application of Newton's theory to the
raising of the tides, the complex motion of the Moon, the prediction
of eclipses, the procession of the equinoxes, the flattening of the

Earth (and of Jupiter) at its poles, and the near-parabolic orbits of the comets, though – incomprehensibly – he fails to acknowledge that it was the astronomer Edmund Halley who triumphantly predicted the return of the comet since named after him.

In the last paragraph of his essay, Smith wonders whether his irresistible enthusiasm for the new order may not have led him to betray his own Principles. The natural laws enunciated by Sir Isaac Newton

> Not only connect together most perfectly all the phaenomena of the Heavens, which had been observed before his time, but those also which the persevering industry and more perfect instruments of later Astronomers have made known to us . . .
> *And even we, while we have been endeavouring to represent all philosophical systems as mere inventions of the imagination, to connect together the otherwise disjointed and discordant phaenomena of nature, have insensibly been drawn in, to make use of language expressing the connecting principles of this one, as if they were the real chains which Nature makes use of to bind together her several operations.* Can we wonder, then, that it should have gained the general and complete approbation of mankind, and that it should now be considered, not as an attempt to connect in imagination the phaenomena of the Heavens, but as the greatest discovery that ever was made by man, *the discovery of an immense chain of the most important and sublime truths*, all closely connected together, by one capital fact, of the reality of which we have daily experience. [My italics] (EPS, p. 105)

So were Newton's Mathematical Principles of Natural Philosophy 'mere inventions of the imagination' or were they links in 'an immense chain of the most important and sublime truths?' In short: Was mankind deceived? Or were the Principles misconceived? My own answer to both questions would be 'not entirely'.[3] It would surely be perverse to deny that a system of thought that makes it possible to predict eclipses to within a few seconds in a century, or to guide a space vehicle round the rings of Saturn, must contain a substantial element of truth. Such a system may of course be superseded by another, for certain purposes or in certain respects; but this is not to be taken – though it sometimes is – as an indication of the impossibility of constructing veridical portraits of the world in which we live.

As for the Principles that lead and direct Philosophical

Enquiries, perhaps their least ephemeral message is that science, as we now call it, is a product of the human imagination – a fact that is now taken for granted by psychologists interested in artistic or scientific creativity. In this sense Smith's approach to the history of astronomy was that of a psychologist rather than a philosopher of science as we would now understand those terms. The questions he asks about our responses to alternative cosmologies could equally well be asked about our responses to symphonies or to cathedrals, and the answers would be much the same: a cathedral can certainly evoke Wonder, Surprise or Admiration, and for very similar reasons. But between a cathedral and a cosmology there is a crucial difference, which Smith's enquiry fails to address: a cosmology can fail to correspond with observation in a way that a cathedral cannot. There is, furthermore, no way in which a symphony can be said to predict anything at all, let alone incorrectly; but the distinction is crucial to the acceptability of a scientific theory.

In recent times there have been two contributions to the philosophy of science that would undoubtedly have caught Smith's interest and attention: Sir Karl Popper's account of the logic of scientific discovery,[4] and Thomas Kuhn's essay on the structure of scientific revolutions.[5] Popper argues that the scientific theories we value most are those that make the boldest testable claims and survive the attempt to falsify these claims. Kuhn maintains that unsatisfactory theories are not so much refuted as rejected when a new 'paradigm' emerges – a thesis that has a distinctly Smithian flavour. In defence of Smith's view, Raphael and Skinner point out that the replacement of one theory by another is not always in order to accommodate new empirical facts; but it would be a mistake to infer that scientific theories are no more secure than women's fashions against the whims of Surprise, Wonder and Admiration.

Notes

1. A reference to Descartes' conjecture that the planets are guided round the sun by a system of vortices in a ubiquitous ether (*vide infra*).
2. The motion of bodies on a moving train precisely resembles their motion when the train is at rest – a foreshadowing of the principles of relativity.
3. Raphael and Skinner, in their General Introduction to the Glasgow edition (*vide supra*), give the Principles their more enthusiastic support.

4. Popper (1935 and 1963).
5. Kuhn (1962).

References

Kuhn, T. S. (1962) *The Structure of Scientific Revolutions* (Chicago).
Popper, K. R. (1935; Eng. trans. 1972) *Logik der Forschung* (London).
Popper, K. R. (1963) *Conjectures and Refutations* (London).

Adam Smith 1790: the man recalled;
the philosopher revived

D. D. RAPHAEL

We commemorated in 1990 the bicentenary of Adam Smith's death. The first part of this chapter gives new information about a biographical document written soon after that event. The second part discusses changes in the thought of his last years, as shown in the sixth edition of *The Theory of Moral Sentiments*, revised over the years 1786–9 and published in May 1790, two months before Smith died.

I

The Laing manuscripts in the Edinburgh University Library include a number of papers written by George Chalmers (1742–1825), a lawyer and civil servant who spent his leisure hours on historical and biographical work. He wrote several biographies and evidently contemplated more, since some of the papers in the Laing collection have the form of biographical notes composed after the death of their subjects. One is on Adam Smith (Laing MSS, II. 451/2, f. 429–34). The text is reproduced by permission of the Edinburgh University Library.

Ad. Smith LL.D. B1723–D1790

Mr Callender told me, That Ad. Smith was a *posthumous* child; That he was probably educated at Kirkaldy, where his father was Collector of the Customs & where he was born, (Ad. Smith having once shewn him the House wherein he drew his first breath) & That he went thence to the College of Glasgow and thence to Baliol Col.

Camb., which he did not like and left in disgust. He then returned
to his mother at Kirkaldy; and while he lived with her he made it
his constant practice summer & winter to bathe in the Forth, [p. 2]
Forth, a practice which prevented colds.

Being now idle, he went to Edinburgh about 1750 and privately
taught the Civil Law to students of Jurisprudence.ˣ It was the fame
which he there gained as a Teacher of Law, that induced the patrons
to invite him to the professorship in the College of Glasgow. Such
were the Lectures, which he here gave, that he used to appeal
['appeal' replaces deleted words 'complain (say)'] to Callender That
Dᴿ Robertson had borrowed the first vol. of his histy of Cha. 5 from
them; as every student could testify. Of Robertson he used to say,
That his judgement enabled him to form a good Outline, but he
wanted [p. 3] industry to fill up his plan; That Robertson inverted
morals, by blaming what he should have praised, and praised, what
he should have blamed: That he liked Robertson better when at a
distance than he did upon nearer inspection.

There was a competition between him and Archᵈ Henderson for
the place of Comᴿ of the Customs Edinᴿ; but after the Dk of
Buccleugh had carried it (1777.) for him agᵗ Lord Mountstuart, who
obtained a pension of £400 net for Henderson, Dᴿ Smith proposed
to Exchange his office of £500 a yʳ for Hendersons pension, in order
that he might live at London; but, this was not allowed. When Smith
took his place [p. 4] place at the Board of Customs he in some
measure gave up his books; which his friends observing remon-
strated, particularly R. Cullen, the Lawyer, of whom Smith said,
that he was the best scholar he had ever had.

Mᴿ Callender added, that Dᴿ S. was a plain unreserved speaker
of his real opinion in all companies, whereby he sometimes gave
offence, without meaning it.

On the verso of p. 1, opposite the passage on p. 2 marked with a
superscribed x, there is an addition:

ˣ It was then that he first became acquainted wʰ D. Hume: The
friendship between them continued thro' Life.
Hume reviewed the Moral Sentiments [1759–1760.]

On the verso of the final (blank recto) page, there is a further
entry. The second part of it ('Mr Lumisden says . . .') is in fainter
ink, indicating that this was written at a different time:

D.ʳ Adam Smith
17 July 1790 Died at Edinburgh D.ʳ Ad. Smith, one of the Commissioners of the Customs
Scots Mag. 1790–363.
Pub. Moral Sentiments 1759.

M.ʳ Lumisden says, That D.ʳ A. Smith wrote the prefatory advertisement to W.ᵐ Hamilton of Bangors works which were printed at
Glasgow 1748– The Preface is dated 21 Dec.ʳ 1748–M.ʳ Hamilton told
this to M.ʳ Lumisden.–The Preface to the Edinburgh Edition 1760
was written by David Rae, Lord Eskgrow.

There are several references to this biographical note in W. R.
Scott's book, *Adam Smith as Student and Professor* (Glasgow, 1937).
Scott nowhere says that it was written by George Chalmers;
indeed some of his phrases give the impression that it was actually
written by the 'Mr Callender' who is named at the beginning as
the source of Chalmers' information. I suspect that Scott may have
taken notes when he read the paper and have then forgotten that
it refers to 'Mr Callender' as informant, not as author. Scott
supposed that 'Mr Callender' was John Callander of Craigforth
(an estate near Stirling), an antiquary and agriculturalist who had
qualified as an advocate, though he never practised, and who spent
a fair amount of his time in Edinburgh. He was an almost exact
contemporary of Adam Smith, the years of his birth and death
(1722–1789) being just one year earlier than those of Smith. The
two men were probably acquainted. Smith was a foundation
member of The Literary Society of Glasgow, whose records show
that John Callander of Craigforth, David Hume, and 'Mr [presum-
ably Adam] Ferguson, now I believe in Edinburgh College' were
elected members in the second year of the society's existence,
1753.[1] Scott's inference that this Mr Callander was Chalmers'
informant was mistaken, but it was not unreasonable and could be
pardoned if only Scott had said explicitly that it was no more than
a supposition and that the document from which he was quoting
simply names 'Mr Callender' and does not identify him.

Scott refers to the document on pp. 20, 50, 54–6, and 64 of his
book. Three of the passages include quotations. One of the
quotations is garbled and sadly misleading. Two of Scott's passages
contain surmise that goes further than his evidence warranted. The

evidence that he cites in all four passages is simply the document in the Laing collection of manuscripts. On p. 20 Scott writes of 'the report of John Callander (who had come on a visit to Kirkcaldy either from Edinburgh or Craigforth, and stayed with Adam Smith); he said that Smith "had shown him the house in which he first drew breath".' The statement that Callander had come on a visit from Edinburgh or Craigforth to stay with Smith is pure surmise. So is Scott's statement on p. 50 that Callander was 'an intimate friend of Adam Smith', elaborated on p. 54 to 'who was an intimate friend of Adam Smith and who attended the final course of the Edinburgh lectures'. That exercise of imagination is followed by faulty quotation: 'He said that "Adam Smith taught Civil Law to students of Jurisprudence, such were the lectures which he here gave".' The absence of points of omission after 'Jurisprudence' and of an initial capital for 'such' led Scott, and lead the reader, to think that the words, 'such were the lectures which he here gave', refer to the Edinburgh lectures and are intended simply to repeat the earlier statement that their content was Civil Law.

The real identity of 'Mr Callender' can be inferred from another of George Chalmers' manuscript notes in the Laing collection. Several of them begin with the phrase 'Mr Callender [or 'Callendar'] told me', but one, containing information about David Hume, begins 'Mr Callendar told me from what he had heard his Uncle Ramsay say'. Mr Tatsuya Sakamoto of Keio University came upon this document when doing some research on Hume. His attention was arrested by a statement in it that Hume reviewed Adam Smith's *Theory of Moral Sentiments* in the *Critical Review* of 1759 or 1760. Remembering that, in a recently published article, Dr David Raynor (now of the University of Ottawa) had argued from internal evidence that Hume was the author of an anonymous notice of Smith's book in the *Critical Review* of 1759, Mr Sakamoto discussed Chalmers' note with me. We followed up the problems which it raised and eventually wrote a joint paper, 'Anonymous Writings of David Hume', now published in the *Journal of the History of Philosophy*, 28: 2 (1990), pp. 271–81. In the course of our research we found decisive evidence for concluding that Chalmers' informant was not John Callander of Craigforth but David Callander of Westertown (1742–98), a nephew of Michael Ramsay of Mungale and a pupil of Adam Smith at Glasgow University. I should add that we received invaluable assistance from Dr David Raynor, who among other things told us of two letters which he had discovered, written by Michael Ramsay to forward the interests of his nephew David Callander, whom he described as enjoying the high regard and support of his former teacher Adam Smith and of David Hume. Michael Ramsay was a close friend of Hume and that is why Callander's information about Hume is based on what he had heard from his Uncle Ramsay. Although Chalmers' references to Mr Callander in other notes do not carry a similar identifying phrase, it is inconceivable that they could refer to a different Mr Callander without distinguishing him from the Mr Callander of the note on Hume. In any event there is now enough evidence about relations between David Callander and Adam Smith to show that this Mr Callander was a likely source of information about Smith, while the only evidence for relations between John Callander of Craigforth and Smith is the record of their common membership of The Literary Society of Glasgow.

Even if one has no knowledge of the note on Hume with its mention of Callander's Uncle Ramsay, the note on Smith taken by itself should induce some doubt whether Chalmers' informant could have been John Callander of Craigforth. The form of the note indicates that it was written after Adam Smith's death; the heading gives the dates of birth and death, and the whole text is couched in the past tense, implying that Smith is no longer alive. John Callander of Craigforth died in September 1789, nine months before Smith, and so could not have 'told' Chalmers about Smith at the time when Chalmers wrote it down. Chalmers might, of course, be recalling what was told to him some time ago, but that seems unlikely. I at any rate was puzzled about this feature of the note even before acquiring enough evidence to eliminate Callander of Craigforth as a nephew of Michael Ramsay.

Some considerable time after the article written by Mr Sakamoto and myself had been accepted for publication, I was enabled by fortunate chance to read an uncompleted draft typescript of a book about associates of Adam Smith by Dr Jeremy J. Cater of Royal Holloway and Bedford New College, University of London. One of Dr Cater's numerous discoveries coincided with ours about the identity of George Chalmers' informant. Starting off from deficiencies in W. R. Scott's book, Dr Cater had independently, and indeed at an earlier date, concluded that the informant could not have been John Callander of Craigforth and should instead be identified as Adam Smith's former pupil David Callander. He has examined in depth a number of related biographical issues. So far as Chalmers' note on Smith is concerned, I am indebted to Dr Cater for enlightening me on two points. On a couple of others we had reached similar views, and on yet another we disagree.

David Callander was the youngest of the five children of Alexander Callander of Westertown, a Writer (i.e. solicitor),[2] and Margaret Ramsay, a sister of Michael Ramsay of Mungale. They married in 1734 and the husband died in April 1742, leaving four young children, two sons and two daughters, with a fifth child on the way. The posthumous child was David, born on 17 September 1742. It is not surprising that Michael Ramsay should have rallied round and done his best, for years on end, to help his sister's family, and especially his three nephews, to establish themselves in life. Indeed family correspondence[3] shows Michael Ramsay to have been an exceptionally altruistic man altogether (despite adverse comments on his character expressed and reported by James Boswell[4]). He arranged for the oldest of the three nephews, John, to be articled to his lawyer, a Writer to the Signet in Edinburgh. John found both the lawyer and the tedious hack work assigned to him extremely disagreeable, and after some years Ramsay acceded to his desire to join the Army and bought a commission for him. John eventually rose to the rank of Lieutenant-Colonel and then became a Member of Parliament and a Baronet. The second son, Alexander, went out to the East India Company, again through the good offices and with the financial help of Michael Ramsay. He was very successful and was able to give extensive financial assistance to virtually all the members of his family when they needed it. On his return to Britain he became a merchant in London and then an MP well before his elder brother John. In this latter period of his life he seems to have employed his younger brother David as a personal assistant.

David was reckoned to be the brains of the family. He was sent to Glasgow University in 1756 and matriculated as a member of Adam Smith's ethics class on 14 November 1757, 'annum jam in Academia agens secundum'.[5] He proceeded to Balliol College, Oxford, with the Snell Exhibition in 1760, took the Oxford degree of BA in 1764, and proceeded to MA in 1772. According to Michael Ramsay, he spent six years at Oxford.[6] Like other talented but penurious scholars, he hoped to secure a post as tutor to a young nobleman. Michael Ramsay goes on to say that David Hume (no doubt at Ramsay's instigation) had proposed him for such a post while he was still a student at Oxford. Eventually he did obtain two tutorial posts, both of which took him to France. The first was in 1769–70 as tutor to the two sons of Sir Thomas Burnet (or Burnett) who were also nephews of Sir Alexander Ramsay, mentioned more than once in Michael Ramsay's letters as a helpful kinsman. In the second post, which lasted from December 1774 to the late summer of 1776, David Callander acted as tutor to Lord Vaughan, son and heir of Viscount Lisburne. Judging from reports in John's letters to Alexander, David greatly enjoyed the experience of travelling in France on both occasions, but in writing of the second appointment John regrets that it provided only for an allowance during the period of tutorship and did not include a 'settlement', no doubt meaning a subsequent pension such as Adam Smith and Adam Ferguson enjoyed. Apart from these two happy periods of congenial employment, David Callander had no luck in getting a job and evidently had long bouts of depression in consequence.

His brother John, like his uncle Michael Ramsay, made strenuous efforts on his behalf. Among other things, John visited Adam Smith in London on at least four occasions in 1773–4 to seek help and advice for David. On one of these (reported in a letter from John to David dated 7 July 1773), Adam Smith told John that 'he had had an offer of going abroad with Lord Clive's son, but that at the desire of the Duke of Bucklugh he refused accepting it'. Smith went on to say that he had then mentioned David Callander but found that Lord Clive had already settled on a substitute if Smith himself were unwilling. Smith assured John that he kept David Callander constantly in mind and would do all he could for him if opportunity offered. In a later letter John wrote that Adam Smith was a 'sincere friend' to David and was ready to recommend him for a possible post in India.[7] John himself tried to get David a job in India, or elsewhere abroad, as secretary to some important person in the diplomatic or military establishment. At one time he suggested the Church and pulled strings with a friend among the county gentry. At another he offered to buy David a commission in the Army. Neither of these two last suggestions were to David's taste, and eventually he insisted that the time for a tutorship had gone by. In 1784 his brother Alexander, still in India, accepted the advice of a good friend, Mr J. Cheape, and provided £3,000 to be invested so as to yield an annual income of £180 for David. Cheape, who had praised David's self-reliance, was then taken aback to find him saying that 'an employment . . . is neither consonant with my inclinations, nor my time of life'[8] (he was forty-one at the time). He just wanted to get on with his 'literary pursuits', though they do not seem to have resulted in any published work of his own. John in one of his letters puts it all down to David's education and says that it is better nowadays to be bred a tailor than a scholar. He could have said the same today.

Michael Ramsey's letter of 1768 to the Lord Privy Seal spoke of Adam Smith as well as Hume. It said that David Callander had enjoyed the particular approbation and friendship of Smith at Glasgow and that Smith had been 'his warm and affectionate friend ever since' and had recently given him advice about a proposed visit to France. John Callander's letters of 1773–4 show that Smith's concern for his former pupil continued over the years. David was a reserved character and John had to press him to write to and call on Smith. There is no definite record of his having done so (no letters written by David himself are preserved in the family archives), but it seems very likely that they did meet on more than one occasion, in London or Scotland or both. David Callander spent a good part of his mature years in London and he was frequently in Scotland too. I have no independent evidence showing that Callander and Chalmers were acquainted. Chalmers corresponded with Adam Smith from London in 1785–6 and may possibly have met Smith at Edinburgh in 1789.[9] His biographical interests will no doubt have led him to look out for people with personal knowledge of his subjects. One possible link with David Callander might be indicated by a family letter addressed to him in 1781 at the house of a Mr Mitchell in London. Chalmers' notes refer more than once to information given to him by a Mr Mitchell. But the coincidence of names may be pure chance.

The decisive piece of evidence for identifying Chalmers' 'Mr Callender' is the reference to his Uncle Ramsay in the note about Hume. (A letter of Ramsay to Hume about his 'eldest Callander nephew' rules out the possibility that John Callander of Craigforth might also have been a nephew of Ramsay.) One then needs to ask whether David Callander is likely to have been a reliable informant. Mr Sakamoto and I, in our paper about the note on Hume, concluded that much of its information was reliable, though we had reservations about its leading item. Having now read a number of Michael Ramsay's letters, I am a little more sceptical about the accuracy of his memory. He seems inclined to use rose-tinted spectacles when looking at his relations and friends. But I have not found reason to distrust the accuracy of Callander. Another of Chalmers' notes reports a description by Callander of Hume's drawing-room. It is unusually detailed and gives the impression of clear-cut accuracy. The note on Adam Smith contains one obvious error – the location of Balliol College in Cambridge; but it is equally obvious that this error cannot have been due to Callander, who spent six years at the place. Dr Cater tells me that there is another error in the first name of Smith's rival for the post of Commissioner of Customs. Chalmers' note calls him Archibald instead of Mathew Henderson. A venial error, I think, whether it emanates from Callander or from Chalmers.

Dr Cater sees a more serious error in the statement that Smith taught 'the Civil Law' at Edinburgh. Strictly this should mean Roman Law and Smith was not competent to teach a course specifically in that discipline. I take a different view of the statement. Although the term 'civil law' primarily meant Roman Law, it was also used more generally. Even in the seventeenth century, Hobbes regularly employs the term to mean the whole of positive law as contrasted with natural law. Adam Smith himself, in his lectures on jurisprudence, speaks of 'the civilians' both when he is referring to writers on Roman Law and when referring to the treatment by continental writers of general jurisprudence, including political theory.[10] In the latter instance he calls these writers 'civilians' because they are trained in the continental tradition of civil law (*based* on Roman Law) as contrasted with common law. Chalmers' statement is one of two pieces of evidence that Smith's lectures at Edinburgh went beyond the original course on rhetoric and belles lettres. The more important piece of evidence is Smith's paper of 1755, described in Dugald Stewart's 'Account of the Life and Writings of Adam Smith' (IV. 25). This does not say explicitly that the additional course of lectures was on jurisprudence, and indeed John Rae[11] took it to mean that Smith gave a course simply on economics; but it does connect the Edinburgh lectures of 1750–1 with the Glasgow lectures of 1751–2 that Smith gave to

'Mr Craigie's class'. We know from Smith's correspondence that he was asked to stand in for Craigie on the 'Natural Jurisprudence and Politics' parts of the Moral Philosophy course.[12] In the circumstances, W. R. Scott[13] took 'Civil Law' in the Chalmers note to mean jurisprudence, and I think that is reasonable. It is most unlikely that Adam Smith himself would have used the term 'the Civil Law' when speaking of these lectures, but Callander or Chalmers may well have thought it a suitable description for lectures that do, after all, include a good deal about the principles of Roman Law.

Scott was, however, at fault in his garbled quotation. For one thing, he omits the statement that 'it was the fame which [Smith] there [i.e. at Edinburgh] gained as a Teacher of Law that induced the patrons to invite him to the professorship in the College of Glasgow'. For another, Scott treats the following phrase, 'Such were the Lectures, which he here gave', as still referring to the Edinburgh lectures. Dr Cater has observed (and has kindly allowed me to use his observation) that the word 'here' in this phrase must mean Glasgow, not Edinburgh; it refers back to the immediately preceding words, 'in the College of Glasgow'. That is why, Dr Cater notes, the report can go on to say that Smith used to appeal to Callander, one of the Glasgow students who could testify from their knowledge of the jurisprudence lectures, for confirmation that William Robertson had borrowed Smith's thoughts for his general excursus on the progress of society.

Whether there is any justice in Smith's complaint about Robertson is a matter that I am not competent to discuss. Dr Cater has examined it in detail. But I think we can take the report as a reliable indication of what Smith felt. It says that Smith 'used to appeal to Callender', implying that he did so more than once – not the sort of thing that a fallible memory would invent.

What about the statement that Smith's appointment at Glasgow was induced by his fame as a teacher of law in Edinburgh? He gave the jurisprudence lectures in Edinburgh during the winter of 1750–1. He was elected to the Glasgow Chair of Logic on 9 January 1751,[14] when he was half way through the course. It was quick work for his fame as a teacher of law to have made a mark so soon – though, to be sure, he had been a successful teacher of *students* of law (and theology) for the preceding two years with his lectures on rhetoric. His sponsors, especially Henry Home, may well have read the lectures on jurisprudence before they were delivered. They have a wider and more striking appeal than the lectures on rhetoric and could have led to an immediate rise in acclaim by the cognoscenti.

A few other remarks in Chalmers' note call for brief comment. The underlining of the word 'posthumous' in the first sentence probably indicates emphasis by Callander, who was himself a posthumous child and is likely to have felt a special affinity with Adam Smith on that account. Smith for his part may have shared the feeling when he learned that one of his brighter pupils had, like himself, never known a father. Perhaps this contributed to the affectionate friendship of Smith which Ramsay describes. So far as I know, there is no other report that Smith proposed exchanging his appointment as Commissioner of Customs with the rival candidate's pension 'in order that he might live at London'. It would not be out of character for him to have contemplated this. The added statement that 'Hume reviewed the Moral Sentiments [1759–60]' is probably an abbreviated repetition of the similar statement in the note on Hume. Having had occasion to add that Smith became acquainted with Hume in the period of the Edinburgh lectures, Chalmers must have recalled his earlier report from Callander that Hume reviewed Smith's first book. Likewise the paragraph in fainter ink on the final page, reporting Andrew Lumisden's testimony that Smith wrote the original preface to William Hamilton's poems, is probably a later addition repeating a similar report in the hand of George Chalmers, dated 20 May 1794, in another of the Laing MSS in Edinburgh University Library.[15]

II

The Theory of Moral Sentiments was first published in 1759. It went through six editions in Adam Smith's lifetime. The second edition of 1761 includes some substantial revision in order to answer two criticisms put to Smith, one by Gilbert Elliot on the relation of conscience to social mores, the other by David Hume on the relation of approval to sympathy. The revision clarifies rather than amends the views that Smith had expounded in edition 1. The third edition of 1767 contains an additional work, 'A Dissertation on the Origin of Languages', which is quite independent of the thought of *The Theory of Moral Sentiments*. Changes in this edition are minimal, but they include slight alterations in two passages about religion which seem to suggest a more detached attitude towards conventional religious doctrine. The fourth edition of 1774 and the fifth of 1781 contain only light revision with no effect on the thought of the book. Edition 4, however, has an added sub-title, to which I shall refer again when I come to discuss the major addition to edition 6.

The sixth edition of 1790 is a greatly expanded book. It takes further the elaboration, begun in edition 2, of Smith's view of conscience and of the relation between moral approval and sympathy. On this occasion he does not simply clarify what he had written before, but modifies some of his views. While emphasising further the capacity of conscience to be independent of common social reactions, Smith is at the same time more cautious about the reliability and efficacy of conscience in the face of adverse social opinion. As for approval and sympathy, he now sees the moral danger as well as the social utility of the sympathetic admiration for the rich and the great which supports class distinction. The expanded treatment of conscience is connected with an expanded treatment of the role of self-command, and that in its turn is connected with an expanded account of the ethical thought of the Stoics. There are also certain revisions and additions on the topic of religious belief which afford evidence both that Smith had abandoned specifically Christian doctrine and that he still retained an attachment to the fundamentals of religion. The most striking change of all (which includes some of the new material on self-command) is a wholly new Part VI, 'Of the Character of Virtue'. This calls for special attention.

The new Part VI divides the virtues into three categories: prudence, which concerns the happiness of oneself; justice and beneficence, which concern the happiness of other people; and self-command, without which no virtue can reach perfection. Prudence, beneficence, and self-command are each treated at length in separate sections. There is no such section for justice. Smith explains the omission in his introduction to the second section (VI. ii. intro. 2): first, the principles of positive justice, permitting action that restrains or punishes, are the subject of the 'particular science' of jurisprudence and so need no detailed account in a book on ethics; second, the general principle of negative justice, forbidding action that hurts or disturbs the happiness of others, is so obvious as to need no further explanation. Smith's first remark, about positive or legal justice, probably implies that he had written at length about it in his uncompleted book on jurisprudence. He had also already included a fair amount about the basic concept of justice in Part II of *The Theory of Moral Sentiments*, where an initial statement of differences between justice and beneficence is followed by discussion of the links between justice and the main topic of Part II, merit and demerit. In contrast with this excursus on justice, beneficence and prudence had not received detailed description in the original book but had rather been taken for granted as virtues that are plainly intelligible.

The new Part VI, then, repairs an omission in adding sections on prudence and beneficence. The same thing is true of the section on self-command. Just as the original book had contrasted justice and beneficence, it had likewise emphasised differences between benevolence (or 'humanity') and self-command. This was in Part I, Section i, Chapter 5, 'Of the amiable and respectable virtues'. The language was influenced by Hume, and that is why Smith wrote in this place of 'humanity' rather than 'benevolence'. His intention was to contrast the Christian virtue of love or benevolence with the Stoic virtue of self-command and to set them up as equal partners in an overall plan of the virtues.

> And hence it is, that to feel much for others and little for ourselves, that to restrain our selfish, and to indulge our benevolent affections, constitutes the perfection of human nature; . . . As to love our neighbour as we love ourselves is the great law of Christianity, so it is the great precept of nature to love ourselves only as we love our neighbour, or what comes to the same thing, as our neighbour is capable of loving us.
> (I. i. 5. 5)

This gives self-command a cardinal role among the virtues, and when Smith came to elaborate his account of the character of virtue in the new Part VI, he was bound to highlight self-command as much as beneficence. In fact self-command is made more prominent still in edition 6. It is not only the subject of a section in the added Part VI but is also the main topic of a new chapter in Part III, 'Of the Influence and Authority of Conscience'. The first part of this new chapter had been added (to the preceding chapter) in edition 2 as an answer to Gilbert Elliot's criticism of Smith's view of conscience. But the major part of the new chapter is a disquisition on self-command. One is almost inclined to say that the role of self-command has now become superior to that of Christian love.

But this would be going too far. Smith retained the passage, quoted above, which gives equal status to Christian love and Stoic self-command. If he had been asked to rate his cardinal virtues in a relative order of value, I believe he would have said that one cannot assign higher and lower value to justice, beneficence, and self-command. Justice is the essential basis; beneficence and self-command are the apexes; all three are of equal importance.

The same cannot be said of Smith's remaining cardinal virtue, prudence. It is given more prominence than in the earlier version of the book, and the late Professor A. L. Macfie and I were led to say, in our Introduction to *The Theory of Moral Sentiments*, that this 'increased attention to prudence in edition 6 is natural from the more mature Adam Smith who had pondered on economics for so long'.[16] No doubt that is true, but the section on prudence in the new Part VI is there to repair an omission, as is the section on beneficence. It does not imply that Smith now valued prudence more highly or that he placed it on a level with justice, beneficence, and self-command. Indeed he explicitly says twice that approval of the self-interested virtue of prudence is limited to 'cold esteem' (VI. i. 14, VI. concl. 5). To be sure, this self-interested virtue is also called the 'inferior' or 'vulgar' (i.e. common) form of prudence, as contrasted with a 'superior' prudence that presupposes 'the utmost perfection of all the intellectual and of all the moral virtues' (VI. i. 15, VI. concl. 5); but the 'superior prudence' is not a species of the virtue that forms the subject and the title of Part VI, Section i, namely 'the Character of the Individual, so far as it affects his own Happiness'. When Smith writes of 'superior prudence' (VI. i. 15), he is referring to the use of the word 'prudence' to describe wise policy for the public interest. 'Wise and judicious conduct, when directed to greater and nobler purposes than the care of the health, the fortune, the rank and reputation of the individual, is frequently and very properly called prudence. We talk of the prudence of the great general, of the great statesman, of the great legislator.'

Dr Laurence Dickey of Columbia University has argued in a recent article[17] that Smith's evaluation of prudence is lower in edition 6 than in edition 1. His argument turns on the ascription of 'cold esteem' (and of the adjective 'vulgar', which he misunderstands) to prudence in edition 6, as contrasted (so he thinks) with much higher praise in edition 1. Dr Dickey is mistaken on the latter point. He quotes a passage from the earlier material which contrasts the qualities admired in the rich and the great with the more worthy qualities that can be achieved by 'the man of inferior rank' or 'private man'. Dr Dickey thinks that this 'private man' can also be described as 'the prudent man' and that Smith's warm praise of such a character in 1759 is replaced by 'cold esteem' in 1790. But the virtue of the 'private man' of the 1759 passage is not confined to prudence. The passage comes from the chapter entitled 'Of the origin of Ambition, and of the distinction of Ranks'. The paragraph concerned (I. iii. 2. 5) begins with the foolish emphasis placed by 'the great' on politeness of behaviour. It contrasts this with 'the most perfect modesty and plainness' to be sought by 'the man of inferior rank' or 'private man', and then goes on to say that if such a man 'hopes to distinguish himself, it must be by more important virtues' (note the plural). He must acquire various talents, superior knowledge and industry in his profession. 'He must be patient in labour, resolute in danger, and firm in distress. . . . Probity and prudence, generosity and frankness, must characterize his behaviour upon all ordinary occasions'; but he must also be keen to engage in special situations that call for 'the greatest talents and virtues'. To suggest that this passage fastens upon prudence is clearly misguided. Prudence is mentioned simply as one of a number of desirable qualities recommended to the 'private man'.

It remains true that the term 'cold esteem' occurs only in edition 6: 'Prudence . . . commands a certain cold esteem, but seems not entitled to any very ardent love or admiration' (VI. i. 14). Does this imply that Smith thought less well of prudence in 1790 than in 1759, as Dr Dickey claims? I doubt it. When Smith, in edition 1, made the case, against Hutcheson, for prudence as a virtue, he classified it as one of 'the inferior virtues' and said that a lack of prudence was a failing which calls for pity rather than contempt (VII. ii. 3. 15–16). That is the other side of the coin which shows approval of prudence as cold esteem, not ardent love or admiration. The later description fills out but does not alter the earlier one.

There is, however, one passage of the earlier version which speaks in warmer terms of prudence. This is because Smith there stresses the element of self-command in prudence. The 'eminent esteem' of which he writes is directed at the self-command. The spectator, we are told, 'knows from experience, how few are capable of this self-command' in abstaining from present for future pleasure, and therefore he admires it. 'Hence arises that eminent esteem with which all men naturally regard a steady perseverance in the practice of frugality, industry, and application, though directed to no other purpose than the acquisition of fortune. The resolute firmness . . . necessarily commands our approbation' (IV. 2. 8). If, as Smith says a little earlier (IV. 2. 6), the virtue of prudence 'consists' in the union of rational foresight of advantage with the self-command of abstention, then there is an inconsistency between this characterisation of prudence and that found in the other quoted passages, which confine prudence to the status of inferior virtue and cold esteem. But I do not think it is an inconsistency of attitude between 1759 and 1790. The lower opinion of ordinary prudence is expressed in 1759 too, as we have seen. It appears that the higher opinion of IV. 2. 8 is meant to refer to a relatively rare form of prudence ('The spectator . . . knows . . . how few are capable of this self-command'). If so, Smith made a mistake when he wrote in IV. 2. 6 as if all prudence, common as well as rare, includes self-command.

In any event, the character of Smith's account in all the relevant passages precludes the idea that his personal evaluation of prudence had changed in 1790. All the passages are presented as sociological reports. When Smith writes of prudence as an inferior virtue which commands only cold esteem, and of its absence as a failing which arouses mere pity, he is telling us what he takes to be the common reaction. He is doing the same thing again when he writes that 'all men naturally' feel eminent esteem for the exceptional self-command of sustained frugality, etc. He himself shares these common attitudes, but they are not expressed as his personal views. If the 'cold esteem' passages did reflect a change, it would have to be a change in (Smith's perception of) social attitudes, not a change in Smith's individual scale of values. In fact, of course, it was always true and remains true that self-interested prudence is generally approved in a cool manner, and not with the warmth that greets beneficence or justice.

I have said that the new Part VI, 'Of the Character of Virtue', was inserted in edition 6 to make good an omission. Yet it also fails to do the most important part of the task required. To understand why, we need to look at the earlier version of the book.

We find there a theory built up by careful stages from a simple base. Part I explains judgements of propriety and impropriety (that is to say, simple judgements of right and wrong) made about the actions of other people. Part II explains the rather more complex judgements of merit and demerit, again as made about the actions of other people. Part III explains moral judgements made about one's own actions; it claims that these are more complex still, because they depend upon a knowledge of judgements about others. Part IV, focusing upon the concept of utility, shows the relevance of aesthetic judgement both to ethics and to economics. Part V continues the broadening of perspective by examining the sociological background of aesthetic and moral judgement. That completes the theory. The final part of the book (VI in editions 1– 5, VII in edition 6) is a survey of the history of moral philosophy, classifying and criticising the main types of theory with the aim of showing how Smith's own theory accounts for the element of truth in earlier theories while avoiding their weaknesses.

After an introductory paragraph, the final part of the book begins its serious business with a statement of the task of moral philosophy. 'In treating of the principles of morals there are two problems to be considered. First, wherein does virtue consist? . . . And, secondly, by what power or faculty in the mind is it, that this character, whatever it be, is recommended to us? (VII. i. 2). This statement reads like the opening of a treatise or discourse, and when editing the text of *The Theory of Moral Sentiments* I suggested that the first version of Smith's lectures probably began at this point, with a critical survey of earlier theories before developing Smith's own views. I now think there is a further reason for supposing that the statement was taken over from the start of Smith's lectures and was not written after Parts I–V had been composed in book form. The statement specifies two problems for moral philosophy, the nature of virtue and the nature of moral judgement; but the preceding five parts of the book have focused on the second problem alone. There is an elaborate, systematic theory of moral judgement. But while there are some incidental remarks about particular virtues, there is nothing remotely resembling a systematic theory of the nature of virtue. In short, the book does not live up to the programme set for moral philosophy.

Smith himself may have realised the discrepancy when he came to revise the work for edition 4 (1774), since the original title, 'The Theory of Moral Sentiments', was there supplemented by a sub-title, 'or An Essay towards an Analysis of the Principles by which Men naturally judge concerning the Conduct and Character, first of their Neighbours, and afterwards of themselves'. This is a precise description of Smith's method of handling his main theme, moral judgement. I think that the new Part VI, added to edition 6, is intended to repair the omission of a treatment of the other main problem announced in the programme of the final part. But it seems unlikely that Smith had the task consistently in mind from 1774 onwards. Edition 5 (1781) contains no revisions of real substance. Smith wrote on 21 April 1785 to his publisher, Thomas Cadell, welcoming the information that a new edition of *The Wealth of Nations* was called for, and added: 'If a new edition of the theory is wanted I have a few alterations to make of no great consequence which I shall send to you.'[18] He then mentioned a projected new edition in a letter of 1 November 1785 to the Duc de La Rochefoucauld. This too does not suggest any extensive revision and says that Smith hoped to do the work 'before the end of the ensuing winter'.[19] On 14 March 1786 he asked Cadell what demand there still was for the book.[20] Then on 15 March 1788, in another letter to Cadell, Smith wrote of 'giving the most intense application' to a revision of *The Theory of Moral Sentiments*, 'to all parts of which I am making many additions and corrections'. Even at that stage, however, he does not mention a new Part VI. On the contrary, he says: 'The chief and the most important additions will be to the third part, that concerning *the sense of Duty* and to the last part concerning *the History of Moral Philosophy*.'[21] The idea of adding the new Part VI evidently came later. Smith refers to it in a further letter to Cadell dated 31 March 1789: 'Besides the Additions and improvements I mentioned to you; I have inserted, immediately after the fifth part, a compleat new sixth part containing a practical system of Morality, under the title of the Character of Virtue.'[22]

'A practical system of morality': that is a fair description of the new Part VI. But what has happened to Smith's original requirement that a treatise of moral philosophy should explain the nature of virtue? The requirement did indeed include the content of virtue, which is what we are now given; but the essential problem was to find a theory that explains that content, just as the second problem assigned to moral philosophy was to find a theory that explains moral judgement.

In the old Part VI (now Part VII), Smith's statement of the two problems is immediately followed by a summary of three theories about the first problem and four theories about the second. On the first problem, Hutcheson had said virtue consists in benevolence, Samuel Clarke had said 'acting suitably to the different relations we stand in', others had said a prudent pursuit of our own happiness (VII. i. 3). The next section then spells out these three types of theory, but in a different order. The first chapter deals with 'those Systems which make Virtue consist in Propriety'. It begins with three theories of the ancient world, those of Plato, Aristotle, and the Stoics. It then proceeds to the 'modern systems' of Samuel Clarke, his follower William Wollaston, and (oddly enough) the third Earl of Shaftesbury, who was in fact a thinker of a very different stamp. Smith bundles these strange bedfellows together because they all (as he thinks) say that an action is virtuous because its motive is proper or suitable to its object or to nature. The second chapter deals with 'systems' that make virtue consist in prudence, the prime example being that of Epicurus; and the third chapter is on the benevolence theory, with Hutcheson as the prime example. Smith then says that all theories of virtue can be reduced to one or other of the three he has discussed. In the final paragraph of the third chapter (VII. ii. 3. 21), he says that Hume's theory (that qualities of the mind are virtuous if agreeable or useful) is a form of the propriety theory because it implies that 'virtue consists not in any one affection, but in the proper degree of all the affections'. He then ends by saying that his own theory is in the same boat, the only difference being that Hume's theory 'makes utility, and not sympathy, or the correspondent affection of the spectator, the measure of this proper degree'. (Edition 6 says 'the natural and original measure'.)

So there you have it. The correct theory, that virtue consists in propriety, is shared by Plato, Aristotle, the Stoics, Clarke, Wollaston, Shaftesbury, Hume, and Smith. The earlier forms of the theory are, however, inadequate in not specifying how propriety or suitability is measured; Smith remedies the defect with his theory of moral judgement based on sympathy. As a solution of what is supposed to be one of the two main problems of moral philosophy, this achieves nothing, in stark contrast to Smith's ingenious and well-constructed solution of the second problem. The theory that virtue consists in propriety is too vague to be an explanation and too wide to differentiate it from the rival theories, for it is very easy to argue that a policy of prudence is pre-eminently acting conformably or suitably to nature, and it is not difficult to mount a similar argument for benevolence. This propriety theory of virtue also sits ill with distinctions drawn elsewhere between propriety and virtue. In Part I (I. i. 5. 7–8), Smith says there is 'a considerable difference between virtue and mere propriety', the former calling for admiration, the latter for simple approval; and in Part VII itself (VII. ii. 1. 50), he says that propriety is a necessary condition of all virtue but not a sufficient condition of virtues such as beneficence that call for a 'superior degree of esteem' going beyond approval. The plain fact is that Smith has not thought out an answer to the first problem set by his programme. When he came to write the new Part VI, he tried to repair the omission after a fashion but still did not come to grips with the original problem.

I must now turn back to Dr Laurence Dickey's article. His reasonable suggestion of a change of heart on prudence is only a small part of the subject-matter of his article, and I must say something more about it, both because it criticises, with some absurd misrepresentation, the treatment of 'the Adam Smith problem' in the Glasgow edition of *The Theory of Moral Sentiments*, and because it ends with a fictional hypothesis about Smith's views in 1790.

W. R. Scott's fiction of an intimate friendship between Adam Smith and John Callander of Craigforth went beyond his evidence, but at least it was based on evidence that might have given it support. Dr Dickey's hypothesis has no such excuse. He claims that edition 6 of *The Theory of Moral Sentiments* discloses a new outlook on Smith's part, reflecting a tradition of Christian theology which was specifically opposed to Stoicism and which was developed in English and German Protestant thought of the eighteenth century. The idea that such a theology can be elicited from edition 6 is pure fiction.

Dr Dickey begins with the hoary 'Adam Smith problem' and believes that what he has to say reconstitutes that problem in a more complex and more justifiable form. The original problem was an alleged inconsistency between the psychology and values of *The Theory of Moral Sentiments* and those of *The Wealth of Nations*: the *Moral Sentiments*, it was said, praises altruistic sympathy as the motive of desirable behaviour, while *The Wealth of Nations* praises self-interest. A number of scholars have shown that there is no such inconsistency. They at first concentrated on the fact that prudence or rational self-interest is counted as a virtue in both books. This argument was especially emphasised by the late Professor A. L. Macfie in a paper of 1959[23] and in his contribution to a discussion, made jointly with myself, in the Introduction to the Glasgow edition of *The Theory of Moral Sentiments*.[24] My own contribution to the refutation was to point out that the problem arose from misunderstanding Smith's treatment of certain philosophical issues, especially the role of sympathy in the *Moral Sentiments*: sympathy in Smith's theory is concerned with moral judgement, not moral motivation. Dr Dickey allows that the refutation is sound but he accuses the editors of the *Moral Sentiments* (and two other scholars, Professors T. D. Campbell and Donald Winch) of over-simplifying the problem with their argument that there is continuity between the *Moral Sentiments* and *The Wealth of Nations*.

He makes the absurd charge that 'the continuity argument . . . maintains that the ethical system of *TMS* "contains" the economic argument of *WN*' and 'conceptually insists that *TMS* is the single "motivating center" of Smith's thought'.[25] It would be tedious to spell out in detail the errors in his representation of statements made by the four scholars concerned. (I sent a detailed account to Dr Dickey when his article appeared.) It will be sufficient to note here the origin of the words in double quotation marks which give the impression of authentic reproduction. First, the quoted word 'contains' has been extracted from two sentences of Professor Winch, who wrote that *The Theory of Moral Sentiments* 'contains Smith's general theory of morality or psychology' and that *The Wealth of Nations* applies to 'economic action . . . the general theories of social (including economic) behaviour contained in the earlier work'.[26] That innocuous statement is a far cry from Dr Dickey's report of a view that the *ethical system* of the *Moral Sentiments* contains the *economic argument* of *The Wealth of Nations*. Secondly, the quoted phrase 'motivating center' does not come from any of the four scholars criticised, but from Eric Voegelin, who, Dr Dickey tells us in a note, uses it when 'discussing the different historical layers of the Old Testament'. The phrase itself is obscure; but to transfer it from Voegelin on the Old Testament to four plain-speaking writers on Adam Smith is beyond reason.

Dr Dickey proceeds to contrast the 'continuity argument' with the view of Jacob Viner that there is a discontinuity (but on a different topic) between the *Moral Sentiments* and *The Wealth of Nations*, and with a third view that there is continuity together with change. He says that the first view takes the *Moral Sentiments* as the motivating centre of Smith's work, the second takes *The Wealth of Nations*, and the third takes both works as 'rival centers of meaning'. Dr Dickey thinks that all three are inadequate and should be replaced by his own view that there are three motivating centres. What this means, in plain English, is that both *The Wealth of Nations* (1776) and the sixth edition of *The Theory of Moral Sentiments* (1790) show important changes in Adam Smith's thought. It would be surprising if this were not true, but of course there is room for difference of opinion whether the changes imply inconsistency with Smith's earlier thought of 1759. The subsequent and major part of Dr Dickey's article in fact says almost nothing about *The Wealth of Nations* but concentrates upon changes that edition 6 of the *Moral Sentiments* makes to the text of edition 1.

I have already considered what Dr Dickey has to say about prudence; the fact that 'cold esteem' occurs only in edition 6 does afford prima facie evidence of a change of thought. But he goes much further. He is surprised that the editors of *The Theory of Moral Sentiments*, after noting major changes in edition 6, then 'curiously insist' that 'In general [Part VI] rounds out and clarifies, rather than changes, Smith's ethical theory'.[27] Evidently he did not understand that 'ethical theory' meant what it said. He went on subsequently to claim that edition 6 of the *Moral Sentiments* is 'a manifestation of "coy theology"' found in English Protestant thought of the late eighteenth century and in German metaphysical thinkers of the same period. In his own study of this tradition, which he calls 'the theology of the divine economy', Dr Dickey has learned that it 'originally developed in opposition to Stoic materialism', and he therefore 'takes exception' to the view of the editors of the *Moral Sentiments* that some of the new content of edition 6, like the old of edition 1, shows the influence of Stoic ethics.[28]

But why should anyone suppose that Adam Smith in 1790 had come to be influenced by English Protestant theology and German metaphysics? Dr Dickey's only argument is drawn from a long paragraph in the new Part VI of *The Theory of Moral Sentiments* (VI. iii. 25) about the wise and virtuous man. He italicises one clause, one sentence, and two phrases, each of which reminds him of what

he has read of his particular Protestant theology. The clause refers
to 'the great demigod within the breast' – typical Smith language
for the exclusively Smithian theory of conscience. The phrase
'demigod within the breast' appears also in III. 2. 32, a
paragraph written for edition 6 but replacing similar language in
a passage written in 1759 and added to edition 2 (1761), which
describes conscience as the 'substitute of the Deity' (TMS, p. 130).
Dr Dickey's second and third italicised passages say that the wise
and virtuous man endeavours 'to assimilate' his character to an
'archetype of perfection', whereby 'he imitates the work of a divine
artist'. The word 'assimilate' reminds Dr Dickey of his 'mainline
Protestant theology shaped in the image of the theology of the
divine economy'.[29] He adds in a note that he believes the English
line of this tradition might have begun with the Cambridge
Platonists. So far as Adam Smith is concerned, it would be more
relevant to observe that Smith had a sketchy knowledge of the
Cambridge Platonists but a more detailed knowledge of *their*
archetype, Plato. The passage quoted from Smith is probably an
echo of Plato's doctrine in the *Republic* and the *Timaeus*, both of
which Smith knew well, as we may see from the *Moral Sentiments*
VII. ii. 1. 2–11 and the essays on Ancient Physics and Ancient
Logics. Dr Dickey's fourth and final passage says that the wise and
virtuous man is aware of his imperfection and his 'distant approx-
imation to rectitude'. Here again Dr Dickey is reminded of
language in his Protestant theology about 'approximationism' and
humility. One does not have to go to a particular form of Christian
theology, or even any Christian theology, to find praise of humility
and a recognition that the virtue attained by human beings falls
far short of perfection. The general subject of Smith's paragraph,
'the *wise and* virtuous man', is not a specifically Christian ideal but
owes at least as much to Greek thought. I would not say it is
necessarily Stoic, since it stems from Socrates and Plato; but the
paragraph does, after all, form part of the section on the Stoic
virtue of self-command. To object, as Dr Dickey does, to the idea
of Stoic influence because his pet Protestant theology 'originally
developed in opposition to Stoic materialism' is ludicrous. Smith
had little interest in Stoic materialism. Stoic ethics was what
fascinated him. Its influence is as plain as a pikestaff from the text
itself. The extent of that influence has been traced in more striking

detail by an Italian scholar, Professor Gloria Vivenza, in an excellent book, *Adam Smith e la Cultura Classica* (Pisa, 1984), which examines the influence of the ancient world on the whole of Smith's thought, including his economics.

The mere similarity between a few phrases in one paragraph of *The Theory of Moral Sentiments* and some specialised terms in a body of theological doctrine affords no real evidence of causal connection. Facts about Smith's life are more to the point. There is ample evidence that Smith abandoned a belief in Christian doctrine (while retaining a form of natural religion) long before 1790. There is no reason to suppose that he returned to it in the last years of his life. If he had done so, he would certainly not have deleted from edition 6 of *The Theory of Moral Sentiments* a celebrated passage about Christ's Atonement and substituted for it a detached comment on 'every religion and . . . every superstition that the world has ever beheld' (II. ii. 3. 12). The idea of a return to Christianity in the form of English Protestantism or German metaphysics simply adds to the absurdity. Smith spent his last years in Edinburgh among his friends of the Scottish Enlightenment. If he had thought that deeper enlightenment was to be found, after all, in revealed religion, he would not have gone to *English* theologians for it. As for contemporary German metaphysics, he never showed the slightest interest in such a thing. He read widely in Greek, Latin, French, and Italian, but he seems to have had no knowledge of German, and the catalogue of his library includes only two books in the German language – German translations of *The Theory of Moral Sentiments* and *The Wealth of Nations*. He knew works of jurisprudence by German-speaking scholars, but they were written in Latin.

A final word about the Adam Smith problem. To deny inconsistency between *The Theory of Moral Sentiments* and *The Wealth of Nations*, or between the first and sixth editions of the *Moral Sentiments*, is not to deny the existence of tension between ethics and economics in the thought of Adam Smith. The benefits of the market and of its driving force, prudent self-interest, are countered by the risks of harm to the moral fabric and of illusion about the value of luxuries. Smith shows his awareness of this in *The Theory of Moral Sentiments* and *The Wealth of Nations* alike. He saw the tension because he was a clear-sighted man. That tension is not an Adam Smith problem but a problem of the real world.

Notes

1. W. J. Duncan (1831), p. 133.
2. The matriculation entry for David Callander at Glasgow University describes his father as 'quondam Scriba'.
3. I wish to record my gratitude to Mr Richard Callander of Prestonhall, the present head of the family, for allowing me to consult these and other letters relevant to the life of David Callander.
4. See Ernest C. Mossner (1980), p. 60.
5. W. Innes Anderson (1913), p. 56, entry 1806.
6. Letter of 7 March 1768 to the Lord Privy Seal for Scotland; quoted in 'Anonymous Writings of David Hume', *Journal of the History of Philosophy*, 28: 2, p. 276.
7. I am indebted to Dr David Raynor for telling me of these particular letters in which John Callander writes of visits to Adam Smith.
8. Letter from David Callander to J. Cheape, transcribed in a letter of 24 May 1784 from Cheape to Alexander Callander.
9. Corr., pp. 287–91, 322.
10. Adam Smith, LJ (1978), pp. 86, 401.
11. John Rae (1895), p. 36.
12. Corr., p. 5; letter no. 9, to William Cullen, dated 3 September 1751.
13. W. R. Scott (1937), pp. 54–5.
14. Minute of University meeting reproduced in W. R. Scott (1937), pp. 137–8.
15. Chalmers-Laing MS *Notes*, 'Index to the Scots Poets', Laing MSS, p. 359; described and quoted in Nelson S. Bushnell (1957), p. 132, n. 17, and p. 136, n. 15.
16. Adam Smith, TMS (corrected reprint, 1991), p. 18.
17. Laurence Dickey (1986), pp. 579–609.
18. Corr., p. 281; letter no. 244.
19. *Ibid.*, p. 286; letter no. 248.
20. *Ibid.*, p. 293; letter no. 257.
21. *Ibid.*, pp. 310–11; letter no. 276.
22. *Ibid.*, p. 320; letter no. 287.
23. A. L. Macfie (1967), essay 4.
24. Raphael and Macfie, TMS, pp. 18, 20–5.
25. L. Dickey, pp. 584–5.
26. Donald Winch (1978), p. 10; quoted by L. Dickey, p. 584, but with the misleading omission of the words 'or psychology', 'theories of', and 'including economic'.
27. L. Dickey, p. 588; Raphael and Macfie, TMS, p. 18.
28. L. Dickey, pp. 605–7; 592, n. 85.
29. *Ibid.*, p. 608.

References

Anderson, W. Innes (1913), *The Matriculation Albums of the University of Glasgow from 1728 to 1858* (Glasgow).
Bushnell, N. S. (1957), *William Hamilton of Bangour* (Aberdeen).
Dickey, L. (1986), 'Historicizing the "Adam Smith Problem": Conceptual, Historiographical, and Textual Issues', *Journal of Modern History*, vol. 58.

Duncan, W. J. (1831), *Notices and Documents illustrative of The Literary History of Glasgow* (Glasgow).

Macfie, A. L. (1967), 'Adam Smith's *Moral Sentiments* as Foundation for his *Wealth of Nations*', *Oxford Economic Papers*, October 1959; reprinted in *The Individual in Society* (London), essay 4.

Mossner, E. C. (1980), *The Life of David Hume*, second ed. (Oxford).

Rae, John (1895), *Life of Adam Smith* (London).

Raphael, D. D., and Sakamoto, T. (1990), 'Anonymous Writings of David Hume', *Journal of the History of Philosophy*, vol. 28.

Scott, W. R. (1937), *Adam Smith as Student and Professor* (Glasgow).

Winch, D. (1978), *Adam Smith's Politics: An essay in historiographic revision* (Cambridge).

6

Ethics and casuistry in Adam Smith

R. S. DOWNIE

In the final section of the *The Theory of Moral Sentiments* Adam Smith criticises the practice of casuistry and concludes unambiguously: 'The two useful parts of moral philosophy, therefore, are Ethics and Jurisprudence: casuistry ought to be rejected altogether' (TMS VII. iv. 34). In taking this strong line Smith was expressing the accepted view on casuistry in the second half of the eighteenth century. As a result of this onslaught by Smith and others, the practice of casuistry, explicitly so-called, largely died out, at least in academic circles. Curiously, however, it has appeared again during the last decade in the form of a growing interest in such matters as medical ethics, business ethics, environmental ethics, and other related specialisms within the general area of 'applied ethics'. Sometimes, it is true, 'applied ethics' is simply moral philosophy using realistic problems as specific examples. But often there is an attempt in these areas, by philosophers and others, to answer practical moral problems, 'dilemmas' as they are often called. Indeed, there have grown up in the US specialists called 'ethicists' who are sometimes attached to hospitals and are consulted by medical specialists, rather as biochemists might be consulted for specialist advice. Hence, if we think of casuistry as being concerned with what are still called 'cases of conscience' or as arising out of 'nice and delicate situations in which it is hard to determine whereabouts the propriety of conduct may lie' (TMS VII. iv. 17) there is little doubt that there has been a resurgence of casuistry. It is therefore of contemporary relevance as well as of historical interest to consider the arguments which Adam Smith among others urged against casuistry. If he is correct, then a great deal of what is written as 'applied ethics' must in some ways be misleading to those who turn to it for help. This chapter will therefore be concerned with what Adam Smith meant by casuistry, how he distinguished it from ethics and from jurisprudence (which together for him make up moral philosophy proper), and with an assessment of his arguments against casuistry and their relevance to the contemporary casuistry of applied ethics.[1]

Smith's account of casuistry

In *The Theory of Moral Sentiments* Smith distinguishes moral precepts of two sorts: rules of justice and other virtues. Rules of justice are precise and accurate, whereas the other virtues are loose and indeterminate. He tells us that those authors who have attempted to systematise the rules of morality have been influenced by the particular sort of rules with which they have been mainly concerned:

> and one set has followed through the whole that loose method to which they were naturally directed by the consideration of one species of virtues; while another has as universally endeavoured to introduce into their precepts that sort of accuracy of which only some of them are susceptible. The first have wrote like critics, the second like grammarians. (TMS VII. iv. 2)

He finds the first method practised especially among the ancient philosophers such as Aristotle or Cicero. This method seems to be partly psychological, 'to ascertain . . . wherein consists the sentiment of the heart, upon which each particular virtue is founded'; it is partly what we would now call 'conceptual' – 'what sort of internal feelings or emotion it is which constitutes the essence of friendship, of humanity, of generosity, of justice, of magnanimity, and of all the other virtues, as well as of the vices which are opposed to them'; and it is partly what we might call 'behavioural' – we must ascertain 'what is the general way of acting, the ordinary tone and tenor of conduct to which each of those sentiments would direct us, or how it is that a friendly, a generous, a brave, a just, and a humane man, would, upon ordinary occasions, chuse to act' (TMS VII. iv. 3–4). These, then, are the connected aspects of the method of enquiry which Smith calls 'Ethics', a science which is both 'highly useful and agreeable'.

> By the vivacity of their descriptions they inflame our natural
> love of virtue, and increase our abhorrence of vice: by the
> justness as well as delicacy of their observations they may
> often help both to correct and to ascertain our natural
> sentiments with regard to the propriety of conduct, and
> suggesting many nice and delicate attentions, form us to a
> more exact justness of behaviour, than what, without such
> instruction, we should have been apt to think of. (TMS VII.
> iv. 6)

This strongly normative function of ethics is emphasised again later
(TMS VII. iv. 34). By way of contrast, we should note that
casuistry is said to abound in abstruse and metaphysical distinctions but is 'incapable of exciting in the heart any of those emotions
which it is the principal use of books of morality to excite' (TMS
VII. iv. 33).

As a comment here it can be remarked that moral philosophers
who recognise a normative function in ethics will regard it as
mainly concerned with reaching by argument conclusions about
the *content* of what ought to be done, rather than with the exciting
in the heart of emotions. But it is worth noting that some writers
on medical ethics give it a 'consciousness-raising' function, and this
is similar to what Smith means by the exciting of emotions. This
point will be discussed again below. Curiously, whatever Adam
Smith may say is the point of ethics, his own writing in *The Theory
of Moral Sentiments* seems to be more plainly descriptive and
theoretical than 'exciting'.[2]

The second sort of moralist treats moral precepts like a grammarian, in that the aim is not, as with the first sort, to characterise
virtue and vice in a general sort of way, but 'to lay down exact and
precise rules for the direction of every circumstance of our
behaviour' (TMS VII. iv. 7). Moralists of this second sort are both
the casuists and those who treat of what Smith calls 'natural
jurisprudence'. The proper concern of these moralists is with
justice, because Smith thinks that it 'is the only virtue with regard
to which such exact rules can properly be given'. But although both
casuists and jurisprudentialists try to write precisely about justice,
they do so in different ways. The difference is an interesting one.

> Those who write upon the principles of jurisprudence, con-
> sider only what the person to whom the obligation is due,
> ought to think himself entitled to exact by force; what every

impartial spectator would approve of him for exacting, or what a judge or arbiter, to whom he had submitted his case, and who had undertaken to do him justice, ought to oblige the other person to suffer or to perform. The casuists, on the other hand, do not so much examine what it is, that might properly be exacted by force, as what it is, that the person who owes the obligation ought to think himself bound to perform from the most sacred and scrupulous regard to the general rules of justice, and from the most conscientious dread, either of wronging his neighbour, or of violating the integrity of his own character. It is the end of jurisprudence to prescribe rules for the decisions of judges and arbiters. It is the end of casuistry to prescribe rules for the conduct of a good man. (TMS VII. iv. 8)

To illustrate the two points of view, Smith takes the case of a highwayman who by the fear of death obliges a traveller to promise him a sum of money. The question is whether such a promise, extorted by force, ought to be regarded as obligatory. Smith argues that if we view the matter as a question of jurisprudence there is no problem; the traveller could not be held to be legally bound by his promise. This was Hume's view.[3] But if we take it as a problem in casuistry the answer is not so easy. The good man might feel himself bound by the promise – it all depends on the circumstances, how much the sum was, how the traveller was treated by the highwayman, and so on. But the important point, Smith stresses, is that

whenever such promises are violated, though for the most necessary reasons, it is always with some degree of dishonour to the person who made them . . . Our imagination therefore attaches the idea of shame to all violations of faith, in every circumstance and in every situation . . . Fidelity is so necessary a virtue, that we apprehend it in general to be due even to those to whom nothing else is due, and whom we think it lawful to kill and destroy. (TMS VII. iv. 13)

An up-to-date example of this point is the case of the IRA man who forced his Protestant hostages to promise on their Bible not to give evidence to the police. The hostages were later advised by their minister that they had an obligation to keep the promise.

These illustrations are clearly important for bringing out a difference between the jurisprudential and casuistical points of view. But apart from the specific point that the matter of duress seems more complex from the point of view of casuistry than from that of jurisprudence, what exactly is the difference? The answer might at first seem to be that jurisprudence is concerned with the rules of justice, whereas casuistry is concerned with those of beneficence, with 'rules for the conduct of a good man'. There is no doubt that Smith does maintain this distinction, but in this context the relevant distinction seems not to be that between justice and beneficence, but to be a distinction within justice. Smith suggests several ways of drawing the distinction. First, it seems to be a distinction between the view obtained by concentrating on the attitudes of those who possess rights and are owed duties, and that obtained by concentrating on the attitude of those who owe the duties – being, according to Smith, the points of view of jurisprudence and of casuistry respectively. But this way of drawing the distinction is unsatisfactory in that it would have the consequence of restricting the scope of good men to their approach to the performance of their duties, whereas sometimes goodness could consist in the waiving of rights. Secondly, and more plausibly, he suggests that it is a distinction between legal justice (the sphere of 'judges and arbiters') and moral justice (the sphere of a 'good man' who is concerned with 'the integrity of his own character').

Having drawn the distinction, Smith then goes on to point out the failure of writers on justice to take note of it:

> But though this difference be real and essential, though these two sciences propose quite different ends, the sameness of the subject has made such a similarity between them, that the greater part of authors whose professed design was to treat of jurisprudence, have determined the different questions they examine, sometimes according to the principles of that science, and sometimes according to those of casuistry, without distinguishing, and, perhaps, without being themselves aware when they did the one, and when the other. (TMS VII. iv. 15)

The practice of judges and other proponents of 'jurisprudence' pronouncing on matters of social and moral importance far beyond the bounds of law has continued to the present day. Smith, however, confines himself to a discussion of casuists who go beyond consideration of what a conscientious regard to the general rules of justice would demand of us and consider wider aspects of morality. The origins of this he finds in 'auricular confession' in times of barbarism and ignorance. His point is that people with burdens on their conscience wish to confide and to be persuaded that they are still worthy of regard. A group of clergy therefore emerged as confessors with a reputation for judging on all matters of moral right and wrong. But in order to become qualified as a confessor it was helpful to study 'cases of conscience', or 'nice and delicate situations in which it is hard to determine whereabouts the propriety of conduct may lie . . . and hence the origin of books of casuistry' (TMS VII. iv. 17). The duties which casuists chiefly considered were those governed by general rules, and where failure may be accompanied by punishment or remorse. In other words, the casuists were not mainly concerned with the supererogatory. Smith is obviously correct in explaining this by saying that we are all more concerned with our infringements of rules than we are with our failure to be as generous, friendly or otherwise as virtuous as we ought.

There were three sorts of duty which fell into the principal category. First, there were 'breaches of rules of justice', as we have seen. Secondly, there were breaches of the rules of chastity. Smith notes that the latter might also be breaches of justice, since they might involve injury to some other. At other times they might simply be a breach of decorum, but characteristically they are 'violations of a pretty plain rule'. Hence they bring ignominy and shame, and therefore fall within the sphere of casuistry. Thirdly, there are breaches of the rules of veracity. As with casuistry, such breaches may involve injustice, but they do not necessarily harm others. Nevertheless, they are always 'a breach of a very plain rule', and therefore bring shame.

Smith proceeds to a discussion of various aspects of veracity and of related virtues and vices. For example, he warns us against the dangers of being too credulous, while at the same time he notes that the 'desire of being believed seems to be one of the strongest of all our natural desires'. Indeed, he speculates that it is 'perhaps, the instinct upon which is founded the faculty of speech, the characteristical faculty of human nature' (TMS VII. iv. 25). Having already warned us against being too credulous, he proceeds to note that it is always mortifying not to be believed, and indeed, that 'to tell a man that he lies, is of all affronts the most mortal'. This leads him to consider related qualities of character, and he compares the man of reserve with the man of openness and frankness. It might be said that Smith is here indulging in many normative moral recommendations of the sort that he is shortly going to criticise the casuists for making. But this is unfair to Smith. What he is doing in these pages is to describe qualities of character and virtues and vices in the general sort of way which he regards as proper for the science of Ethics. He is not directing us to what is right or wrong in specific cases.

We can sum up his account of the nature of casuistry in his own words:

> The chief subjects of the works of the casuists, therefore, were the conscientious regard that is due to the rules of justice; how far we ought to respect the life and property of our neighbour; the duty of restitution; the laws of chastity and modesty; and wherein consisted what, in their language, are called the sins of concupiscence; the rules of veracity, and the obligations of oaths, promises, and contracts of all kinds. (TMS VII. iv. 32).

Smith's criticism of casuistry

Let us now turn from Smith's account of the nature and origin of casuistry to his criticisms of it. He makes two main critical claims: one is concerned with the casuists' treatment of the *content* of what we ought to do, and the other with the effect of casuistry on our *motivation*.

The first claim involves three connected points. The first of these is that the casuists 'attempted, to no purpose, to direct by precise rules what it belongs to feeling and sentiment only to judge of' (TMS VII. iv. 33). Smith's point here is not that rules are never appropriate – it will be remembered that they are the main subject matter of natural jurisprudence – but that the casuists use them for the looser virtues where rules are inappropriate. The second point is that in any event it is not possible to ascertain by rules what is required in many cases, for there cannot be rule-like dividing lines between, for example, a delicate sense of justice and a weak scrupulosity of conscience, or between reserve and dissimu-lation – 'what would hold good in any one case would scarcely do so exactly in another'. A third and connected point is that even although books of casuistry contain many cases, 'yet upon account of the still greater variety of possible circumstances' it would only be a matter of chance if a case was found which was exactly parallel to the one being considered. Hence, books of casuistry not only try to do the impossible, but are also useless. These connected criticisms concern the content of what we ought to do.

The second claim involves criticisms which concern our motivation towards duty. First, books of casuistry, because of their style, do not 'tend to animate us to what is generous and noble . . . or soften us to what is gentle and humane'. Secondly, and more dangerously, they 'tend rather to teach us to chicane with our own consciences, and by their vain subtilties serve to authorise innumerable evasive refinements with regard to the most essential articles of our duty' (TMS VII. iv. 33). In view of these criticisms it is not surprising that Smith concludes that 'casuistry ought to be rejected altogether' and that the 'two useful parts of moral philosophy, therefore, are Ethics and Jurisprudence' (TMS VII. iv. 34). He does note that some philosophers, such as Cicero, have produced doctrines not unlike the casuists, in that they have attempted to provide 'rules for our conduct in many nice cases'. But such philosophers are not really casuists because they have not attempted to provide complete systems, but have used the cases simply to illustrate that in some situations it is not clear what are the rules of duty.

It will be remembered that Smith regards Jurisprudence as a respectable branch of moral philosophy, and he therefore concludes his account of casuistry by discussing the relationship between it and systems of positive law. Jurisprudence does allow of precision, like the rules of a grammarian, and Smith seems to hold that it would be possible to work out a complete system of natural jurisprudence, or of rules of ideal justice. But for many reasons, such as the interest of the government or of those who tyrannise government, or 'rudeness and barbarism', or 'the unfortunate constitution of their courts of judicature', the positive laws of many nations do not exactly coincide with the dictates of natural justice. Indeed, 'In no country do the decisions of positive law coincide exactly, in every case, with the rules which the natural sense of justice would dictate' (TMS VII. iv. 36).

Smith completes his account of casuistry by looking forward to a work he intended to write but never completed. He notes that philosophers who have treated of justice in the past such as Plato, Aristotle and Cicero, have not attempted to provide a detailed enumeration of the rules of justice, but have treated justice in the general sort of way they have treated other virtues. Grotius is said to be an exception and to be the only author who has attempted in a systematic way to give a detailed account of the laws and institutions which might be expected to give effect to the more general principles of justice. He himself hopes in another book to carry out a similar project (TMS, advertisement).

The historical context

Before discussing Smith's arguments against casuistry I shall place them in a wider historical context. For although Smith gives his own slant to the arguments, he is writing in a climate which was increasingly hostile to casuistry. Why was this so? To understand the answer to this question we must consider some aspects of the history of casuistry.

It is generally supposed that casuistry is peculiarly a practice of the Roman Catholic Church. Certainly it is true that it originated in its distinctively modern form in the writings of the Church from the thirteenth century onwards. Smith is correct here in seeing the origins of casuistry in the challenges faced by the clergy when they had to deal with the many problems of individuals who came to confession. These problems generated a literature dealing with a wide range of religious, institutional and moral problems. But such preoccupations were by no means confined to the Roman Catholic Church and many casuistical works were produced by Protestants in Germany and England in the first part of the seventeenth century. The word 'casuistry', however, retains its connections with the Roman Catholic Church, and especially with the Jesuits. By the time Smith was writing, the word had acquired the pejorative associations which it has kept ever since. Indeed, a century earlier, in the mid-1650s, Pascal was able to ridicule casuistry in the *Lettres Provinciales*. We shall consider in the final section whether there is anything worthwhile in casuistry, despite its bad name, but let us first look at the typical problems discussed by the casuists.

The typical problems discussed were of four main kinds. First, there were those of the interpretation of the Scriptures or Church teaching. Such questions were naturally to be expected, as Smith notes, during periods of widespread ignorance. Secondly, there were problems of applying general rules to particular cases. For example, a great deal of literature was concerned, again as Smith notes, with the question of what constitutes telling lies. The early

Church Fathers disputed as to whether there could be circumstances in which lying was permissible, and Aquinas distinguished
between officious, jocose, and pernicious lies, or those intended to
benefit another person, those told as a joke, and those intended to
harm. Only lies in the last class were mortal sins.[4] Many other
general principles invited this kind of refinement over their application in particular cases. Thirdly, casuists were concerned with
problems of conflict between principles. Some duties were held to
be absolute, such as those deriving from the Ten Commandments,
or others deriving from practices of the church, such as the duty of
the confessor to keep a secret learned in the confessional. But
difficulties could arise if these absolute duties clashed, as when
telling the truth would lead to murder. Casuists acquired a bad
name for their discussion of such conflicts, but the problem is
genuine enough and discussion has continued among the learned
of this century as to how it should be resolved.[5] Fourthly, there
were problems of reconciling the ideals of moral behaviour as
specified in these absolute duties with the realities and necessities
of life. A duty not to steal might be laid down by the Church as
an absolute duty, but if times were hard there were difficulties for
the poor which, to their credit, the casuists recognised. Casuistry
provided a way of reconciling the absolute demands of the truly
religious life with the necessities of the fallen world.

Granted that these are some of the typical problems addressed
by the casuists, we can now consider why a climate developed
which was hostile to casuistry. The first reason is the socio-
economic changes which took place in the second half of the
seventeenth century. Let us illustrate this by looking at the
treatment by Smith, and later by Kant, of the problems of
reconciling the demands of duty with the necessities of life, which
as we have seen was a problem addressed by the casuists. Smith
writes:

> The thief imagines he does no evil, when he steals from the
> rich, what he supposes they may easily want, and what
> possibly they may never even know has been stolen from them
> . . . When once we begin to give way to such refinements, there
> is no enormity so gross of which we may not be capable. (TMS
> III. vi. 6. 10).

Kant considers the same kind of example – that of a person who holds someone else's property in trust. Here is Kant's statement of the case:

> Suppose, for instance, that someone is holding another's property in trust (a deposit) whose owner is dead, and that the owner's heirs do not know and can never hear about it. Present this case even to a child of eight or nine, and add that, through no fault of his, the trustee's fortunes are at their lowest ebb, that he sees a sad family around him, a wife and children disheartened by want. From all of this he would be instantly delivered by appropriating the deposit. And further that the man is kind and charitable, while those heirs are rich, loveless, extremely extravagant spendthrifts, so that this addition to their wealth might as well be thrown into the sea. And then ask whether under these circumstances it might be deemed permissible to convert the deposit to one's own use. Without doubt, anyone asked will answer 'No!' – and in lieu of grounds he can merely say: 'It is wrong!', i.e. it conflicts with duty.[6]

This example, like that of Smith, is very much in the tradition of casuistry, but it is now a Protestant casuistry influenced by a stress on the importance of protecting property. It has been argued by many that this is characteristic of the values of bourgeois society.[7] We may say, then, that the first factor in the creation of a climate hostile to casuistry from the end of the seventeenth century and on through the eighteenth century is the rise of 'possessive individualism' reflected in the writings of Smith, Kant and many others. Casuistry was seen as a threat to that social order and had therefore to be rejected. Kant's moral ideal of a Kingdom of Ends is in fact a kingdom of those able to exercise free, rational and *economic* choice.

It will be remembered that Smith, while rejecting the attempts of casuists at finding precise rules, recognised as legitimate the efforts of those engaged in natural jurisprudence to produce precise rules. In this he was again influenced by an intellectual current of some strength – the rise of Protestant natural law jurisprudence. This was a movement which both incorporated elements of casuistry and was hostile to it, for the reason that both groups were engaged in similar sorts of reasoning. Let us look first at the influence of casuistry on natural law and jurisprudence.

One influence of casuistry on natural law jurisprudence was

through the casuists' doctrine of 'probabilism'. The doctrine can be explained as follows. As we have already seen it was important to the Church – more specifically in the Counter-Reformation, to the Jesuits – that laymen by means of the confessional should be directed on a path through the world which accommodated Church law to worldly needs. Now these experts, the Jesuits, sometimes differed in their opinions. If, therefore, a layman strayed from the path laid down by one Jesuit he could not fairly be blamed, for it was always 'probable' that the vagrant path followed had been mentioned by another Jesuit. A confessor therefore had the duty of finding a 'probable' opinion which could be cited to relieve the burden on a penitent's conscience. This practice is satirised, as was said, by Pascal.

Despite its abuses, however, the doctrine of 'probablism' did have a profound influence on writers on jurisprudence, and in particular it has been argued that the doctrine of 'probablism' is the origin of the doctrine of 'reasonable doubt' in English law. It was in fact not until the second half of the seventeenth century that 'reasonable doubt' could be invoked in the assessment of evidence in English law. The seventeenth-century judge and writer on law, Sir Matthew Hale, attacked the mathematical model of legal reasoning as found in Hobbes and defended the accumulation of past probabilistic experience. He wrote that: 'since the Subject of Laws are Morall Actions, there cannot be expected that precise certaintie or Evidence thereof, as there is to be found in Mathematicks' . . . 'The great variety of Circumstances which Accompany moral Actions . . . Strangely diversify the application of the Generall Laws'. The reasoning typical of casuistry is then depicted by Hale as more appropriate for law and morality:

> the decisions are more difficult and inevident, and the variety of Mens judgements give different Theorys and make different Conclusions touching them: And therefore to settle and determine these is required much Exercise of the reasoning Faculty, much Judgement and advertence which doth not so commonly fall under ordinary Capacities, this we may easily perceive in the Curious and Subtile Works of Many writers of Morall Philosophy and the Schoolmen and Casuists of this and former Ages.[8]

The writers on jurisprudence therefore borrowed from the casuists, but many also expressed hostility to casuistry and saw it as the job of the *lawyer* to determine particular cases in everyday life. What then was the place of the divines? The answer given by many, such as Locke and Grotius, was that the clergy had an educative role; but the defender of everyday morality through the common law was to be the lawyer. Locke writes that: 'The business of true religion is something quite different. It is not made for outward pomp, nor for ecclesiastical dominion, let alone for force; but for regulating men's lives in accordance with virtue and piety.' The role of the lawyer or magistrate, on the other hand, is to ensure through the civil laws 'the just possession of these things that belong to this life'.[9]

For the purpose of this chapter the important point is that writers on jurisprudence took on the mantle of casuistry while rejecting the suggestion that it was casuistry that they were engaged in. Smith himself notes the ambiguity. He observes that writers on both casuistry and jurisprudence had slid from one to the other without noting that they had done so. My second point, then, is that an atmosphere hostile to casuistry was created, in that those writing in the tradition of Protestant natural law perceived themselves as having exclusive rights to this sort of probabilistic argument. The lawyers had replaced the Jesuits as the new 'experts'. The third factor was a change, or a making explicit, of a moral outlook. The central characteristic of this outlook was its emphasis on the autonomy of the individual moral conscience. Many philosophers throughout the second half of the seventeenth century expressed this in a variety of ways and contexts. For example, Thomas Rainborough of the Leveller faction expresses the idea in a political context when he is concerned about suffrage: 'Every man born in England cannot, ought not, neither by the Law of God nor the Law of Nature, to be exempted from the choice of those who are to make laws for him to live under, and for him, for aught I know, to lose his life under.'[10] Again, in 1690 John Locke expresses the idea in a context in which he is stressing the importance of the exercise of individual judgement.

> The fourth and last wrong measure of probability I shall take notice of, and which keeps in ignorance or error more people than all the others together, is that which I have mentioned in the foregoing chapter; I mean the giving up our assent to the common received opinion, either of our friends or party, neighbourhood or country. How many men have no other

ground for their tenets, than the supposed honesty, or learning, or number of those of the same profession? . . . This at
least is certain, there is not an opinion so absurd, which a man
may not receive upon this ground; there is no error to be
named, which has not had its professors: and a man shall
never want crooked paths to walk in, if he thinks that he is in
the right way, whenever he has the footsteps of others to
follow.[11]

By the early eighteenth century the idea is widespread. Bishop
Butler expresses it as a moral point as follows:

And from all these things put together, nothing can be more
evident, than that, exclusive of revelation, man cannot be
considered as a creature left by his Maker to act at random,
and live at large up to the extent of his natural power, as
passion, humour, wilfulness, happen to carry him; which is the
condition brute creatures are in; but that *from his make,
constitution, or nature, he is in the strictest and most proper sense a law*
to himself. He hath the rule of right within: what is wanting
is only that he honestly attend to it.[12]

It is important to notice that this doctrine of the autonomy of
the individual will can, and historically did, take one or other of
two forms. For some writers individual conscience is expressed
through judgements of individual reason. This tradition was to
culminate in Kant's doctrine of pure practical reason or rational
will. For other writers conscience is expressed through feeling. This
version of it is developed in the 'moral sense' or 'moral sentiment'
school of British empiricism, and it is this version which Smith
expresses. 'It may be said in general of the works of the casuists
that they attempted, to no purpose, to direct by precise rules what
it belongs to feeling and sentiment only to judge of' (TMS VII. iv.
33).

A point related to the idea of individual conscience as moral
sense or rational faculty concerns the *immediacy* which is to be
expected from moral judgements and was thought to be lacking in
the devious writings of the casuists. If the conscience is indeed a
special faculty then we would expect that, like our other senses, it
would pronounce immediately. Butler again is clearly tilting at the
casuists when he writes that:

In all common ordinary cases we see intuitively at first view
what is our duty, what is the honest part. This is the ground

of the observation, that the first thought is often the best. In these cases doubt and deliberation is itself dishonest: as it was in *Balaam* upon the second message. That which is called considering what our duty is in a particular case, is very often nothing but endeavouring to explain it away. Thus those courses, which, if men would fairly attend to the dictates of their own consciences, they would see to be corruption, excess, oppression, uncharitableness; these are refined upon – things were so and so circumstantiated – great difficulties are raised about fixing bounds and degrees: and thus every moral obligation whatever may be evaded.[13]

Smith himself frequently uses the term 'chicane' for this process of considering what our duty is in a particular case. 'A man often becomes a villain the moment he begins, even in his own heart, to chicane in this manner' (TMS VII. iv. 10). Again, the works of the casuists do not 'tend to animate us to what is generous and noble . . . but tend rather to teach us to chicane with our own consciences' (TMS VII. iv. 33). To 'chicane' for Smith is to depart from immediate pronouncements and engage in 'abstruse and metaphysical distinctions'.

At this point a question can be raised as to why Smith allowed the practice of natural jurisprudence, which involves 'abstruse distinctions' if not chicaning, while rejecting casuistry. The answer is that law was seen as something external to the newly-discovered individual self. Certainly, there were problems of collisions between individual conscience and law, and an important aspect of the history of jurisprudence is that of recording successive attempts to keep law and conscience in harmony. But to the extent that law was perceived to be external to the self, it was regarded as legitimate for there to be 'experts' who considered precise applications of natural jurisprudence in systems of positive law.

My claim in this section has been that Adam Smith was able to write with confidence against the casuists because he was writing in an intellectual climate affected by the rise of possessive individualism with its emphasis on property rights, by the rise of a strong school of Protestant natural rights theory, and, most importantly, by the emergence of the distinctively modern idea of the importance of the individual conscience – a faculty which, whether predominantly rational or sentimental or a mixture, was capable of immediate awareness of what ought to be done.

Smith's criticisms and modern casuistry

Let us now in this final section consider Adam Smith's arguments against casuistry outside their historical context, as arguments in their own right. Are they persuasive, and in particular, what force, if any, do they have against the rise of casuistry in our own time in the form of medical ethics, business ethics and the like? It might be helpful to address three questions. I shall consider in the light of Smith's arguments, and contemporary practice, whether casuistry is possible, whether it is desirable, and whether it is a legitimate part of moral philosophy.

Note to begin with that any discussion of casuistry presupposes that there is a correct answer to a moral question, that in some sense of the ambiguous term 'objective', moral judgements are objective. This hardly needs saying if we are dealing with the casuistry of the Counter-Reformation, or that of the Protestant tradition of natural law. All the thinkers of the seventeenth and eighteenth centuries accepted some version of an objective view. The possible exception is Hume, who is often interpreted as the founder of what has come to be known as 'emotivism'. But even Hume accepts a modified doctrine of natural law, at least in his account of the origins of justice.

Nowadays, however, many philosophers espouse some form of emotivism, or its developments, such as prescriptivism. For such philosophers casuistry must be a pointless procedure for, in terms of such a view, there is nothing that objectively one ought to do anyway, so there is no point in worrying, far less 'chicaning', in the process of deciding. Indeed, the 'angst' of the Existentialist writers is located in a contradiction: they reject any form of objectivity while at the same time they stress the importance of making a morally responsible choice. But if a choice can in no sense be objectively right or wrong, it cannot be said to matter how one chooses. Why, then, the anguish? Be that as it may, it can be argued that the casuistry of medical ethics does presuppose some sort of objectivity in that the arguments – 'case conferences' – take place against a background of codes of medical ethics which have a quasi-legal status. Let us now consider the extent to which Smith's arguments are valid against this distinctively modern form of casuistry.

His first argument, it will be recalled, was that casuists attempted 'to no purpose, to direct by precise rules what it belongs to feelings and sentiment only to judge of'. We noted that there are several points here. One is that casuists seek for rules when it is not appropriate. Now, in so far as we think of medical ethics as discussed against a background of codes, then a search for precise rules might be appropriate. For example, most codes contain rules enjoining confidentiality. But can a doctor tell a colleague what a patient has told him in confidence if the transmission of such information will be for the benefit of the patient? This kind of question is similar to those discussed both by the casuists of the Counter-Reformation and by those of the Protestant natural law tradition.

Before we accept modern casuistry as legitimate, we must consider the force of the second and third points which come out of Smith's first argument – that there cannot be clear rule-like dividing lines between closely similar cases, and that books of cases are useless because of the even greater variety of possible circumstances. These points are relevant to modern discussion in view of the dominant 'case conference' method of teaching and discussing medical ethics.[14]

The answer to Smith here is to point out that what is taking place in such discussions is a form of what he calls 'natural jurisprudence'. It is an attempt to translate into case law, to give concrete application to, the ideals contained in codes. If natural jurisprudence is a legitimate activity, so too is this.

It might be objected that such discussions are assuming that there can be moral experts, and that such an assumption is incompatible with the assumption of the moral importance of individual autonomy which underlies the anti-casuistry arguments. The answer to this is that indeed some conception of expertise is being presupposed. If we consider many of the complex issues which are faced in medical ethics, such as problems of surrogacy, genetic engineering, the transplanting of foetal tissue to mitigate the effects of Parkinson's disease and so on, we are dealing with problems where both the technical and the moral issues are so complex that something approaching an expertise is involved. An example of modern casuistry which illustrates this is the Warnock Report on Human Reproduction.[15] But the need for expert opinion does not mean that we do not also require autonomous judgement; the judgement is the more autonomous through being informed by a rational expertise. We can conclude that medical ethics is possible in so far as it approximates to what Smith means by natural jurisprudence; in so far as it is a kind of natural jurisprudence, it does not violate individual autonomy because it is providing guidelines which are external to the self.

Smith's second group of arguments against casuistry were to the effect that it does not 'animate us to what is generous and noble' but rather teaches us 'to chicane with our consciences'. Smith is certainly correct in claiming that casuistry is concerned mainly with what is required or forbidden, that is, with rules, rather than with questions of motivation. And medical ethics is predominantly concerned with similar questions. We noted that the chief problems the casuists addressed were the interpretation of the Scriptures and Church teaching, the application of rules to particular cases, conflicts between general principles, and the reconciling of ideals or principles with the necessities of life. Medical ethics is predominantly concerned with a range of similar questions. As we have seen, there are problems of interpreting codes and BMA teaching, applying these general principles to particular cases, reconciling conflicts (many writers assume that all problems in medical ethics are 'dilemmas'), and finally reconciling the ideals of medical practice with the necessities, often economic necessities, of modern life. What bearing do the arguments in Smith's second group of criticisms have on these endeavours?

To deal first with the second part of Smith's criticism, we can say that it does not follow that to discuss such important and difficult questions is to begin to 'chicane' with our conscience. Many moral problems are of such complexity that it is not possible to pronounce immediately on them. Smith lived in a simpler age, although he perhaps underestimated the complexity of the moral problems even of his own age.

As for the first part of his criticism, that casuistry does not 'animate us to what is generous and noble', we might reply that this is not a legitimate function of ethics. Even those philosophers who allow that ethics has a normative function draw the line before this. If ethics can assist in discovering what we should do, then this is as far as it can reasonably go; to motivate is another matter entirely.

It may be, however, that Smith's point can be restated as one about awareness, rather than motivation: what in modern parlance might be called 'consciousness-raising'. It is true that the casuistry of Smith's times and earlier tended not to deal with that, but many modern writers on casuistry, especially in the area of medical ethics, are concerned with it.[16] For example, they are sometimes concerned with raising the awareness of doctors of the indignities and impersonality of high-technology medicine. There is therefore a similarity between one aspect of modern casuistry and one aspect of what Smith means by ethics, as distinct from what he means by casuistry. Despite Smith's arguments, then, casuistry is possible, and medical ethics illustrates a modern form of casuistry which has similarities both to casuistry (and natural jurisprudence) in his sense and to one aspect of ethics in his sense.

Is casuistry desirable? It would be undesirable if it did indeed teach us to chicane with our conscience. But this is surely not inherent in the activity. The logic of Smith's use of the term casuistry is as follows: helpful and worthwhile attempts to interpret complex doctrines, apply rules to particular cases, resolve conflicts and adapt the ideal to the real are to be applauded and called 'natural jurisprudence'; unhelpful or unsuccessful attempts at the same are to be called 'casuistry'. The criticism of Smith is a little unfair, because the casuists he criticises, as some who nowadays write on medical ethics, did attempt to find precision where it cannot be found. But this overzealous approach is not intrinsic to the casuistical process. In so far as casuistry confines itself to seeking precision where it *can* be found it can be regarded as a desirable undertaking, and the same is true of its modern counterpart, medical ethics.

There is another aspect of casuistry, the desirableness of which might be questioned. Does casuistry take from us the burden of individual responsibility and hand us over to moral experts? We have already touched on this question. It will be remembered that we argued that indeed there are areas where the concept of the expert is not inappropriate. For example, moral problems of the natural environment are complex, and so too are some moral problems in medicine. Reference to a moral expert committee therefore makes some sense, and need not threaten autonomy. On the other hand, there is a tendency, especially in the USA, for doctors to turn to 'ethicists' as they are called, rather as they might turn to a biochemist, for an expert opinion. This is surely to be rejected as a legitimate procedure. The ethicist may have the legitimate function of clarifying for the doctor some of the complex moral issues with which medicine must deal. But in the end it is the doctor and the patient together who must decide. Provided they do not attempt to bypass autonomy, then casuistry and medical ethics are desirable forms of intellectual activity.

Finally, we can raise the question of whether casuistry, granted that it is possible and can be desirable, is a branch of moral philosophy. We can ask the same of medical ethics. There is no one answer to this question because fashions change as to what is or is not a legitimate function of moral philosophy. There is, however, one objection to the view that casuistry is a legitimate branch of moral philosophy which is based on a misunderstanding. The objection is that the judgements of casuistry are directed at reaching decisions in *particular* cases, whereas moral philosophy is concerned with *types* of case. Smith himself certainly held that moral philosophy was concerned with types, for it belonged to what he called 'didactic discourse'. Didactic discourse was concerned with putting 'the arguments on both sides of the question in their true light, giving each its proper degree of influence, and has it in view to persuade no further than the arguments themselves appear convincing' (LRBL i. 149). This type of discourse is contrasted on the one hand with rhetoric which attempts to persuade, and on the other hand with 'narrative discourse' (such as historical discourse) which is concerned with particular events or actions. Philosophy, like the sciences, is a form of didactic discourse and is directed at types of event or action. 'In every case, therefore, Species or Universals, and not Individuals, are the objects of Philosophy' (EPS, p. 119, Logics and Metaphysics).[17] If we assume this view of philosophy, then it will follow that if casuistry is directed at reaching decisions in particular cases it cannot be a branch or moral philosophy.

This kind of objection has been discussed, perhaps surprisingly, by G. E. Moore.[18] He agrees that casuistry is much more detailed and particular than ethics,

> but that means that they differ only in degree and not in kind
> . . . Both alike deal with what is general, in the sense in which
> physics and chemistry deal with what is general . . . Casuistry
> aims at discovering what actions are good, *wherever they occur*
> . . . For just as physics cannot rest content with the discovery
> that light is propagated by waves of ether, but must go on to

discover the particular nature of the ether-waves corresponding to each several colour; so Casuistry, not content with the
general law that charity is a virtue, must attempt to discover
the relative merits of every different form of charity. Casuistry
forms, therefore, part of the ideal of ethical science: Ethics
cannot be complete without it.

In so far as we accept this view of casuistry – that it attempts to
produce refined rules which may help in deciding individual cases
– it will fit with Smith's view of philosophy as concerned with
species or types of action. Smith's own objection to the use of
refined rules was rather that they tend to usurp our own decisions
in particular cases. But, as we have seen, to use precise rules is not
to dispense with the need for individual autonomous judgement in
particular cases.

We are now in a position to sum up. It will be remembered that
Smith depicted moral philosophy as follows:

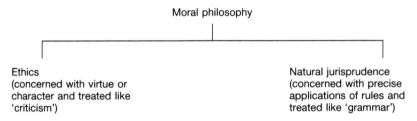

Moral philosophy

Ethics
(concerned with virtue or
character and treated like
'criticism')

Natural jurisprudence
(concerned with precise
applications of rules and
treated like 'grammar')

Casuistry was rejected as useless and pernicious. I have argued
that what Smith is really rejecting is what we might call the
pathology of casuistry. The valuable aspects of it can be assimilated
into broad interpretations both of what he calls 'ethics' – the
'consciousness-raising' aspects of ethics – and of what he calls
'natural jurisprudence'; and this is true of that modern form of
casuistry which is medical ethics. If we accept this argument then
the diagram must be extended as follows:

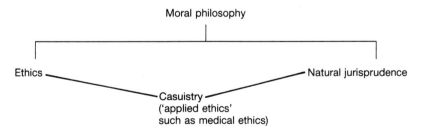

Moral philosophy

Ethics

Natural jurisprudence

Casuistry
('applied ethics'
such as medical ethics)

Notes

1. My views on the history of casuistry have been influenced by the chapters by Edmund Leites, Margaret Sampson and H. D.-Kittsteiner in Leites, ed. (1988). I am also indebted to Elizabeth Telfer for commenting on my views on casuistry.
2. For an illuminating account of Smith's views on the nature of philosophy see T. D. Campbell (1971), chapter 1.
3. David Hume, *Treatise of Human Nature*, III, ii. V.
4. Thomas Aquinas, *Summa Theologica*, translated by English Dominican Province (1922), 2.2, ques. 110, art. 1–4. Helpful passages on moral attitudes to lying are contained in S. Bok (1978).
5. Cf. W. D. Ross (1939), chap. 4.
6. I. Kant, *On the Old Saw: That may be Right in Theory, but it Won't Work in Practice*, tr. E. B. Ashton (1974), p. 53. There is an interesting discussion of Kant's views on casuistry in H. D.-Kittsteiner, 'Kant and Casuistry', in Leites (1988).
7. C. B. Macpherson (1962).
8. The quotations are from *Reflections by the Lord Chief Justice Hale on Mr Hobbes, his Dialogue of the Law*, published by W. Holdsworth (1921). I am indebted for this source to Margaret Sampson, 'Laxity and Liberty' in Edmund Leites (1988), pp. 86–8.
9. John Locke (1667) translated by J. W. Gough (1968), p. 60.
10. A. S. P. Woodhouse (1950), p. 56.
11. John Locke, *Essay Concerning Human Understanding* (1690), IV. xx. IV.
12. Joseph Butler (1726), ed. W. R. Matthews (1949), Sermon III, para. 3.
13. Butler, *op. cit.*, Sermon VII, para. 14.
14. There are many examples of this in the literature of medical ethics, but a good example of this form of modern casuistry is Baruch Brody (1988).
15. *Report of the Committee of Inquiry into Human Fertilisation and Embryology* (1984).
16. See, for example, Rosemary and Victor Zorza (1980), and G. Pence (1980).
17. There is a discussion of Smith's views on different types of discourse in T. D. Campbell (1971), ch. 1.
18. G. E. Moore (1903), pp. 4–5.

References

Ashton, E. B., transl., *Kant, On the Old Saw* (Philadelphia, 1974).
Bok, S., *Lying* (Sussex, 1978).
Brody, B., *Life and Death and Decision Making* (Oxford, 1988).
Campbell, T. D., *Adam Smith's Science of Morals* (London, 1971).
Gough, J. W., transl., John Locke, *A Letter on Toleration* (Oxford, 1968).
Holdsworth, W., 'Sir Matthew Hales on Hobbes; an Unpublished MS', *Law Quarterly Review*, 37, pp. 286, 290.
Kittsteiner, H.-D., 'Kant and Casuistry', in Leites (1988).
Leites, E., ed., *Conscience and Casuistry in Early Modern Europe* (Cambridge, 1988).

Macpherson, C. B., *The Political Theory of Possessive Individualism* (Oxford, 1962).

Matthews, W. R., ed., *Joseph Butler, Fifteen Sermons* (London, 1949).

Moore, G. E., *Principia Ethica* (Cambridge, 1903).

Pence, G., *Ethical Options in Medicine* (New Jersey, 1980).

Report of the Committee of Enquiry into Human Fertilisation and Embryology, the Warnock Report (London, HMSO, 1984).

Ross, W. D., *Foundations of Ethics* (Oxford, 1939).

Sampson, M., 'Laxity and Liberty', in Leites (1988).

Woodhouse, A. S. P., ed., *Puritanism and Liberty, Being the Army Debates (1647–49) from the Clarke Manuscripts with Supplementary Documents* (London, 1950).

Zorza, R., V., *A Way to Die* (London, 1980).

7

Adam Smith: ethics and self-love

ANDREW S. SKINNER

Introduction

Modern preoccupations with certain matters of policy have given Smith's economic analysis and associated prescriptions renewed prominence. The psychological judgements on which *The Wealth of Nations* is apparently based have also attracted attention and made familiar Smith's classic statement that:

> It is not from the benevolence of the butcher, the brewer, or the baker, that we expect our dinner, but from their regard to their own interest. We address ourselves, not to their humanity but to their self-love, and never talk to them of our own necessities but of their advantages. Nobody but a beggar chuses to depend chiefly upon the benevolence of his fellow citizens. Even a beggar does not depend upon it entirely. (WN I. ii. 2)

Economists have interpreted this statement to mean that Smith was dealing with a restricted range of human experience in *The Wealth of Nations* – what Alfred Marshall was later to describe as the study of mankind 'in the ordinary business life' (1956, p. 12). Looked at in this way, the suggestion that men act in a self-interested manner can be seen as an hypothesis which makes the task of economic analysis more manageable. Exactly this point was made by Smith's contemporary, Sir James Steuart, when be observed: 'The principle of self-interest will serve as a general key to this enquiry; and it may, in one sense, be considered as the ruling principle of my subject, and may therefore be traced throughout the whole. This is the main spring . . . ' (1966, p. 142). Yet Smith's position is more complex than this line of argument might be taken to imply. To begin with there is an historical or 'genetic' dimension to the argument, which is also to be found in the work of Sir James Steuart and David Hume. In Smith's case the argument features the deployment of four 'stages' or modes of subsistence; the stages of hunting, pasture, agriculture and commerce. These stages help Smith to establish a precise set of linkages between types of economy and corresponding social structures or forms of dependence. In *The Wealth of Nations*, the argument is deployed in Book V where he addresses the problems of defence and justice in a variety of historical settings. But perhaps the most striking example is provided in Book III where Smith sets out to trace the gradual emergence of the present establishments in Europe starting from the collapse of the Roman Empire in the West. In so far as Smith wrote as an economist, he was concerned with an institutional structure with a history.

The argument had been first stated in Smith's *Lectures on Jurisprudence*. But in the *Lectures* Smith adopted a wider historical sweep as compared to *The Wealth of Nations* and concentrated more on the broadly constitutional implications which were involved. Adopting a more pluralist approach than is evident in the sociological analysis, Smith tried to bring out the relationship between economic development and the form of government, thus explaining the background to the Revolution Settlement (cf. Skinner, 1982). While the historical process unfolded by virtue of the activities of individuals who were unconscious of the ends which these actions served to promote, the result was a new environment, economic and political, wherein the active disposition of man was to find new and profoundly significant forms of expression.

The claim of freedom was not narrowly based. Smith also insisted that there was a *moral* dimension in suggesting that men *ought* to be permitted to enjoy the fruits of their own efforts, especially in the context of the fourth economic stage which had effectively broken down the bonds of dependence which characterised the feudal/agrarian situation. Smith went on to argue that the individual in the pursuit of his own interests should do so in a way which respects the interests and needs of others. He went further in suggesting that *all* actions, including the 'economic actions' of individuals or of corporations, are continually subject to the scrutiny of ourselves and others while being subject, further, to the discipline of accepted rules of social conduct, albeit with varying degrees of success.

Smith probably assumed that readers of *The Wealth of Nations* would have read *The Theory of Moral Sentiments*. It is certainly to this book that we must turn before the dimension of Smith's thought to which we have just alluded can be illuminated. It is only in the *Moral Sentiments* that we confront a full treatment of the complex psychology of self-love. This is to be found throughout the work, but especially in Part VI which was added to the sixth edition in 1790.

It will be convenient to begin with Smith's account of the way in which we judge the behaviour of ourselves and others, before exploring some of the implications of the argument for our understanding of Smith's approach to certain economic, moral and political questions.

The process of moral judgement: the background

Smith's *Theory of Moral Sentiments*, which owes a great deal to Hutcheson and Hume, might well be regarded as an extensive commentary on the text: 'There is no virtue without propriety, and wherever there is propriety some degree of approbation is due. But . . . though propriety is an essential ingredient in every virtuous action, it is not always the sole ingredient' (TMS VII. ii. 1. 50). In expounding on this text, Smith first explains what is meant by the concept of propriety, before going on to draw a distinction between propriety and virtue, and propriety and merit. In fulfilling these tasks it may be argued that he initially considers actions or expressions of feeling which do not have consequences for others, before going on to examine the more complex case where a judgement has to be formed with regard both to the actions of the agent and the reactions of the subject. We may take these in turn.

On Smith's argument, the process by which we distinguish between objects of approval or disapproval involves a complex of abilities and propensities which include sympathy, imagination, reason and reflection. To begin with, he stated that man is possessed of a certain 'fellow-feeling': 'How selfish soever man may be supposed, there are evidently some principles in his nature, which interest him in the fortune of others, and render their happiness necessary to him, though he derives nothing from it except the pleasure of seeing it' (TMS I. i. 1. 1). This fellow-feeling, or interest in the fortune of others, permits us to feel joy or sorrow, as it were on their behalf, and to form a judgement as to whether or not the circumstances faced by an individual contribute to a state of pleasure or of pain. An expression of sympathy (broadly defined) for another person thus involves an act of reflection and imagination on the part of the observer or spectator, in the sense that we can only form a judgement with respect to the situation faced by another person 'by changing places in the fancy' with him.

The question of propriety becomes relevant when we go beyond the consideration of the circumstances facing the subject, to examine the extent to which his actions or 'affections' (i.e. expressions of feeling) are appropriate to the conditions prevailing or to the objects which they seek to attain. Smith thus defined propriety or impropriety as consisting in 'the suitableness or unsuitableness, in the proportion or disproportion which the affection seems to bear to the cause or object which excites it' (TMS I. i. 3. 6).

Given the principles so far established, it follows that where the spectator of another man's conduct seeks to form an opinion as to its propriety, he must 'bring home to himself' both the circumstances and the 'affections' of the person judged. As before, Smith argued that such a judgement on the part of the spectator must involve an effort of the imagination, since 'When we judge in this manner of any affection, as proportioned or disproportioned to the cause which excited it, it is scarce possible that we should make use of any other rule or canon but the corresponding affection in ourselves' (TMS I. i. 3. 9). The argument suggests that the actions of all men are judged by the spectator of their conduct, and that 'When the original passions of the person principally concerned are in perfect concord with the sympathetic emotions of the spectator, they necessarily appear to this last just and proper' (TMS I. i. 3. 1).

The argument raises two distinct but connected problems, affecting the person judged and the person who judges. In the first place it is evident that the spectator can only 'enter into' the situation of another to a limited degree; the problem being that we have 'no immediate experience of what other men feel'. As Smith pointed out: 'Mankind, though naturally sympathetic, never conceive, for what has befallen another, that degree of passion which naturally animates the person principally concerned' (TMS I. i. 4. 7). It was in recognition of this point that Smith went on to argue that the degree to which the spectator can 'enter into ' the feelings of the subject can involve a virtue – the 'soft and amiable' virtue of sensibility or humanity.

Secondly, it is evident that if the reactions of the spectator provide the means by which the conduct of others is judged, and if the spectator has no immediate experience of what other men feel, then it follows that an action which is considered to be 'proper' by the spectator must involve an element of restraint on the part of the agent. In other words, the person *judged* can only attain the agreement, and thus the approval of the spectator 'by lowering his passion to that pitch, in which the spectators are capable of going along with him. He must flatten, if I may be allowed to say so, the sharpness of its natural tone, in order to reduce it to harmony and concord with the emotions of those who are about him' (TMS I. i. 4. 7).

It thus follows that before actions or expressions of feeling can be approved by the spectator, an element of restraint must be present: a certain mediocrity of expression with which Smith associated the 'awful and respectable' virtue of self-command. In this way Smith made due allowance for both sets of virtues, and in so doing illustrated what he meant by saying that propriety was an essential, but not the sole, ingredient of virtue. As he noted, 'the virtues of sensibility and self-command are not apprehended to consist in the ordinary, but in the uncommon degrees of those qualities' (TMS I. i. 5. 6). There is, in short, a considerable difference between 'those qualities and actions which deserve to be admired and celebrated, and those which simply deserve to be approved of' (TMS I. i. 5. 7).

The latter points serve to introduce the second side of Smith's account, namely, his interest not merely in the judgement of an action in relation to the 'cause or object which excites it', but also in relation to the end proposed or the effects produced. In this connection, Smith argued that the merit or demerit of an action would depend on the beneficial or hurtful effects which it tended to produce, and that judgement in such cases would involve framing an opinion as to the propriety of the action of the agent and of the reaction of the subject. More specifically, Smith argued that our sense of the merit of an action 'seems to be a compounded sentiment, and to be made up of two distinct emotions; a direct sympathy with the sentiments of the agent, and an indirect sympathy with the gratitude of those who receive the benefit of his actions' (TMS II. i. 5. 2). It then follows that 'In the same manner as our sense of the impropriety of conduct arises from a want of sympathy, or from a direct antipathy to the affections and motives of the agent, so our sense of its demerit arises from what I shall here . . . call an indirect sympathy with the resentment of the sufferer' (TMS II. i. 5. 4). Smith emphasised three points which derive from this argument.

He noted first that our estimate of the merit or demerit of an action must be linked to our understanding of the motives of the agent, and not merely to an appreciation of its consequences. 'We do not . . . thoroughly and heartily sympathise with the gratitude of one man towards another, merely because this other has been the cause of his good fortune, unless he has been the cause of it from motives which we entirely go along with' (TMS II. i. 4. 1). Nor, he points out, can we sympathise entirely with the resentment which one man feels for another 'unless he has been the cause of it from motives which we cannot enter into'.

Secondly, Smith argued that actions which are judged to have the quality of 'merit' dispose us to reward the perpetrator of them by virtue of our fellow-feeling with both the agent and the subject.

> But when to the hurtfulness of the action is joined the impropriety of the affection from whence it proceeds, when our heart rejects with abhorrence all fellow-feeling with the motives of the agent, we then heartily and entirely sympathise with the resentment of the sufferer. Such actions seem then to deserve, and, if I may say so, to call aloud for, a proportionable punishment; and we entirely enter into, and thereby approve of, that resentment which prompts to inflict it. (TMS II. i. 4. 4).

Thirdly, it is argued that 'the greater and more irreparable the evil that is done, the resentment of the sufferer runs naturally the higher; so likewise does the sympathetic indignation of the spectator' (TMS II. ii. 2. 2). Hence, loss of life arouses the highest degree of resentment, followed by loss of liberty or property, which is followed in turn by breach of contract – on the gound that to 'be deprived of that which we are possessed of, is a greater evil than to be disappointed of what we have only the expectation' (*ibid.*).

It will be evident that Smith's argument is in large measure designed to explain the manner in which we form judgements as to the propriety or merit of actions taken by ourselves or others, and that such judgements always have a 'social' reference. Or, as Smith put it:

> Were it is possible that a human creature could grow up to manhood in some solitary place, without any communication with his own species, he could no more think of his own character, of the propriety or demerit of his own sentiments and conduct, of the beauty or deformity of his own mind, than of the beauty or deformity of his own face . . . Bring him into society, and he is immediately provided with the mirror which he wanted before. (TMS III. 1. 3)

The basic point is that men generally react to the images thus presented in a way which suggests that they are important to them: it is for this reason, for example, that we seek a certain mediocrity of expression in our expression of feeling. As Smith noted:

> Nature, when she formed man for society, endowed him with an original desire to please, and an original aversion to offend his brethren. She taught him to feel pleasure in their favourable, and pain in their unfavourable regard. She rendered their approbation most flattering and most agreeable to him for its own sake; and their disapprobation most mortifying and most offensive. (TMS III. ii. 6.).

Yet at the same time, Smith observed that this general disposition may be insufficient of itself to secure adequate levels of control over our passions or expressions of feeling, for reasons which are connected with the basic mechanisms by virtue of which judgements are formed, namely, the spectator of our conduct, who is required to be at once impartial and well informed.

In the case of the *actual* spectator it is evident that the accuracy of judgement must be a function of the *information* available, and that information with respect to the feelings of a person external to him, can never be complete. Smith's point is that we can generally acquire a level of information which is at least sufficient to permit us to arrive at an informed judgement, when contemplating the observed circumstances of an individual or his reaction to them. But at the same time there is evidently one area where it is particularly difficult to get access to the necessary information, namely, that which relates to the motives which prompt a person to act in a particular way. This is obviously an important problem, given Smith's contention that knowledge of motive is essential to the decision as to whether or not an action partakes in any degree

of merit. Smith formally recognised the point in the discussion of
justice when noting that men typically judge 'by the event and not
by the design', observing that in this lay some advantage: 'That
necessary rule of justice . . . that men in this life are liable to
punishment for their actions only, not for their designs and
intentions, is founded upon this salutary and useful irregularity in
human sentiments concerning merit or demerit, which at first sight
appears so absurd and unaccountable' (TMS II. iii. 3. 2). Yet at
the same time it is evident that while this 'irregularity' may be
useful in one sense, in another it may have a contrary tendency in
that it constitutes a 'great discouragement' to virtue.

Hence the prominent importance in Smith's theory of the
'supposed' or '*ideal*' spectator of our own conduct (that is, the
spectator whom we visualise as being always well-informed with
regard to our own motives), and his argument that we are really
subject to two sources of judgement – that of the 'man without'
and that of 'the man within' (cf. TMS p. *17*). 'The jurisdiction of
the man within, is founded altogether in the desire of praise-
worthiness, and in the aversion to blame-worthiness' (TMS III. 2.
32).

The second aspect of Smith's problem arises from the fact that
man is presented as an active, and frequently self-regarding being,
who is unlikely to be wholly impartial in judging his own actions.

Self-love and approbation

Self-love (which for the purpose of the *present* argument I take to
be synonymous with self-interest) represents a thread which runs
through the argument which we have just considered and reflects
Smith's recognition of the point that 'Every man, as the Stoics used
to say, is first and principally recommended to his own care' (TMS
VI. ii. 1. 1). Smith objected to Francis Hutcheson's assertion that
self-love was a principle 'which could never be virtuous in any
degree or in any direction' (TMS VII, ii. 3. 12). Against this
position Smith argued that a regard 'to our own private happiness
and interest . . . appear upon many occasions very laudable
principles of action' (TMS VII. ii. 3. 16) and added that:

> whatever may be the case with the Deity, so imperfect a
> creature as man, the support of whose existence requires so
> many things external to him, must often act from many other
> motives. The condition of human nature were peculiarly hard,

if those affections, which, by the very nature of our being, ought frequently to influence our conduct, could upon no occasion appear virtuous, or deserve esteem and commendation from anybody. (TMS VII. ii. 3. 18)

But Smith also consistently argued that actions of a self-interested nature frequently reflect that desire for approval which is central to the ethical dimension of *The Theory of Moral Sentiments*, and further that such actions will take place at any given point in time within a particular social and economic environment. The theme is elaborated in Part VI of the work where Smith describes the roles which we play in the context of the 'subaltern societies' to which we typically belong – such as the immediate and extended family, circles of friends, place of employment and professional associations. Self-love also has its part to play in the political area where Smith noted that:

> Men desire to have some share in the management of publick affairs chiefly on account of the importance which it gives them. Upon the power which the greater part of the leading men, the natural aristrocracy of every country, have of preserving or defending their respective importance, depends the stablity and duration of every system of free government. (WN IV. vii. c. 74)

Major applications of Smith's psychological assumptions are also to be found in his treatment of questions which are more explicitly economic in character.

To begin with, Smith addressed the issue of utility or the sources of satisfaction which are attainable by virtue of man's command over resources. In *The Wealth of Nations*, for example, he drew attention to the fact that beauty and scarcity help to explain the value which we place upon commodities such as the precious metals or stones: 'The demand for the precious stones arises altogether from their beauty. They are of no use, but as ornaments; and the merit of their beauty is greatly enhanced by their scarcity' (WN I. xi. c. 32).[1] The argument builds upon that of the *Lectures on Jurisprudence* where Smith drew attention to the 'taste of beauty, which consists chiefly in the three following particulars, proper variety, easy connexion, and simple order' (LJ(B) p. 208) and elaborated on the significance of qualities such as colour and imitation.[2] He summarised the argument in the statement that:

> These qualities, which are the ground of preference and which

give occasion to pleasure and pain, are the cause of many insignificant demands which we by no means stand in need of. The whole industry of human life is employed, not in procuring the supply of our three humble necessities, food, cloaths, and lodging, but in procuring the conveniences of it according to the nicety and delicacey of our taste. To improve and mutiply the materials which are the principal objects of our necessities, gives occasion to all the variety of the arts. (LJ(B), p. 209)

The analysis was stated most fully in *The Theory of Moral Sentiments* Part IV and especially in Chapter 1 which is entitled 'Of the beauty which the appearance of utility bestows upon all the productions of art, and of the extensive influence of this species of beauty'. In this chapter Smith accepted Hume's suggestion that the utility of any object 'pleases the master by perpetually suggesting to him the pleasure of conveniency which it is fitted to promote ... The spectator enters by sympathy into the sentiments of the master, and necessarily views the object under the same agreeable aspect' (TMS IV. 1. 2). But Smith felt that the point could be further developed:

> But that this fitness, this happy contrivance of any production of art, should often be more valued, than the very end of which it was intended; and that the exact adjustment of the means for attaining any conveniency or pleasure, should frequently be more regarded, than that very conveniency or pleasure, in the attainment of which their whole merit would seem to consist, has not, so far as I know, been yet taken notice of by any body (TMS IV. 1. 3)

As the editors of the *Moral Sentiments* have observed, Smith 'sets great store by this observation not only for its originality but also because it forms a link, in his view, between ethics and political economy'. There are two links with the economic analysis which may be noted here. First, Smith uses the argument to explain the demand for commodities or for 'conveniences' (TMS IV. 1. 6). Secondly, he employs the argument to illustrate the point that: 'Power and riches appear then to be, what they are, enormous and operose machines contrived to produce a few trifling conveniencies to the body, consisting of springs the most nice and delicate' (TMS IV. 1. 8).

Smith went on to make two points both of which are associated with the argument developed thus far. He suggests that the 'rich' have an important function with regard to the distribution of the product. In a passage which contains a notable reference to the invisible hand, Smith remarked that:

> The homely and vulgar proverb, that the eye is larger than the belly, never was more fully verified than with regard to him. The capacity of his stomach bears no proportion to the immensity of his desires, and will receive no more than that of the meanest peasant. The rest he is obliged to distribute among those, who prepare, in the nicest manner, that little which he himself makes use of . . . They consume little more than the poor, and in spite of their natural selfishness and rapacity, tho' they mean only their own conveniency, tho' the sole end which they propose from the labour of all the thousands whom they employ, be the gratification of their own vain and insatiable desires, they divide with the poor the produce of all their improvements. They are led by an invisible hand to make nearly the same distribution of the necessaries of life, which would have been made, had the earth been divided into equal portions among all its inhabitants, and thus without intending it, without knowing it, advance the interest of the society, and afford means to the multiplication of the species. (TMS IV. 1. 10)

It should also be noted that Smith attached great importance to the point that the active pursuit of riches and of the imagined conveniences of wealth is a self-sustaining process which involves a deception, in the sense that realised satisfaction rarely equals that which had been expected. He added:

> It is well that nature imposes upon us in this manner. It is this deception which rouses and keeps in continual motion the industry of mankind. It is this which first prompted them to cultivate the ground, to build houses, to found cities and commonwealths, and to invent and improve all the sciences and arts, which ennoble and embellish human life, which have entirely changed the whole face of the globe, have turned the rude forests of nature into agreeable and fertile plains, and made the trackless and barren ocean a new fund of subsistence, and the great high road of communication to the different nations of the earth. The earth, by these labours of mankind has been obliged to redouble her natural fertility,

and to maintain a greater number of inhabitants. (TMS IV.
1. 10)

The references offered so far in addressing issues of an 'economic'
nature concentrate on motives which relate to *self* and trace some
of their consequences. But Smith went further in arguing that the
(self-interested) pursuit of wealth has a *social* reference.

In this context, Smith contended that 'a person appears mean-
spirited' who does not pursue the 'more extraordinary and important objects of self-interest', and contrasted the 'man of dull
regularity' with the 'man of enterprise', going on to remark that
'those great objects of self-interest, of which the loss or acquisition
quite changes the rank of the person, are the objects of the passion
properly called ambition' (TMS III. 6. 7). Smith concluded:

> it is chiefly from this regard to the sentiments of mankind, that
> we pursue riches and avoid poverty. For to what purpose is
> all the toil and bustle of this world? What is the end of avarice
> and ambition, of the pursuit of wealth, of power, and prehemi-
> nence [sic]? Is it to supply the necessities of nature? The wages
> of the meanest labourer can supply them. . . . From whence,
> then, arises that emulation which runs through all the different
> ranks of men, and what are the advantages which we propose
> by that great purpose of human life which we call bettering
> our condition? To be observed, to be attended to, to be taken
> notice of with sympathy, complacency, and approbation, are
> all the advantages which we can propose to derive from it. It
> is the vanity, not the ease, or the pleasure, which interests us.
> But vanity is always founded upon the belief of our being the
> object of attention and approbation. (TMS I. iii. 2: 1)[3]

The reference to vanity reminds us that the TMS affords some
interesting (if 'splenetic') perspectives on a basic human drive. In
at least one place Smith cited the case of the individual 'whom
heaven in its anger has visited with ambition' (TMS IV. i. 8).
Elsewhere he drew attention, with ironic wit, to 'place, that great
object which divides the wives of aldermen', as being the 'end of
half the labours of human life'. (TMS I. iii. 2. 8)

Yet Smith recognised that the pursuit of *place* and wealth was a
basic human drive which was linked to the desire to better our
condition, 'a desire which, though generally calm and dispassionate, comes with us from the womb, and never leaves us till we go
into the grave' (WN II. iii. 28); a drive which involves 'unrelenting

industry' (TMS IV. 1. 8) and sacrifices which are supported by
the approbation of our fellows. 'The habits of oeconomy, industry,
discretion, attention and application of thought, are generally
supposed to be cultivated from self-interested motives, and at the
same time are apprehended to be very praiseworthy qualities,
which deserve the esteem and approbation of every body' (TMS
IV. 2. 8). Hence, he continued, 'that eminent esteem with which
all men naturally regard a steady perseverance in the practice of
frugality, industry and application, though directed to no other
purpose than the acquisition of fortune'.[4] He added that it 'is the
consciousness of this merited approbation and esteem which is
capable of supporting the agent in this tenour of conduct', since
normally the 'pleasure which we are to enjoy ten years hence
interests us so little in comparison with that which we may enjoy
today' (TMS IV. 2. 8)[5]. In short, we admire both the ends (riches)
and the means of attaining them, where both refer to the opinions
of our fellows.

Self-love and constraint

What is most interesting about the argument is the repeated
emphasis on the point that the fundamental drive to better our
condition is rooted in a desire to be approved of or at least to be
admired. But Smith made a different, if related, point when he
observed that the individual in the pursuit of his own ends must
take account of the interests and opinions of his fellows. If the
individual:

> would act so that the impartial spectator may enter into the
> principles of his conduct, which is what of all things he has
> the greatest desire to do, he must, upon this, as upon all other
> occasions, humble the arrogance of his self-love, and bring it
> down to something which other men can go along with. They
> will indulge it so far as to allow him to be more anxious about,
> and to pursue with more earnest assiduity, his own happiness
> than that of any other person. Thus far, whenever they place
> themselves in his situation, they will readily go along with
> him. In the race for wealth, and honours, and preferments, he
> may run as hard as he can, and strain every nerve and every
> muscle, in order to outstrip all his competitors. But if he
> should justle, or throw down any of them, the indulgence of

the spectators is entirely at an end. It is a violation of fair play, which they cannot admit of. (TMS II. ii. 2. 1)

Smith added a further gloss to the argument in suggesting that the objectives of actions based upon self-love could be realised by practising the virtue of prudence, which is essentially rational self-love. In this context Smith cited Epicurus who rested his case on two main propositions: first, that in 'ease of body . . . and in security or tranquility of mind, consisted . . . the most perfect state of human nature' (TMS VII. ii. 2. 7) and, second, that bodily pleasure and pain were the sole ultimate objects of natural desire or aversion. In this system temperance can be seen as prudence with regard to pleasure, and caution as prudence with regard to tranquility – a state of mind which is attained only in so far as our actions do not cause others to regard us with indignation.

Smith rejected the general tenor of the approach partly on the ground that it too gave too little emphasis to the 'soft and amiable' virtues, in celebrating the importance of 'the habits of caution, vigilance and sobriety'. He also rejected an argument which seemed to suggest that an action could only be regarded as virtuous in so far as it contributes to some end, thus echoing the earlier criticism (TMS IV) of Hume's alleged reliance on utility as the basis of approbation.

Smith recognised that 'success or disappointment in our under-takings must very much depend upon the good or bad opinion which is commonly entertained of us, and upon the general disposition of those we live with, either to assist or to oppose us' (TMS VII. ii. 2. 13). Yet, as he observed:

> Prudence, . . when directed merely to the care of the health, of the fortune, and of the rank and reputation of the individual, though it is regarded as a most respectable, and even, in some degree, as an amiable and agreeable quality, yet it is never conceived as one, either of the most endearing or of the most ennobling of virtues. It commands a certain cold esteem, but seems not entitled to any very ardent love or admiration. (TMS VI. i. 14)

A general desire to avoid being treated with 'indignation' or to be approved of by others is unlikely to be sufficient to ensure an adequate level of control, especially given the assumption that men are above all active in the pursuit of their own interests. The basic problem which arises is that we may upon particular occasions fail to judge our own actions with the required degree of impartiality. As Smith put it:

> There are two different occasions upon which we examine our own conduct and endeavour to view it in the light in which the impartial spectator would view it: first, when we are about to act; and secondly, after we have acted. Our views are apt to be very partial in both cases; but they are apt to be most partial when it is of most importance that they should be otherwise. (TMS II. 4. 2)

First, 'When we are about to act, the eagerness of passion will seldom allow us to consider what we are doing, with the candour of an indifferent person ' (TMS III. 4. 3). Secondly, Smith noted that while we are likely to be able to judge our own actions in a clearer light after the event, this is of little benefit to those who may suffer from them, and that even here 'it is so disagreeable to think ill of ourselves, that we often purposely turn away our view from those circumstances which might render that judgement unfavourable' (TMS III. 4. 4). The argument suggests that there will be many occasions on which men are unlikely to be able to form accurate judgements with respect to their own activities, and that they would therefore be unlikely to be able to impose on themselves the kind of restraint which the 'inhabitant within the breast' would normally recommend. As Smith remarked in a passage which is likely to have attracted the attention of Robert Burns: 'this self-deceit, this fatal weakness of mankind, is the source of half the disorders of human life. If we saw ourselves in the light in which others see us, or in which they would see us if they knew all, a reformation would generally be unavoidable. We could not otherwise endure the sight' (TMS III. 4. 6; see Macfie (1967), p. 66). The problem has a particular, but not an exclusive, relevance for the discussion of economic issues.

Smith's solution to the problem just identified involves no principle in addition to those already considered:

> Nature . . . has not left this weakness, which is of so much importance, altogether without a remedy; nor has she abandoned us entirely to the delusions of self-love. Our continual observations upon the conduct of others, insensibly leads us to form to ourselves certain general rules concerning what is fit and proper either to be done or to be avoided. (TMS III. 4. 7)

In short, Smith suggests that our capacity to form judgements in particular cases permits us to frame general rules by the process of induction – thus *formally* admitting reason to the discussion of morality:

> It is thus that the general rules of morality are formed. They are ultimately founded upon experience of what, in particular instances, our moral faculties, our natural sense of merit and propriety, approve, or disapprove of. We do not originally approve or condemn particular actions; because, upon examination, they appear to be agreeable or inconsistent with a certain general rule. The general rule, on the contrary, is formed, by finding from experience, that all actions of a certain kind, or circumstanced in a certain manner, are approved or disapproved of. (TMS III. 4. 8)

Reason, it will be observed, is not the *original* source of the distinction between what is fit and proper to be done or to be avoided, but merely the means of elucidating general principles from a number of particular judgements, each one of which initially depends on the exercise of our moral sentiments.

These general principles or rules become, in turn, yardsticks against which we can judge our own conduct under all circumstances and are thus of 'great use in correcting the misrepresentations of self-love concerning what is fit and proper to be done in our particular situation' (TMS III. 4. 12). Indeed, Smith went so far as to argue that without a regard to general rules of behaviour, 'there is no man whose conduct can be much depended upon' (TMS III. 5.2).

Given that general rules may be formulated in the way described, Smith went on to argue that men would be disposed to obey them for two reasons. First, he noted that the voice which commands obedience is that of conscience or duty: 'a principle of the greatest consequence in human life, and the only principle by which the bulk of mankind are capable of directing their actions' (TMS III. 5. 1). It is not the 'soft power of humanity' which ensures that we impose some control over our own passions or activities, rather it is the desire to be praiseworthy; it is 'reason, principle, conscience, the inhabitant of the breast, the man within, the great judge and arbiter of our conduct' (TMS III. 3.4).

Secondly, it is suggested that our disposition to obey is 'still further enhanced by an opinion which is first impressed by nature, and afterwards confirmed by reasoning and philosophy, that those important rules of morality are the commands or laws of the Deity, who will finally reward the obedient, and punish the transgressors of their duty' (TMS III. 5.3). Smith added that:

> The sense of propriety too is here well supported by the strongest motives of self-interest. The idea that, however we may escape the observation of man, or be placed above the reach of human punishment, yet we are always acting under the eye, and exposed to the punishment of God . . . is a motive capable of restraining the most headlong passions. (TMS III. 5. 12)

The rules of behaviour which Smith identifies vary in character. Those which are related to justice may often hinder us 'from hurting our neighbour'; they may only involve restraint from injury and may thus be fulfilled by 'sitting still and doing nothing', while other rules may embody a more comprehensive and positive guide. The essential difference which emerges is that between the negative and positive virtues of justice and beneficence. As Smith put it:

> The rules of justice may be compared to the rules of grammar; the rules of the other virtues to the rules which critics lay down for the attainment of what is sublime and elegant in composition. The one, are precise, accurate, and indispensable. The other, are loose, vague and indeterminate, and present us rather with a general idea of the perfection we ought to aim at, than afford us any certain and infallible directions for acquiring it. (TMS III. 6. 11).

It thus appears that while both sets of rules are useful to society, they must each, taken separately, be compatible with different levels of social experience. Smith notes that where men act with an eye to the positive rules of moral conduct, where their behaviour is marked by beneficence with regard to others (which is perfectly consistent with the pursuit of the objects of self-interest), then that society 'flourishes and is happy'. If on the other hand justice alone is the rule, then life in society may be characterised by nothing more than 'a mercenary exchange of good offices according to an agreed valuation' (TMS II. ii. 3. 2). Smith plainly regarded the first situation as the more typical and as involving a higher level of achievement than the second, although he was in no doubt as to which set of rules was the most important from the standpoint of social order:

> Though Nature, therefore, exhorts mankind to acts of benefi-

cence, by the pleasing consciousness of deserved reward, she has not thought it necessary to guard and enforce the practice of it by the terrors of merited punishment in case it should be neglected. It is the ornament which embellishes, not the foundation which supports the building, and which it was, therefore, sufficient to recommend, but by no means necessary to impose. Justice, on the contrary is the main pillar that upholds the whole edifice. It if is removed, the great, the immense fabric of human society, that fabric which to raise and support seems in this world, if I may say so, to have been the peculiar and darling care of Nature, must in a moment crumble into atoms.

He continued:

Men, though naturally sympathetic, feel so little for another, with whom they have no particular connexion, in comparison of what they feel for themselves; the misery of one, who is merely their fellow creature, is of so little importance to them in comparison even of a small conveniency of their own; they have it so much in their power to hurt him, and may have so many temptations to do so, that if this principle did not stand up within them in his defence, and overawe them to a respect for his innocence, they would, like wild beasts, be at all times ready to fly upon him; and a man would enter an assembly of men as he enters a den of lions. (TMS II. ii. 3.4)

Smith added a further condition in noting that:

As the violation of justice is what men will never submit to from one another, the public magistrate is under a necessity of employing the power of the commonwealth to enforce the practice of this virtue. Without this precaution, civil society would become a scene of bloodshed and disorder, every man revenging himself at his own hand whenever he fancied he was injured. (TMS VII. iv.36).

While this subject is explicitly addressed in the *Lectures on Jurisprudence*, Smith noted elsewhere that the final condition required for social stability and economic order was a system of positive law embodying current conceptions of the rules of justice, to be administered by some system of magistracy.

Some implications of the argument

This paper has not addressed the question of 'wherein does virtue consist' and has touched only slightly on the second problem to which Smith devoted so much attention in the *Theory of Moral Sentiments*, namely, 'how and by what means does it come to pass, that the mind prefers one tenour of conduct to another'. (TMS. VII. i. 2) Rather the purpose has been to identify areas of concern in the ethics which touch upon the interests of students of Smith's political economy.

Some areas of interest are immediately obvious, most notably the attention given to the analysis of the sources of utility in Part IV which throws important light on the issue of subjective preference as it affects the problem of the demand for commodities. Equally significant is the fact that it is in the *Theory of Moral Sentiments* rather than the *Wealth of Nations* that Smith fully explained the psychological drives which support man's desire to better his condition; an argument which is linked in turn to the pursuit of wealth; the desire for status and the admiration of our fellows. It is not difficult to see in this argument an anticipation of modern concerns with sociological factors as they affect economic behaviour – or even an anticipation, however rudimentary, of a kind of life-cycle hypothesis where the behaviour of the individual actively seeking to better his condition is first dominated by frugality before enjoying the conspicuous consumption which is the possible outcome of success.

Equally important is Smith's analysis of self-interest and the need for constraint, where he established the point that men are led as if by an invisible hand to generate barriers against their unsocial passions by natural as distinct from artificial means. This branch of the work is marked by the prominence which Smith gave to the impartial spectator and to the generation of rules of behaviour, of which the rules of justice are the most important at least in the context of social order. But it will be noted that man's capacity to erect barriers against his self-interested passions, which is so essential for the orderly conduct of *economic* affairs, depends critically on his capacity for *moral* judgement.

In the *Theory of Moral Sentiments* Smith also described a wide range of human behaviour. He offers, for example, an account of the prudent, the vain and the proud man (notably in Part VI) but really intended to make the point that men typically manifest both selfish and other-regarding propensities (cf. Wilson, 1976) which find expression as it were at one and the same time. The point is clearly made when Smith remarked that:

Concern for our own happiness recommends to us the virtue

of prudence; concern for that of other people, the virtue of justice and beneficence; of which, the one restrains us from hurting, the other prompts us to promote that happiness. Independent of any regard either to what are, or what ought to be, or to what upon a certain condition would be, the sentiments of other people, the first of these three virtues is orginally recommended to us by our selfish, the other two by our benevolent affections (TMS VI, conclusion)

The student of Smith's economics is thus reminded that our selfish affections represent only one facet of human nature. Even if it is useful to be able to concentrate on the self-regarding propensities in some spheres of economic analysis, Smith does not rule out the possibility that the butcher, the brewer or the baker may, as men, be capable of acts of benevolence in ways which could affect the conduct of their (economic) affairs.

The ethics, in short, remind us that there is a moral dimension to Smith's treatment of (economic) man in society; a point which has enabled Donald Winch and others to argue that Smith's political economy is informed throughout by this consideration (cf. Winch, 1978, Billet, 1976 and Teichgraeber, 1986).

Traditional economic analysis presents a simpler picture. Rational economic man acting as producer maximises efficiency by so arranging his use of factors as to bring to equality their weighted marginal productivities. The rational consumer maximises satisfaction by so arranging his purchases as to bring to equality the weighted marginal utilities of the products which he chooses. In neither case is concern expressed as to the consequences which these decisions may have for the individual or for other people.

Seen in this light, Smith's perspective generates real complications. The producer who seeks to make the best use of resources may contribute to economic efficiency and yet attract unfavourable judgement if, for instance, the wages paid or the conditions of employment offered are perceived by the spectator to involve some degree of exploitation. The consumer in choosing what he believes to be the 'best' use of available resources could do so in a way which attracts a charge of impropriety from the spectator and which may also reflect the presence of a defective telescopic faculty (cf. WN V. ii. g. 4; V. ii. k. 50). Our choice of butcher, brewer or baker may be affected by judgements as to their behaviour on matters other than quality or price. Whom we buy from is as

interesting a decision as what we buy. Such concerns open up
complex questions and suggest that Smith's emphasis upon the
central issue of propriety, may find some interesting applications
in addressing the wider questions of choice in the sense that
'economic' decisions may be socially constrained.

Smith stated, but did not develop, the interesting possibilities
which are presented by this argument. But he did make use of
related points in dealing effectively with an important problem of
the time, namely Bernard Mandeville's 'licentious' doctrine (cf. W.
F. Campbell, 1967, Macfie, 1967, p. 81). The *Fable of Bees*, first
published in 1714 had advanced a doctrine which caused uproar.
As F. B. Kaye remarked:

> The *Fable* was twice presented by the Grand Jury as a public
> nuisance; ministers alike denounced it from the pulpit. The
> book, indeed, aroused positive consternation, ranging from the
> indignation of Bishop Berkeley to the horrified amazement of
> John Wesley, who protested that not even Voltaire could have
> said so much wickedness. In France the Fable was actually
> ordered to be burned by the common hangman. (1924, p. cxvi)

Yet as Hume observed, 'to imagine, that the gratifying of any sense,
or the indulging of any delicacy in meat, drink, or apparel, is of
itself a vice, can never enter a head, that is not disordered by the
frenzies of enthusiasm' (1955, p. 19; 1987, p. 268).

Smith echoed his friend's calm assessment of Mandeville's
position:

> If the love of magnificence, a taste for the elegant arts and
> improvements of human life, for whatever is agreeable in
> dress, furniture or equipage, for architecture, statuary, paint-
> ing and music, is to be regarded as luxury, sensuality and
> ostentation, even in those whose situation allows, without any
> inconveniency, the indulgence of these passions, it is certain
> that luxury, sensuality and ostentation are public benefits;
> since without these qualities upon which he thinks it proper
> to bestow such opprobious names, the arts of refinement could
> never find encouragement and must languish for want of
> employment. Some popular ascetic doctrines which had been
> current before his time, and which placed virtue in the entire
> extirpation and annihilation of all our passions, were the real
> foundation of this licentious system. It was easy for Dr
> Mandeville to prove, first, that this entire conquest never

actually took place among men; and secondly, that, if it was to take place universally, it would be pernicious to society, by putting an end to all industry and commerce, and in a manner to the whole business of human life. By the first of these propositions he seemed to prove that there was no real virtue, and that what pretended to be such, was a mere cheat and imposition upon mankind; and by the second, that private vices were public benefits, since without them no society could prosper or flourish. (TMS VII. ii. 4. 12)

While admitting that Mandeville's argument 'could never have imposed upon so great a number of persons, nor have occasioned so great an alarm among those who are friends of better principles, had it not in some respects bordered upon the truth' (TMS VII. ii. 4. 14), Smith's point was a simple one: namely that the pursuit of gratification is not inconsistent with propriety – and indeed should be consistent with it. It was an important point to make in the sense that the whole process of economic development was seen to be inextricably linked with the natural and insatiable wants of man; a thesis which was central to the explanation of growth in the eighteenth century and in respect of which it was necessary to regain the high moral ground which Mandeville's attack had threatened.

Such sentiments catch the spirit of Hume's essay 'Of refinement in the Arts' where two additional and important arguments were led. First, Hume contended that '*industry, knowledge* and *humanity* are linked together by an indissoluble chain and are found, from experience, as well as reason, to be peculiar to the more polished, and, what are commonly denominated, the more luxurious ages' (1955, p. 23; 1987, p. 271). Yet Smith might have demurred in respect of Hume's use of the term 'humanity' bearing in mind his analysis of the costs of economic development as stated in the *Wealth of Nations*.

While Smith's recommendation that the state should ensure the provision of compulsory education, to offset the psychological effects of the division of labour, seems limited in view of the extent of the problem now perceived (what Karl Marx described as a 'homoeopathic dose') the fact remains that the true extent of the difficulty which is identified in the *Lectures on Jurisprudence* and in the *Wealth of Nations* can only be fully understood when seen against the background of Smith's ethics, thus providing a further example of the inter-dependence of the two books (cf. Freeman, 1969). But there is more to the issue than an element of interdependence in the sense that Smith was suggesting in effect that while economic development was consistent with material benefit, it could also erode that capacity for moral and other forms of judgement which the analysis of the *Theory of Moral Sentiments* had shown to be so important (cf. WN V. i. f. 50). Improvements in the level of real income (i.e. command of utilities) were not, in Smith's view, a wholly adequate measure of welfare; a point which the analysis of the *Theory of Moral Sentiments* taken as a whole helps to confirm (cf. Gee, 1968).

Hume's second point also presented Smith with a difficulty. Smith agreed with his friend's judgement that economic growth would draw authority and consideration to the 'middling rank' and as clearly rejoiced in a situation which had brought to the House of Commons a superior degree of influence. But at the same time, Smith noted that the same historical forces which had elevated the House of Commons to such a degree of influence had also made that body a focal point for sectional interests (cf. WN, I. ix. p. 10), that is, a focal point for the deployment of collective as opposed to individual self-interest. Smith contended that the whole mercantile system had been designed to benefit business rather than national or individual interests. Donald Winch in particular has drawn attention to the distinction 'between the individual pursuit of self-interest under competitive conditions, when the rules of fair-play and strict justice are being observed, and the collective pursuit of self interest through combination, monopoly, and extra-Parliamentary pressure group activity' (1989. p. 24).

The point has been emphasised by students of Smith's politics and of his treatment of the historical origins of the 'present establishments' in Europe (see WN III). But the concern with collective self-interest also finds an echo in the *Theory of Moral Sentiments*, significantly in Part VI which was added in 1790, the year of Smith's death. In these passages Smith described the roles which men play in the context of the 'subaltern' societies to which they typically belong – such as the immediate and extended family, circles of friends, places of employment, or professional and commercial associations. Smith was increasingly conscious, it would seem, of the role of collective interests but offered his readers less assurance that such interests can be readily controlled as compared to his narrower treatment of the working of the exchange economy (cf. Haakonssen, 1980, Winch, 1983), depending as it does on the pursuit of individual interests within a given legal framework. We thus return to the point made at the outset, namely, that Smith intended his published works to be seen as the parts of a wider whole. In lecturing to his students on ethics, jurisprudence and economics, in that order, he provided them and later readers with separate but inter-related lenses through which they could view the activities of man in society.

Notes

This chapter is based in part on an essay entitled 'Moral philosophy and civil society' as published in Skinner (1979). I am indebted to D. D. Raphael and Donald Winch for a number of helpful comments. The usual disclaimer applies.

1. Smith stated the famous paradox of value in WN I. iv. 13. For comment see note 31 to chapter iv in the Glasgow Edition.
2. See also Smith's essay, 'Of the Nature of that Imitation which takes place in what are called the Imitative Arts', in EPS.
3. Cf. TMS VI, i. 3: 'Though it is to supply the necessities and conveniencies of the body, that the advantages of external fortune are originally recommended to us, yet we cannot live long in the world without perceiving that the respect of our equals, our credit and rank in the society we live in, depend very much upon the degree in which we possess, or are supposed to possess, these advantages. The desire of becoming the proper objects of this respect, of deserving and obtaining this credit and rank among our equals, is, perhaps, the strongest of all our desires, and our anxiety to obtain the advantages of fortune is accordingly much more excited and irritated by this desire, than by that of supplying all the necessities and conveniences of the body, which are always very easily supplied.'
4. C. TMS VI. i. 11: 'In the steadiness of his industry and frugality, in his steadily sacrificing the ease and enjoyment of the present moment for the probable expectation of the still greater ease and enjoyment of a more distant but more lasting period of time, the prudent man is always both supported and rewarded by the entire approbation of the impartial spectator, and of the representative of the impartial spectator, the man within the breast.'
5. Cf. TMS I. iii. 5 and VI. i. 7–15 where Smith celebrates the role of the prudent (and economic) man.

Sources

Commentaries on TMS which the present writer has found especially helpful include: T. D. Campbell (1971); V. Foley (1977); J. R. Lindgren (1973); A. L. Macfie (1967); G. Morrow (1928) and D. D. Raphael (1985).

Recent articles which explore the relationship between TMS and WN include W. F. Campbell (1967); J. Evensky (1987) and A. Gee (1968). Others which bear directly upon the argument include R. Anspach (1972), R. W. Coase (1976); P. L. Danner (1976); W. Gramp (1948) and S. Hollander (1977).

References

Anspach, R. (1972), 'The Implications of the *Theory of Moral Sentiments* for Adam Smith's Economic Thought', *History of Political Economy*, 4. Reprinted in Wood (1984), i, 438.

Billet, L. (1976), 'The Just Economy: The Moral Basis of the *Wealth of Nations, Review of Social Economy*, 34. Reprinted in Wood (1984), ii, 205.

Campbell, T. D. (1971), *Adam Smith's Science of Morals* (London).

Campbell, W. F. (1967), 'Adam Smith's Theory of Justice, Prudence and Beneficence', *American Economic Review*, 57. Reprinted in Wood (1984), i, 351.

Coase, R. H. (1976), 'Adam Smith's View of Man', *Journal of Law and Economics*, 19. Reprinted in Wood (1984), i, 546.

Danner, P. L. (1976), 'Sympathy and Exchangeable Value: Keys to Adam Smith's Social Philosophy', *Review of Social Economy*, 34. Reprinted in Wood (1984), i, 628.

Evensky, J. (1987), 'The Two Voices of Adam Smith: Moral Philosopher and Social Critic', *History of Political Economy*, 19.

Freeman, R. D. (1969), 'Adam Smith: Education and Laisser-Faire', *History of Political Economy*, I. Reprinted in Wood (1984), i, 378.

Foley, V. (1977), *The Social Physics of Adam Smith* (Durham).

Gee, A. (1968), 'Adam Smith's Social Welfare Function', *Scottish Journal of Political Economy*, 15. Reprinted in Wood (1984), iv, 84.

Gramp, W. (1948), 'Adam Smith and the Economic Man', *Journal of Political Economy*, 56. Reprinted in Wood (1984), i, 250.

Haakonssen, K. (1980), *The Science of the Legislator* (Cambridge).

Hollander, S. (1977), 'Adam Smith and the Self-Interest Axiom', *Journal of Law and Economics*, 20. Reprinted in Wood (1984), i, 680.

Hume, David (1955), *Economic Writings*, ed. E. Rotwein (London).

Hume, David (1987), *Essays Moral Political and Literary*, ed. E. Miller (Indianapolis).

Kaye, F. B. ed. (1924), *The Fable of the Bees* (Oxford).

Lindgren, J. R. (1973), *The Social Philosophy of Adam Smith* (The Hague).

Macfie, A. L. (1967), *The Individual in Society* (London).

Marshall, A. (1956), *Principles of Economics* (London).

Morrow, G. (1928), 'Adam Smith: Moralist and Philosopher', in *Adam Smith, 1776–1926* (Chicago).

Raphael, D. D. (1985), *Adam Smith* (Oxford).

Skinner, A. S. (1979), *A System of Social Science* (Oxford).

Skinner, A. S. (1982), 'A Scottish Contribution to Marxist Sociology?', in *Classical and Marxian Political Economy*, eds. I. Bradley and M. Howard (London).

Steuart, Sir James (1966), *Principles of Political Economy* (1767), ed. A. S. Skinner (Edinburgh and Chicago).

Teichgraber, R. (1986), *Free Trade and Moral Philosophy: Rethinking the Sources of Adam Smith's Wealth of Nations* (Durham).

Wilson, T. (1976), 'Sympathy and Self-Interest', in *The Market and the State*, eds. T. Wilson and A. S. Skinner (Oxford).

Winch, D. (1978), *Adam Smith's Politics* (Cambridge).

Winch, D. (1983), 'Science and the Legislator: Adam Smith and After', *Economic Journal*, 93.

Winch, D. (1989), 'Adam Smith: Moral Philosopher as Political Economist' (unpublished).

Wood, J. C. (1984), *Adam Smith: Critical Assessments* (Beckenham).

8

The influence of Smith's jurisprudence on legal education in Scotland

JOHN W. CAIRNS

Legal education and natural law

On 8 January 1760, it was moved before the Faculty of Advocates that they should recommend those proposing to join their number to attend the lectures given in the University of Edinburgh on the law of nature and nations. The Faculty noted that regular lectures on that topic were now given in the University and expressed satisfaction with 'the merit and abilities' of the professor (Robert Bruce), and accordingly recommended all those who intended to become 'Candidates for the office of Advocate, to apply to the study of the law of Nature and Nations', because 'it concerns the honour of the Faculty that their members should be versant in every part of polite Literature and particularly in the law of Nature and Nations, the fountain of Justice and equity'.[1] After noting on 5 January 1762 that this resolution had not been adhered to, and establishing a committee to consider how to make it effective, the Faculty resolved as follows on 24 November:

> The Dean and Faculty of Advocates considering that they by their Resolution dated the 8th January 1760 recommended it to all young Gentlemen who intended to offer themselves Candidates for the office of Advocate to apply to the study of the Law of Nature and Nations, And considering that it concerns the Honour of the Faculty that their members should be versant in every part of polite literature and more particularly in those parts of Learning which are immediately connected with the Roman Law and the Law of Scotland. They therefore recommend to the private Examinators in both

Branches of the Law from and after the twelfth Day of June next to examine Candidates upon the Law of Nature and Nations in so far as it is connected with the Civil Law or the Law of this Country. And they hereby appoint That a Copy of this their Resolution to be sent to all the professors in the University of Edinburgh in order that the same may be intimated to the Students at their respective Colleges.[2]

This requirement was a new departure for the Faculty of Advocates. Until 1750, intrants to the Faculty had been examined on either Scots law or Civil (Roman) law, and, after 1750, on both.[3] These proposals in the 1760s must be seen in the context of the Advocates' attempts after 1750 to respond to the impact of Enlightenment thought in Scotland;[4] and in 1748 Lord President Dundas had already recommended to the Faculty that those intending to come to the bar should be 'careful to learn thoroughly the principles of the Roman Law and the Laws of Nature and Nations', and should not 'neglect Academical learning' before studying the laws of their own country.[5]

The chair of Public Law and the Law of Nature and Nations had been founded in 1707, and was the oldest chair in law in the University of Edinburgh.[6] Most of its holders had at least attempted to lecture.[7] The legal profession does not appear, however, to have been particularly interested in the discipline of Grotian natural law which its holders taught,[8] and Dundas's encouragement of study of the law of nature and nations as preparation for practice at the bar is the earliest which I have found. In the second half of the seventeenth century, when advocates aimed at the establishment of chairs in law, what they were concerned with was education in Civil law.[9] In the 1690s, establishment of a chair of law in Edinburgh was considered, but the professor would have taught Civil law and Scots law.[10] The extensive duties of the holder of the chair of law established in Glasgow in 1714 did not include the law of nature and nations.[11]

By the middle years of the eighteenth century, however, natural law thinking had come to dominate the moral philosophy curriculum in the Universities of Edinburgh and Glasgow.[12] Of primary importance in this development was Gershom Carmichael's adoption of Pufendorf's treatise *De officio hominis et civis* in Glasgow in the 1690s.[13] Following Pufendorf, Carmichael redefined moral philosophy as natural law.[14] Other moral philosophers followed this lead.[15] Scots lawyers were also familiar with natural law. James Dalrymple, Viscount Stair's *Institutions of the Law of Scotland*, published in 1681, was influenced by Grotian natural law.[16] For the first half of the eighteenth century, the text most used to teach Scots law was Sir George Mackenzie's *Institutions of the Law of Scotland*.[17] In the title, 'Of Laws in General', Mackenzie briefly alluded in two paragraphs to the law of nature and the law of nations.[18] These two paragraphs inevitably stimulated all the lecturers on Scots law to some comments on natural law and the law of nations; but study of student notes suggests their consideration of the topic was slight.[19]

Thus, from the second half of the seventeenth century, Scots lawyers and moral philosophers were aware of the natural jurisprudence stemming from the work of Grotius and Pufendorf. In classes in moral philosophy and in the lectures of the Professors of Public Law and the Law of Nature and Nations the natural law approach to the basis of moral and legal obligations had become institutionalised by 1750. In the teaching of Scots law, however, natural law had remained of minimal importance. Furthermore, despite Lord President Dundas's initial endorsement of study of the laws of nature and nations in 1748, it had no necessary place in the training of the profession until the bar's enthusiastic adoption of the discipline in the 1760s.

Why, then, did the Faculty of Advocates desire in the 1760s that intrants should have studied natural law? In this chapter I shall argue that Adam Smith's *Lectures on Jurisprudence* showed how law could be taught as a dynamic historical process. Though Smith's lectures were given as part of a course on moral philosophy, they had practical significance for lawyers. Until Smith lectured in Glasgow, law professors had used natural law as an organising framework for expounding rules of law for students to memorise;[20] but Smith demonstrated that natural jurisprudence explained how law developed and ought to be further developed. Smith had turned natural law from an abstract ahistorical discipline into a concrete, historical explanation and critique of law. Thus, the lectures given by the Professor of Public Law and the Law of Nature and Nations assumed a greater potential significance for lawyers: no longer were they merely elegant learning, and it is worth noting that in 1762 the Faculty saw them as closely connected with the study of Civil law and Scots law. This was what made Smith a suitable candidate for that chair in 1758, when his friends David Hume and William Johnstone urged him to seek it (Corr., pp. 24–5). Smith's *Lectures on Jurisprudence* thus came at a crucial juncture in the development of legal education in Scotland, and pointed out a new route for it to take. It is perhaps in this respect no coincidence that, in 1762, John Erskine, Professor of Scots Law in Edinburgh, advised his cousin, Lord Cardross, then a student in Glasgow, to take Smith's moral philosophy class (about which Erskine was obviously not too well informed) along with the class in Civil law.[21] As Dr Phillipson has shown, in the middle years of the eighteenth century the Faculty of Advocates sought a role as law reformers.[22] Smith's *Lectures on Jurisprudence* showed a method of achieving it.

Adam Smith's natural jurisprudence

On 9 January 1751, Smith was elected Professor of Logic in the University of Glasgow.[23] Before he arrived in October 1751, Thomas Craigie, Professor of Moral Philosophy, had become ill, and Smith agreed to teach natural jurisprudence and politics to the absent professor's class (Corr., pp. 4–5).[24] Craigie died in November, and on 22 April 1752 Smith was elected to the vacant chair, the translation taking place on 29 April.[25] Smith's fitness for the post had already been demonstrated by the lectures he had given privately in Edinburgh in 1748–51 on rhetoric and *belles lettres*, and jurisprudence.[26]

According to John Millar, Smith's moral philosophy course was divided into four parts: natural theology; ethics (which he afterwards published as *The Theory of Moral Sentiments*); justice; and political regulations founded on expediency (which he subsequently published as *The Wealth of Nations*; Stewart, pp. 274–5). The last two of these were dealt with in the *Lectures on Jurisprudence* of which we have two sets of student notes dating from the sessions 1762–3 (LJ(A)) and 1763–4 (LJ(B)) respectively. It may be noted that Smith finished with a brief account of the laws of nations (LJ(A), p. 7; LJ(B), pp. 398–9 and 545–54).[27] This four-fold division followed the traditional structure of the Glasgow moral philosophy curriculum.[28] From Dugald Stewart we learn that, after Smith published *The Theory of Moral Sentiments* in 1759, in his remaining four years in Glasgow 'the plan of his lectures underwent a considerable change. His ethical doctrines . . . occupied a much smaller portion of the course than formerly: and accordingly, his attention was naturally directed to a more complete illustration of the principles of jurisprudence and of political economy' (Stewart, p. 300). In the lecture course of 1763–4, Smith altered the structure of his account of jurisprudence, preferring the method of the civilians (LJ(B), p. 401).

That Smith should have changed the structure of his course in the period of his tenure of the chair is hardly surprising. Furthermore, from the pre-1759 fragment identified by Professor Raphael, and the Anderson notes discussed by the late Professor Meek, we can also see that his own views changed: it was in the course of his professorship that he developed the concept of the impartial spectator and the four-stage theory of social development.[29] Although this development raises interesting questions, there is not the time to deal with it here. Accordingly, the following account of his teaching will be based on the fuller evidence we have of the last five years of his tenure provided by the early editions of *The Theory of Moral Sentiments*[30] and the two student reports of his *Lectures on Jurisprudence* in 1762–3 and 1763–4. This will also have the advantage of focusing on his class at the very period when the Faculty of Advocates became seriously interested in natural jurisprudence, when Smith's friends urged him to obtain the Edinburgh chair, and when the University of Glasgow awarded him the degree of LL.D. because of his reputation in letters and particularly because he had taught jurisprudence 'with great applause'.[31]

Smith's general approach

Smith is reported as telling his class that '[j]urisprudence is the theory of the rules by which civil governments ought to be directed' (LJ(A), p. 5; see also LJ(B), p. 397, and TMS VII. iv. 36). His *Lectures on Jurisprudence* therefore attempted to establish 'a system of what might properly be called natural jurisprudence, or a theory of the general principles which ought to run through and be the foundation of the laws of all nations' (TMS VII. iv. 37; see also LJ(B), p. 397). The first aim of governments was to secure justice 'to prevent the members of a society from incroaching on one anothers property . . . . The end proposed by justice is the maintaining men in what are called their perfect rights' (LJ(A), p. 5). The second aim was 'promoting the opulence of the state. This produces what we call police.' This encompassed regulations on trade, commerce, agriculture, and manufacturing. It also covered cleanliness, described as 'two [*sic*] mean and trifling' to be dealt with. Public security also came under this heading in two aspects: first, as security from fires and accidents, also 'too trifling' to be discussed; second, as 'justice of police' which was devoted to policing in the modern sense, the creation of criminal statutes, and the bringing of criminals to justice. This Smith stated he would deal with under 'the former part of jurisprudence', that, is justice, with which it was connected (LJ(A), pp. 5–6). The most important part of police was that relating to commerce and plenty, and this was what he would treat under the heading (LJ(A), pp. 5–6). Government had to cover its expenses, so the third topic to be covered was revenue (LJ(A), p. 6). Finally, the laws of peace and war would be discussed, as the state had to be protected from external threat (LJ(A), pp. 6–7; see also LJ(B), pp. 398–9).

Justice and rights

Smith told his class that '[j]ustice is violated whenever one is deprived of what he had a right to and could justly demand from others, or rather, when we do him any injury or hurt without a cause' (LJ(A), p. 7). This concept of rights drew on the theory of justice Smith expounded in *The Theory of Moral Sentiments*. Justice was 'upon most occasions, but a negative virtue, and only hinders us from hurting our neighbour' (TMS II. ii. 1. 9). He erected his moral philosophy on the empirically observable phenomenon of sympathy. Human beings, through their own experience of pleasure and pain, could imaginatively enter into the pleasure and pain of others (TMS I. i. 1–4; II. i. 5). Thus, when a person saw another assaulted, he could sympathetically appreciate the feelings of both the person attacked and the attacker, and, if fully informed, form a moral judgement of the situation. Should the attacker have no motive or an unworthy one, the assault was unjust (TMS II. ii. 1. 5–7; II. ii. 2. 1–3). Of course, human beings are never fully informed about any situation, and real spectators never detached, so Smith proposed the concept of the impartial spectator as providing the test of ideal justice. Individual human actors judged their own conduct by reference to what they considered would be the reaction of the impartial spectator (TMS II. ii. 2. 1).[32] If by this test an action was unjust, the other party had a right that it not be carried out.

A first point to note is that for Smith, justice was what made social life possible (TMS II. ii. 3. 4 and 6; VII. iv. 36). Justice, however, was not founded on utility, but arose from humankind's abhorrence of injustice (TMS II. ii. 3. 9). Second, certain rights were 'natural': 'Among equals each individual is naturally, and antecedent to the institution of civil government, regarded as having a right both to defend himself from injuries, and to exact a certain degree of punishment for those which have been done to him' (TMS II. ii. 1. 7). This would include not only physical injury, but injury to reputation (TMS VII. ii. 1. 10). Third, the greater the injury, the greater was the resentment of the person injured, the greater the sympathetic indignation of the spectator, and, indeed, the sentiments of guilt and shame of the injurer. This led to a variation in the degree of punishment which there was a right to exact (TMS II. ii. 2. 2). Fourth, that some rights were 'natural', being antecedent to civil government, led to the inference that others were not, and brought about through historical development.

Smith enumerated possible injuries in the *Lectures on Jurisprudence*. A man (to use his term) could be injured in three ways: as a man; as a member of a family; and as a citizen or member of a state (LJ(A), p. 7; LJ(B), p. 399). As a man, he could be injured in his person, reputation or estate. As a member of a family, he could be injured as a father or son, husband or wife, master or servant, guardian or ward. As a member of a state, he could be injured, if a magistrate, by disobedience, or if a subject, by oppression (LJ(A), pp. 7–8; LJ(B), p. 399). Injury to a man's person or reputation was injury to a natural right. Injury to his property, or to him as a member of a family or a state was injury to an adventitious right (LJ(A), p. 8; LJ(B), pp. 399–400). Adventitious rights were those brought into existence by the development of civil government. Smith adopted this terminology of rights from Francis Hutcheson.[33]

Justice, rights, and history

In the *Lectures on Jurisprudence*, Smith used a four-stage theory to explain historical development.[34] In the first stage, humankind supported themselves by hunting and fishing. When natural increase of population made this impossible, humankind would domesticate animals and support themselves as shepherds. When increase of population again made no longer viable this pastoral, second stage of society, humanity would turn to cultivation of the soil to support themselves. In this agricultural stage, as techniques of cultivation improved, society would develop beyond mere subsistence to produce a surplus, which would lead to the exchange of commodities, eventually inaugurating the final stage of commerce (LJ(A), pp. 14–16; LJ(B), pp. 459–60). Smith expounded this in detail in connection with the adventitious right of property. Hunters and fishers had little need of laws of property: the only injury they could suffer was to be deprived of their game. Pastoral society gave rise to laws of property as shepherds owned their flocks: '[i]n this state many more laws and regulations must take place'. In agricultural society, '[t]he laws . . . will be of a far greater number than amongst a nation of shepherds' because 'there are many ways added in which property may be interrupted as the subjects of it are considerably extended'. Finally, '[i]n the age of commerce, as the subjects of property are greatly increased the laws must be proportionally multiplied' (LJ(A), p. 16).

The growth of property and of government went together: 'among hunters there is no regular government; they live according to the laws of nature' (LJ(B), p. 404; see also LJ(A), pp. 201–2). That is, they only had natural rights. 'The appropriation of herds and flocks, which introduced an inequality of fortune, was that which first gave rise to regular government. Till there be property there can be no government, the very end of which is to secure wealth, and to defend the rich from the poor' (LJ(B), pp. 404–5; see also LJ(A), p. 202). The existence of property and regular or civil government gave rise to other adventitious rights. Contracts were obviously dependent on the existence of property. Commercial society greatly increased the scope of actionable contractural rights (LJ(A), pp. 96–7). That the rights relating to families should be adventitious is not so obvious. The union of man and woman was natural and related to care of offspring. Because human beings took so long to mature, the union of their parents must be of long duration (LJ(A), pp. 141–3; LJ(B), p. 438). But in early societies, the authority of the husband was very great, since 'the government is at first in all nations very weak, and very delicate of intermeddling in the differences of persons of different families; they were still less inclined to intermeddle in the differences that happen'd amongst persons of the same family'. So that government might be maintained, the father of the family had absolute authority (LJ(A), pp. 143–4; cf. LJ(B), pp. 439–40). Fathers did not even need to aliment children: to do so was an act of benevolence, not justice (LJ(A), p. 172; LJ(B), p. 449). In *The Theory of Moral Sentiments*, Smith had already pointed out that '[t]he laws of all civilized nations oblige parents to maintain their children, and children to maintain their parents'. In making this provision, the 'civil magistrate' was 'promoting the prosperity of the commonwealth, by establishing good discipline, and by discouraging every sort of vice and impropriety'. Thus, as an act of police, civil government compelled the performance of a duty originally of beneficence (TMS II. ii. 1. 8). The authority of a master over his servants in early society was likewise absolute, as was necessary when governments were weak (LJ(A), pp. 175–6; LJ(B), pp. 450–1). In all these relations, as society developed, law affected the relationship more. Thus these more refined legal rights were adventitious rights.

Smith dealt with crimes as injuries to a man's estate. He pointed out, however, that crimes were of two sorts: first, those infringing natural rights; and secondly, those infringing acquired or adventitious rights (LJ(A), p. 105). He started with wilful murder, for which 'the only proper punishment is the death of the offender' (LJ(A), p. 106; see also LJ(B), p. 476): 'injury naturaly [*sic*] excites the resentment of the spectator, and the punishment of the offender is reasonable as far as the indifferent spectator can go along with it. This is the natural measure of punishment' (LJ(B), p. 475). Death was the natural punishment for murder, but 'amongst barbarous nations the punishment has generally been much slighter', because 'the weakness of government in those early periods of society . . . made it very delicate in intermeddling with the affairs of individualls' (LJ(A), p. 106; see also LJ(B), pp. 476–7). Thus, while dealing with crimes against a person in the discussion of injuries to a person's estate, he was aware that they infringed natural rights. The account is awkwardly placed given Smith's analytical scheme; but this is presumably due to ease of exposition. It is telling that, in early society, infringements of natural rights should not have received their 'natural' punishment because of the weakness of government. It was as societies developed strong governments that the natural punishment might be imposed. While the natural jurisprudence of punishment of infringements of natural rights was always the same, what actually was done varied historically for reasons of utility.

In sum, Smith's discussion of rights was complex: some were natural, but their enforcement might vary according to government. Other rights were only brought about by the existence of civil government; but once created, their enforcement became a matter of justice, judged by the standard of the impartial spectator. Furthermore, Smith used his stadial theory in a thorough fashion only in discussing property; but since it was property which gave rise to government, and government affected all rights, the four stages necessarily informed the discussion of the whole.

Government, sovereignty, and positive law

For Smith, sovereignty consisted of three attributes: the power of making laws; the power 'of trying causes and passing judgement or of settling other judges'; and 'the power of making peace or war'. In monarchical governments the monarch possessed all these three powers; in aristocratic, the aristrocracy; and in democracy, the *'whole body of the people* conjunctly' (LJ(A), pp. 200–1; see also LJ(B), p. 404). In societies of hunters, 'there can be very little government of any sort, but what there is will be of the democratical kind'. Disputes within families were left to the families to resolve; disputes between others were rare, but if occurring and a threat to the community, the community as a whole resolved them by a process of reconciliation rather than a judicial process. The whole community decided on peace and war. 'The legislative power can hardly subsist in such a state; there could be occasion but for very few regulations, and no individuall would think himself bound to submit to such regulations as were made by others, even where the whole community was concerned' (LJ(A), pp. 201–2; see also LJ(B), p. 404).[35] Pastoral society first gave rise to government by creating property and hence disparity of wealth: the poor became dependent on the rich. Furthermore, with the introduction of property, 'many disputes on that head must inevitably occur'. Yet far fewer than 'in the farther advances of society'. Disputes could still be resolved by meetings of the whole community, but the rich men, because of their influence over their dependents, would have most influence in deliberation, and indeed, their authority would soon become hereditary. But, '[t]he legislative [power] is never met with amongst people in this state of society.

Laws and regulations are the product of more refind [*sic*] manners and improved government, and are never found till it is considerably advanced' (LJ(A), pp. 202–5). Nonetheless, though there was no legislation, Smith pointed out a little later that '[s]ettled laws . . . or agreements concerning property, will soon be made after the commencement of the age of shepherds' (LJ(A), p. 209; see also LJ(A), p. 213).

When arts and manufactures were cultivated, the people as a whole could no longer attend trials. Furthermore, their cultivation multiplied 'the causes of dispute'. Accordingly, '[a] certain number of men are chosen by the body of the people, whose business it is to attend on the causes and settle all disputes'. These judges would always include the leading men, and their authority would accordingly grow. As life became more complex, the executive powers of the state were also delegated to this court. Yet, still '[t]he legislative power makes but a very small figure during all this time' (LJ(A), pp. 205–7).

That in pastoral societies there were laws but initially no legislation indicates that Smith envisaged laws as originating in community practices. He stated that '[t]here must indeed be some sort of law as soon as property in flocks commences, but this would be but very short and have few distinctions in it, so that every man would understand it without any written or regular law. It would be no other than what the necessity of the state required.' He again added that written and formal laws were 'a very great refinement of government', and only met in its latest periods (LJ(A), p. 213). Smith appears to have indicated that he would explain the 'progress' of the legislative power (LJ(A), p. 207); but his discussions, as reported, became involved in the politics and history of Greece and Rome, and the rise of allodial and feudal government, and he just assumed legislation was taking place without particularising how this had come about. A little later he returned to the theme of the growth of positive law. He stated: 'The thing which has given occasion to the establishment of laws has always been the generall or partiall institution of judges.' As soon as property had been established judges would soon be required. 'A judge will to such an early nation appear very terrible.' This was beause to 'a rude people' courts of justice 'appear . . . to have an authority altogether insufferable'. The solution was 'to establish laws and rules which may ascertain his [i.e. the judge's] conduct'. Smith is reported as telling his class:

> Laws are in this manner posterior to the establishment of judges. At the first establishment of judges there are no laws; every one trusts to the naturall feeling of justice he has in his own breast and expects to find in others. . . . [Laws] do not ascertain or restrain the actions of private persons so much as the power and conduct of the judge over the people. (LJ(A), pp. 313–14)

This explanation raises difficulties. On the one hand, Smith has already stated that property gave rise to a type of law *before* the creation of courts; on the other, he has here apparently identified law with legislation. Furthermore, in a passage in *The Theory of Moral Sentiments* he wrote that 'those general rules which the sovereign lays down to direct the conduct of his subjects' are 'what are properly called laws' (TMS III. 5. 6).[36] Professor MacCormick has accordingly concluded that Smith 'subscribe[d] to the standard voluntarist notion, later adopted by Benthamite and Austinian "positivists", that the actual positive law of a state is to be identified with the command of the sovereign'.[37]

Part of the answer to this problem must lie in the ambiguity of the terms 'law' and 'legislation'. Smith never completed the 'theory and History of Law and Government' which he still optimistically promised in 1790 (TMS (1790), Advertisement; Corr., pp. 286–7), and in which he would presumably have dealt with such difficulties. The report of Smith's *Lectures on Rhetoric and Belles Lettres* from 1762–3 suggests, however, that his concept of law making was not simply voluntarist. In a discussion of arguments to prove whether or not anything be a law, he pointed out that law could be discovered 'plainly expressed' in a statute, or deduced from a statute, or 'supported as Law by former practise and similar adjudged causes or precedents'. Given that much of his discussion of lawmaking and government in the *Lectures on Jurisprudence* was based on evidence from Greece and Rome, it is notable that he pointed out that precedent 'was not at all used by the antients' in forensic argument. He explained the origin of judges in the need individuals would feel to submit their disputes 'to some impartiall person'. Those eminent people who thus became judges would also typically have been generals (and sometimes legislators). They would have found the task of judging irksome and delegated it to others, who, being of less authority, would have felt more constrained in their decisions in contrast to the first judges who would have been 'very bold in passing sentence'. The newer judges 'would [have been] at pains even to strengthen their conduct by the authority of their predecessors. . . . Whatever therefore had been practised by other judges would obtain authority with them and be received in time as Law' (LRBL, pp. 174–5).[38] Smith, therefore, could conceive of law being created by the practice of the courts.

Smith also expressed a preference for precedent as a mode of law-making. He told his class:

> The Sentences of former Cases [in England] are greatly regarded and form what is called the common law, which is found to be much more equitable than that which is founded on Statute only, for the same reason as what is founded on practise and experience must be better adapted to particular cases than that which is derived from theory only. (LRBL, p. 175)

English law thus had the advantage of 'being more formed on the naturall sentiments of mankind', as Smith told the Jurisprudence class (LJ(A), p. 98), adding later that '[n]ew courts and new laws are . . . great evils. Every court is bound only by its own practise. It takes time and repeated practise to ascertain the precise meaning of a law or to have precedents enough to determine the practise of a court' (LJ(A), p. 287). These remarks confirm not only that Smith recognised that precedent could be a source of law, but also that the enforcement of statutes through legislation was necessarily mediated through the practice of the courts. On the basis of a somewhat different discussion of these (and other) passages, Dr Haakonssen has commented that Smith approved of case law because 'it takes time to find the standpoint of the impartial spectator', which the refinement of law through precedent brought about, especially since 'in [case law] the negative, injustice, is inevitably the matter for consideration – that is what a court case is about'.[39] Statutes were thought up in the abstract, and it was accordingly more difficult to be precise about the requirement of justice.

The need for law to be developed

Governments had to ensure that law conformed as much as possible to justice. While every system of law was, at a certain level, 'a more or less imperfect attempt towards a system of natural jurisprudence', circumstances could prevent this from being so (TMS VII. iv. 36). There are a number of instances of departure of law from justice noted in Smith's *Lectures on Jurisprudence*. One obvious example is his attack on entails in Scotland (LJ(A), pp. 69–71). Less spectacularly, he also suggested that some treason laws enacted under Queen Anne 'might now well be abrogated' (LJ(A), p. 298; see also LJ(B), p. 429). If the law did not develop appropriately in line with the state of the country, not only would opulence be retarded, but injustice would give rise to threatening disturbance. If 'the public magistrate [did not employ] the power of the commonwealth to enforce the practice of [justice] . . . civil society would become a scene of bloodshed and disorder, every man revenging himself at his own hand whenever he fancied he was injured' (TMS VII. iv. 36). A concrete instance of this was the continued practice of duelling: 'For when the law do not give satisfaction somewhat adequate to the injury, men will think themselves intitled to take it at their own hand. The small punishment therefore which is incurred by these affronts according to our law is one great cause of duelling, and is to be accounted a deficientia juris' (LJ(A) p. 124).

Smith and legal education

In his class on moral philosophy, Smith had demonstrated how natural jurisprudence could provide a programme for law reform by treating it as 'that science which inquires into the general principles which ought to be the foundation of the laws of all nations' (LJ(B), p. 397). This was a matter of obvious interest to Scots lawyers, especially when they were contemporaneously involved in projects to abolish entails.[40] Furthermore, there was considerable worry in Hanoverian Britain over the haphazard system of legislation and the disorganised statute book.[41] Legislation was in the hands of politicians, about whom Smith had harsh words to say (LJ(B), p. 539).[42] (In *The Wealth of Nations*, Smith was to draw a sharp distinction between politicians and legislators (WN IV. ii. 39).)[43] Though legislation would be necessary to abolish entails (and in this project the Scots bar lamentably failed because of politicians), Smith's transformation of natural law into historical natural jurisprudence and praise of development through precedent provided lawyers with a plan of action for reform. Not only could they promote legislation 'governed by general principles'

(WN IV. ii. 39; cf. WN IV. introd. 1 and LJ(B), p. 397), and act as legislators at one remove, but they could also use precedent dynamically. In 1758, the Scottish judge Lord Kames remarked that '[l]aw in particular becomes then only a rational study, when it is traced historically, from its first rudiments among savages, through successive changes, to its highest improvements in a civilized society'.[44] Smith, in this sense, had turned law into a rational study, though admitting he himself was not a profound lawyer (Corr., p. 141). In 1777, Kames applied these remarks specifically to legal education, which he criticised as training students to rely on authority rather than reason. What he wished students to learn was historical reasoning about law, which would lead to fruitful modernisation: 'Were law taught as a rational science, its principles unfolded, and its connection with morals and politics, it would prove an enticing study to every person who has an appetite for knowledge. We might hope to see our lawyers soaring above their predecessors; and giving splendor to their country, by purifying and improving its laws.'[45] This is obviously a programme derivable from Smith's natural jurisprudence, and, as Professor Lieberman has shown, Kames envisaged reform through the courts rather than legislation.[46] Whether or not Kames derived these ideas on legal education from Smith is unimportant: it is enough that Smith's natural jurisprudence offered an approach to legal education thought desirable.

This returns us to the Faculty of Advocates' desire in 1760 and 1762 that intending advocates should attend the classes of the Professor of Public Law and the Law of Nature and Nations. Just as the Faculty, in Phillipson's words, made 'claim to the civic leadership of Scottish society',[47] Smith's natural jurisprudence showed one method of achieving their aims of leadership and improvement in the laws. After 1762, the Faculty did not renew their exhortation to attend the class on the law of nature and nations, possibly because the successor to the man in whom they placed confidence did not teach.[48] In the University of Glasgow, however, John Millar, as Professor of Civil Law, expounded Smithian jurisprudence to his classes.[49] And he was an outstandingly successful teacher.[50] In 1779, Allan Maconochie was appointed Professor of Public Law and the Law of Nature and Nations in Edinburgh.[51] In 1788 his class was described thus:

He traces the rise of political institutions from the natural characters and situation of the human species; follows their progress through the rude periods of society; and treats of their history and merits, as exhibited in the principal nations of ancient and modern times, which he examines separately, classing them according to those general causes to which he attributes the principal varieties in the forms, genius, and revolutions of governments. In this manner he endeavours to construct the science of the spirit of laws on a connected view of what may be called the natural history of man as a political agent; and he accordingly concludes his course with treating of the general principles of municipal law, political oeconomy, and the law of nations.[52]

This is the only information about his class; but it indicates that he had adopted an approach at least very similar to Smith's historical natural jurisprudence. Maconochie did not study under Smith. It is, however, intriguing to note that the first known possessor of the second set of notes deriving from Smith's lectures was Maconochie's son. Had his father perhaps obtained them to help prepare his own classes?[53] In Edinburgh as in Glasgow, law students were being equipped with an education to fit them for the task of making the laws of their country a more perfect 'attempt towards a system of natural jurisprudence, or towards an enumeration of the particular rules of justice' (TMS VIII. iv. 36).

Notes

This chapter was originally read at the Nagoya International Symposium to commemorate the Bicentenary of the Death of Adam Smith and is reprinted here with the kind permission of the Adam Smith Society of Japan. I am grateful to my colleague Professor Neil MacCormick for his comments on this paper, and for many general helpful conversations about Adam Smith.

1. National Library of Scotland, F.R.2, Minutes of the Faculty of Advocates, 1751–1783, p. 127. (I am grateful to the Faculty of Advocates for permission to study and cite their records.)
2. *Ibid.*, pp. 147, 156–7 (standard abbreviations in MS expanded).
3. Cairns (1986).
4. *Ibid.*
5. *Minute Book* (1980), p. 225.
6. Grant (1884), vol. I, p. 232.
7. Charles Areskine, professor 1707–34, advertised his lectures in 1711 (see Lorimer (1888), p. 144); William Kirkpatrick was professor for one year only; George Abercromby, professor 1735–59, in 1741 lectured on Grotius' treatise *De jure belli ac pacis* (see (1741) 3 *Scots*

Magazine, pp. 371–4 at 371); Robert Bruce, professor 1759–64, was the teacher referred to by the Faculty of Advocates. For the next two professors, see below, text at notes 48–52.

8. That it was Grotian natural law is indicated both by the title of the chair which reflects the full title of Grotius' work, and by Abercromby's textbook in 1741: see note 7 above. On the spread of similar chairs in Europe, see Tarello (n.d.), pp. 90–3. On the development of Grotian natural law, see, e.g., Haakonssen (1985A).

9. *Minute Book* (1976), pp. 65–6 (12 January 1684).

10. Bower (1817), vol. I, p. 329. In the University of Edinburgh, chairs of Civil Law and Scots Law were created in 1710 and 1722 respectively: Grant (1884), vol. I, pp. 284–8.

11. Coutts (1909), pp. 193–4.

12. And probably in Marischall College, Aberdeen: see Mackinnon (1987).

13. Moore and Silverthorne (1983 and 1984).

14. See *S. Pufendorfii de officio hominis et civis, juxta legem naturalem, libri duo. Supplementis & observationibus in academicae juventutis usum auxit & illustravit Gerschomus Carmichael, philosophiae in academia Glasguensi Professor. Editio secundo priore auctior & emendatior* (Edinburgh, 1724), pp. vi–vii. Carmichael established a curriculum for moral philosophy in Glasgow of natural theology followed by moral philosophy, using for the latter this work of Pufendorf: see his *Synopsis theologiae naturalis, sive notitiae, de existentia, attributis, & operationibus, summi numinis, ex ipsa rerum natura haustae* (Edinburgh, 1729), p. 4.

15. Francis Hutcheson, Carmichael's successor in Glasgow, preserved the same curriculum, and, at least initially, taught Pufendorf's treatise: Wodrow (1843), vol. IV, p. 185. W. Leechman described Hutcheson's moral philosophy class as covering 'Natural Religion, Morals, Jurisprudence, and Government' in 'The Preface, Giving some Account of the Life, Writings, and Character of the Author', in F. Hutcheson, *A System of Moral Philosophy, in Three Books* (2 vols., Glasgow and London, 1755), vol. I, p. xxxvi. See also Hutcheson's *Metaphysicae synopsis: ontologiam, et, pneumatologiam, complectens* (Glasgow, 1742); and *Philosophiae moralis institutio compendiaria, ethices & jurisprudentiae naturalis elementa continens. Lib. III* (Glasgow, 1742). On Hutcheson, see, e.g., Scott (1900); Campbell (1982). In Edinburgh, W. Scott, regent in philosophy, then Professor of, in turn, Greek, and Moral Philosophy, published *Hugonis Grotii de jure belli ac pacis librorum III. compendium, annotationibus & commentaris selectis illustratum. In usum studiosae juventutis academiae Edinensis* (Edinburgh, 1707). Scott's successor in the chair of moral philosophy, John Pringle, taught on the basis of Pufendorf's treatise *De officio*: Grant (1884), vol. I, pp. 273–4; vol. II. pp. 336–7.

16. Stair (1981) (first published in 1681, 2nd edn. 1693, but circulated in MS for twenty years before). On Stair and Grotius, see MacCormick (1979), Stein (1981), and Gordon (1985). On Stair's relationship to the Scottish Enlightenment, see, e.g., MacCormick (1982).

17. G. Mackenzie, *Institutions of the Law of Scotland* (2nd edn., Edinburgh, 1688): on other editions, see Ferguson (1935–8), pp. 30–4.

18. Mackenzie, *op. cit.* above note 17, pp. 2–3.

19. See, e.g., A. Bayne, *Notes, for the Use of the Students of the Municipal Law in the University of Edinburgh: Being a Supplement to Sir George*

Mackenzie's Institutions (Edinburgh, 1731), p. 2; and Edinburgh University Library, MS Gen. 1735 (notes of lectures given by J. Cuninghame), pp. 2–4.

20. For a discussion of methods of teaching, see Cairns (1991).
21. Edinburgh University Library, MS La. II. 238 (letter of 24 November 1762).
22. Phillipson (1976).
23. Scott (1937), pp. 137–8; see also Corr., p. 4.
24. Before Smith arrived, Hercules Lindesay, Professor of Civil Law, taught his class: Scott (1937), p. 139.
25. Scott (1937), pp. 139–40.
26. [A. F. Tytler] (1807), vol. I., pp. 190–1; Scott (1937), pp. 46–61; Campbell and Skinner (1982), pp. 29–39.
27. The relevant section of LJ(A) does not survive.
28. See notes 14 and 15 above. One can trace the resemblance to natural theology followed by a discussion of natural law on the basis of Pufendorf's treatise *De officio*.
29. Raphael (1969); Meek (1976A).
30. What is crucial here are the first two editions of 1759 and 1761 which appeared during Smith's tenure of the Glasgow chair, since I am trying to locate the influence of his theory at a specific time; but the Glasgow Edition may be used as it gives variants. Citations to passages from later editions will be indicated as such for particular purposes.
31. Glasgow University Archives 26645, Minutes of Faculty and Dean of Faculty's Meetings 1732–68, p. 110 (21 October 1762).
32. On Smith's development of this concept, see Raphael (1969 and 1975); see generally on the above, Skinner (1977), pp. 196–202; Campbell (1971), pp. 85–185.
33. Hutcheson, *Philosophiae moralis institutio compendiaria*, above note 15, p. 118 (II. iv. 2); *System*, above note 15, Vol. I, p. 293 (II. v. 1).
34. On the use of stadial theories in the eighteenth century, and the development of the four-stage theory, see Meek (1971 and 1976B); and Stein (1980), pp. 15–50. Stein (1988) points out that we need to be cautious about identifying a four-stage theory when there is really only a three-stage. While I agree with him overall, I am not entirely convinced by his identification of Lord Kames as the originator of the four-stage theory.
35. But cf. LJ(B), p. 407 which appears contradictory to the whole thrust of Smith's argument, and should probably be explained as relating to community regulation of disputes between families on the grounds of utility.
36. On the original placing of this passage, see the editorial note, TMS, p. 161.
37. MacCormick (1981), p. 248.
38. Smith made a similar point about the use of precedent in Rome in WN V. i. f. 44. Given what he has said about 'the antients' not using precedent in LRBL, either he has changed his mind, or more likely, and as I have indicated in my text, was thinking of forensic speeches as the context would imply.
39. Haakonssen (1981), pp. 152–3.
40. See Phillipson (1976), pp. 112–18.

41. Lieberman (1989), pp. 1–28.
42. See generally Winch (1978), pp. 158–60.
43. On Smith's 'science of legislation', see Winch (1978 and 1983); and Burns (1985). On the science of legislation generally, see Burns (1977).
44. [H. Home, Lord Kames], *Historical Law-Tracts* (2 vols., Edinburgh, 1758), vol. I, p. v.
45. [H. Home, Lord Kames], *Elucidations respecting the Common and Statute Law of Scotland* (Edinburgh, 1777), pp. vii–xiii.
46. Lieberman (1989), pp. 144–75; and (1983).
47. Phillipson (1976), p. 112.
48. H. Arnot, *The History of Edinburgh* (Edinburgh, 1779), p. 398. It is notable that the Faculty of Advocates at the same period also encouraged intending members to attend classes in Universal History in Edinburgh. They still encouraged this in 1768 (F. R. 2, above note 1, p. 259). See Cairns (1986), p. 265.
49. See Haakonssen (1985B); Cairns (1988); Cairns (1987), pp. 230 and 233–5.
50. See, e.g., Lehmann (1960), pp. 30–42.
51. Grant (1884), vol. II, pp. 315–16.
52. Arnot, *The History of Edinburgh* (2nd edn., Edinburgh, 1788), p. 398.
53. See the remarks of Cannan in his introduction to Smith (1896), pp. xv–xvii. I am indebted to Professor MacCormick for bringing this to my attention.

References

Bower, A. (1817) *The History of the University of Edinburgh; Chiefly Compiled from Original Papers and Records, Never Before Published*, vol. I, Edinburgh: Alex Smellie, Printer to the University, for Oliphant, Waugh and Innes, Hunter's Square, Edinburgh; and John Murray, Albemarle Street, London.

Burns, J. H. (1977) The Fabric of Felicity: The Legislator and the Human Condition *The Study of Politics: A Collection of Inaugural Lectures*, ed. by P. King, London: Frank Cass, 207–24.

Burns, J. H. (1985) Scottish Philosophy and the Science of Legislation *Royal Society of Edinburgh Occasional Papers* 2–6, 11–29.

Cairns, J. W. (1986) The Formation of the Scottish Legal Mind in the Eighteenth Century: Themes of Humanism and Enlightenment in the Admission of Advocates *The Legal Mind: Essays for Tony Honoré*, ed. by N. MacCormick and P. Birks, Oxford: Clarendon Press, 254–77.

Cairns, J. W. (1987) Eighteenth Century Professorial Classification of English Common Law *McGill Law Journal* 33, 225–44.

Cairns, J. W. (1988) John Millar's Lectures on Scots Criminal Law *Oxford Journal of Legal Studies* 8, 364–400.

Cairns, J. W. (1991) Rhetoric, Language, and Roman Law: Legal Education and Improvement in Eighteenth-Century Scotland *Law and History Review* 9, 31–58.

Campbell, R. H. and Skinner, A. S. (1982) *Adam Smith*, London and Sydney: Croom Helm.

Campbell, T. D. (1971) *Adam Smith's Science of Morals*, London: Allen and Unwin.

Campbell, T. D. (1982) Francis Hutcheson: 'Father' of the Scottish Enlightenment *The Origins and Nature of the Scottish Enlightenment*, ed. by R. H. Campbell and A. S. Skinner, Edinburgh: John Donald, 167–85.

Coutts, J. (1909) *A History of the University of Glasgow From its Foundation in 1451 to 1909*, Glasgow: James Maclehose and Sons.

Ferguson, F. S. (1935–8) A Bibliography of the Works of Sir George Mackenzie Lord Advocate Founder of the Advocates' Library *Edinburgh Bibliographical Society Transactions* 1, 1–60.

Gordon, W. M. (1985) Stair, Grotius and the Sources of Stair's Institutions *Satura Roberto Feenstra sexagesimum quintum annum aetatis complenti ab alumnis collegis amicis oblata*, ed. by J. A. Ankum, J. E. Spruit, and F. B. J. Wubbe, Fribourg: University Press, 571–83.

Grant, A. (1884) *The Story of the University of Edinburgh during its First Three Hundred Years*, vols. I and II, London: Longmans, Green, and Co.

Haakonssen, K. (1981) *The Science of a Legislator: The Natural Jurisprudence of David Hume and Adam Smith*, Cambridge: Cambridge University Press.

Haakonssen, K. (1985A) Hugo Grotius and the History of Political Thought *Political Theory*, 13, 239–65.

Haakonssen, K. (1985B) John Millar and the Science of a Legislator *Juridical Review*, 41–68.

Lehmann, W. C. (1960) *John Millar of Glasgow 1735–1801: His Life and Thought and his Contributions to Sociological Analysis*, Cambridge: Cambridge University Press.

Lieberman, D. (1983) The Legal Needs of a Commercial Society: the Jurisprudence of Lord Kames *Wealth and Virtue: The Shaping of Political Economy in the Scottish Enlightenment*, ed. by I. Hont and M. Ignatieff, Cambridge: Cambridge University Press, 203–34.

Lieberman, D. (1989) *The Province of Legislation Determined: Legal Theory in Eighteenth-century Britain*, Cambridge: Cambridge University Press.

Lorimer, J. (1888) The Story of the Chair of Public Law in the University of Edinburgh *Law Quarterly Review* 4, 139–58.

Maccormick, N. (1979) Law, Obligation and Consent: Reflections on Stair and Locke, *Archiv für Rechts-und Sozialphilosophie* 65, 387–411.

Maccormick, N. (1981) Adam Smith on Law *Valparaiso University Law Review* 15, 243–63.

Maccormick, N. (1982) Law and Enlightenment *The Origins and Nature of the Scottish Enlightenment*, ed. by R. H. Campbell and A. S. Skinner, Edinburgh: John Donald, 150–66.

Mackinnon, K. A. B. (1987) George Turnbull's Common Sense Jurisprudence *Aberdeen and the Enlightenment*, ed. by J. J. Carter and J. H. Pittock, Aberdeen: Aberdeen University Press, 104–10.

Meek, R. L. (1971) Smith, Turgot, and the 'Four Stages' Theory *History of Political Economy* 3, 9–27.

Meek, R. L. (1976A) New Light on Adam Smith's Glasgow lectures on Jurisprudence *History of Political Economy* 8, 439–77.

Meek, R. L. (1976B) *Social Science and the Ignoble Savage*, Cambridge: Cambridge University Press.

Minute Book (1976) *The Minute Book of the Faculty of Advocates Volume I 1661–1712*, ed. by J. M. Pinkerton, Edinburgh: Stair Society.

Minute Book (1980) *The Minute Book of the Faculty of Advocates Volume 2 1713–1750*, ed. by J. M. Pinkerton, Edinburgh: Stair Society.

Moore, J. and Silverthorne, M. (1983) Gershom Carmichael and the Natural Jurisprudence Tradition in Eighteenth-Century Scotland *Wealth and Virtue: The Shaping of Political Economy in the Scottish Enlightenment*, ed. by I. Hont and M. Ignatieff, Cambridge: Cambridge University Press, 73–87.

Moore, J. and Silverthorne, M. (1984) Natural Sociability and Natural Rights in the Moral Philosophy of Gershom Carmichael *Philosophers of the Scottish Enlightenment*, ed. by V. Hope, Edinburgh, Edinburgh University Press, 1–12.

Phillipson, N. T. (1976) Lawyers, Landowners, and the Civic Leadership of Post-Union Scotland: An Essay on the Social Role of the Faculty of Advocates 1661–1830 in 18th-Century Scottish Society *Juridical Review* (N.S.) 21, 97–120.

Raphael, D. D. (1969) Adam Smith and 'The Infection of David Hume's Society': New Light on an old Controversy, together with the Text of a hitherto unpublished Manuscript *Journal of the History of Ideas* 30, 225–48.

Raphael, D. D. (1975) The Impartial Spectator *Essays on Adam Smith*, ed. by A. S. Skinner and T. Wilson, Oxford: Clarendon Press, 83–99.

Scott, W. R. (1900) *Francis Hutcheson: His Life, Teaching and Position in the History of Philosophy*, Cambridge: Cambridge University Press.

Scott, W. R. (1937) *Adam Smith as Student and Professor*, Glasgow: Jackson, Son & Company.

Skinner, A. S. (1977) Adam Smith: Society and Government *Perspectives in Jurisprudence*, ed. by E. Attwool, Glasgow: Glasgow University Press, 195–220.

Smith, A. (1896) *Lectures on Justice, Police, Revenue and Arms, Delivered in the University of Glasgow by Adam Smith, Reported by a Student in 1763*, ed. by E. Cannan, Oxford: Clarendon Press.

Stair, James Dalrymple, Viscount (1981) *The Institutions of the Law of Scotland Deduced from its Originals, and Collated with the Civil, Canon and Feudal Laws, and with the Customs of Neighbouring Nations*, ed. by D. M. Walker, Edinburgh and Glasgow: Edinburgh and Glasgow University Presses.

Stein, P. (1980) *Legal Evolution: The Story of an Idea*, Cambridge: Cambridge University Press.

Stein, P. (1981) The Theory of Law *Stair Tercentenary Studies*, ed. by D. M. Walker, Edinburgh: Stair Society, 181–7.

Stein, P. (1988) The Four Stage Theory of the Development of Societies *The Character and Influence of the Roman Civil Law: Historical Essays*, London and Ronceverte: Hambledon Press, 395–409.

Tarello, G. (n.d.) *Le ideologie della codificazione nel secolo XVIII: Corso di filosofia del diritto*, 3rd edn., Genoa: Edizinoni Culturali Internazionali Genova.

[Tytler, A. F.] (1807) *Memoirs of the Life and Writings of the Honourable Henry Home of Kames, One of the Senators of the College of Justice, and one of the Lords Commissioners of Justiciary in Scotland: Containing Sketches of the Progress of Literature and General Improvement in Scotland During the Greater Part of the Eighteenth Century*, Edinburgh: William Creech, vol. I.

Winch, D. (1978) *Adam Smith's Politics: An Essay in Historiographic Revision*, Cambridge: Cambridge University Press.

Winch, D. (1983) Science and the Legislator: Adam Smith and After *Economic Journal* 93, 501–20.

Wodrow, R. (1843) *Analecta: or, Materials for a History of Remarkable Providences; mostly relating to Scotch Ministers and Christians*, vol. IV, Edinburgh: Maitland Club.

9

Virtue and improvement: the civic world of Adam Smith

JOHN DWYER

I

Adam Smith scholarship has undergone a renaissance in recent years as scholars from a variety of perspectives have challenged many of our most deeply held assumptions about this thinker and the cultural, political and economic environment within which he wrote. The picture of Smith that is beginning to emerge is that of a complex and subtle thinker who was much more aware of the drawbacks of commercial capitalism than many of his later followers. Smith was acutely sensitive, for example, to the human tragedy inseparably connected with the division of labour, and his treatment of the experience of urban workers was seminal to the conceptualisation of alienation (WN V. i. f. 50–5). He was also concerned to assert the domain of politics and law in the face of the ever-increasing influence of merchants and manufacturers (Winch, 1978 and Haakonssen, 1981). And, equally significant, he wanted to ensure that the type of capitalism which developed ensured educational provision and distributive justice for the poorer members of society (Campbell and Skinner, 1976; Hont and Ignatieff, 1986).

One of the most intriguing approaches to the study of Smith and his works is to examine them in the context of that civic humanist vocabulary which John Pocock (1975) has suggested pervaded the literature of the eighteenth century. It is intriguing precisely because it locates the supposed apostle of bourgeois capitalism in relation to a discourse which would appear to have been fundamentally hostile to many of its most basic tenets. The civic humanist prescriptions against 'corruption' in the form of credit, speculation and luxury seem to be diametrically opposed to the new forms for the generation of wealth, which allowed eighteenth-century British society to break through the Malthusian bonds and become the workshop of the western world. The neo-Harringtonian discussion of active citizenship, military prowess, and a devotion to an explicitly public and political domain of virtue seems equally remote from the moral and economic works of Smith which placed so much emphasis upon the prudent self-interest of actors in private life and which argued that the defence of the modern state was best placed in the trained hands of a professional standing army. Moreover, there would seem to be an obvious tension between the civic humanist emphasis upon the independent and complete personality of the *zöon politikon* and Smith's commitment to the division of labour with its concomitant alienation.

Given these obvious contrasts, it is hardly surprising that those scholars who have used the lens of civic humanism in order to illuminate the works of Smith have tended to emphasise the ways in which that thinker either challenged or modified the assumptions of the civic tradition (Teichgraeber, 1982; Robertson, 1983 and 1985; Phillipson, 1986). These and other authors, however, may have been guilty of a degree of anachronism in their treatment of Smith and other eighteenth-century thinkers. Because they are primarily concerned to discover the revolutionary and modern elements in Smith's works, they sometimes obscure the nature and depth of Smith's commitment to a number of concepts which were central to the civic humanist and neo-Harringtonian perspective on national integrity and societal progress. Among these were: the political, social and ethical superiority of land over trade and commerce; the danger of social corruption through faction; the need to control egotism and the profit motive; the fantastical nature of speculation in the forms of excessive credit or paper currency; the debilitating effects of extravagance and empire; and the historical vulnerability of the commercial and imperial state.

In this chapter I want to illuminate the ways in which Smith's major work, *The Wealth of Nations*, continued to reflect a recognisably civic programme. My fundamental argument will be that Smith's great work should be read as an ethical, as well as an economic, tract. Smith sought to construct a recognisably civic polity, based upon the social power of small independent landowners, and to limit the corrupting capacity of commerce. He developed the civic distinction between the natural economy of land and labour and the typically artificial and fantastical character of money and credit. And he deplored the influence which an overgrown commercial empire could have upon public prudence and private morality. While Smith transformed the traditional language of civic humanism, his social and economic vision was true to many of its most central beliefs.

It is my intention to demonstrate the contribution of the civic *mentalité* to Smithean economics. Lest the argument that follows be construed as unduly perverse or heretical, however, I am willing to offer potential critics a few caveats. The first of these is the admission that, while the concept of 'civic humanism' may act as a useful device for exploring the traditional discursive context within which Smith composed his works, it is only a tool for understanding. Like such other conceptualisations as natural juris-prudence or neo-Stoicism, it is an artificial historical construct which reveals certain aspects of Smith's thought at the expense of others. Second, a focus upon the traditional discourse of manly virtue, independence and corruption cannot easily account for what was perhaps most striking and original in Smith's major writings – his appreciation of the subtle workings of sociability and self-interest (cf. Dwyer, 1987). Finally, the civic humanist perspec-tive necessarily obscures that 'scientific' model of a capitalist economy which so many nineteenth- and twentieth-century scho-lars have discovered in *The Wealth of Nations*. I am neither interested in extolling nor negating Smith's contribution to classical economics.[1] What I am concerned to achieve, however, is a more balanced and historical approach to the development of a capitalist ideology.

II

Although the focus of this chapter is socio-ethical rather than economic, it should be noted that its findings reinforce the recent controversial arguments of some economic historians and political scientists. In particular, it supports the so-called 'Brenner thesis' which suggests that modern capitalism originated within an over-whelmingly agrarian context (Brenner, 1982). Brenner argues that the decline of feudalism in England offered novel opportunities for the development of private property and the concomitant ethic of

capitalist accumulation. It was this agrarian capitalism, characterised by rent-paying tenants operating small family farms, which
provided the catalyst for economic specialisation and growth.
Increasing wealth within the relatively stable environment of
English landed society in turn stimulated the production of industrial goods for the home market. Nascent industry and agriculture
evolved within a symbiotic relationship resulting in that 'upward
spiral that extended into the Industrial Revolution' (Brenner, 1982,
p. 113).

Building upon Brenner's insights, the political economist David
McNally has attempted to describe the ways in which economic
thought reflected this agrarian context. In *Political Economy and the
Rise of Capitalism: A Reinterpretation* (1988), the author argues that
it is a mistake to regard Smith as a champion of commercial
capitalism or a properly purified merchant and industrial class.
Smith, he suggests, followed the Physiocrats by grounding his
theories in a world dominated by agriculture. Thus, for example,
he consistently argued that the most accurate determinant of value
was the price of corn and that the most useful social groups were
farmers and labourers. More fundamentally, Smith argued that
economic progress was in large part based upon agricultural
improvement and that any economic doctrines or practices which
deflected capital from agrarian production into industry and
commerce were wrong-headed. The expansion of industry and
commerce were only sustainable and justifiable when they utilised
that agricultural surplus which could not easily be employed within
the agricultural wage fund. Industry and trade, in other words,
properly followed the improvement of the countryside.[2]

So far was Smith from being an advocate of modern capitalism
that, despite his emphasis on the division of labour and the utility
of machinery, his economic analysis allows only a very circum-
scribed role for forms of fixed capital (McNally, 1988, pp. 241–2).[3]
Rather, it was geared to circulating capital in the form of wages;
even a farmer's cows were, to Smith's way of thinking, a sort of
labour whose wages were provided in kind. McNally utilises these
and other insights in order to argue that Smith was not the
defender of commercial or industrial capitalism, but an advocate
for the form of agrarian capitalism which had been long developing
in Great Britain and which Smith and his fellow-Scots hoped would
transform Scotland. For my purposes however, it is just as interesting

to view Smith as establishing a clear economic foundation for the natural hegemony of land over commerce.

What I want to suggest is that this hegemony was as much civic and ethical as it was economic. It was not only the case that land was the most durable form of wealth and that it was the farmer who put into motion the greatest quality of productive labour, but it was also the case that the interest of landed society – the landlord and the farmer – most closely equated with the interest of the 'public' and the 'nation'. The high rents of landlords and the concomitant development of a gentry and yeoman class were symbols of agricultural prosperity. They translated into low grain prices, increased consumption among the labouring classes, a growing and healthy population, and a surplus of labour and capital, some of which could be employed in industry and commerce.

Smith criticised the Physiocrats for constructing a system in which agriculture was considered the only productive activity. He pointed out that industrialists and men of commerce were not a 'barren class'; they too generated national wealth, not only by employing the surplus and producing goods which in turn could be traded, but also by indirectly stimulating agricultural production (WN IV. ix. 29). At the same time, however, Smith made it absolutely clear that the most stable form of national wealth and government revenue was land; that industry and urban development logically followed agricultural development; that a healthy internal trade relied primarily upon the production of corn; and that foreign trade, particularly the 'roundabout' trade with colonies, was inherently precarious (WN II. v. 27–8; III. iv. 24; IV. v. a. 10–14). Smith even computed the latter's utility to the nation, when compared with producing for the home market, in the ratio of one to thirty (WN IV. v. b. 29).

Smith wanted to elevate the status of land above that of commerce and industry. He admitted that the growth of towns and the luxury trade had played a beneficial role in the development of western economies by turning the feudal barons away from war and unprogressive forms of conspicuous consumption into production for the market (WN III. iii). However, this development was accidental and extremely precarious – it represented a 'retrograde order' – as the fate of the Venetian republics and the once-powerful Hanseatic league clearly demonstrated (WN III. i. 9–10; III. iv.

23–4). If Great Britain did not want to follow the example of the declining German states, Smith warned, it needed to tailor its desires more closely to the production of the staple of life and labour – corn. In political terms, this meant consolidating the status and power of the landed interest, which equated most closely with that of the 'public', and controlling those interests which were often opposed to the national interest. The groups which Smith targeted for special criticism were the ones whose profits were not necessarily in the national interest – industrialists and merchants. Moreover, he often compared the latter to their landed counter-parts in a language that had more than a passing resemblance to the moral vocabulary of the civic tradition.

Country gentlemen, wrote Smith, were independent. Not only were they 'dispersed in different parts of the country' but, 'to their great honour', they were the least subject to the 'wretched spirit of monopoly' (WN IV. ii. 21). Merchants and manufacturers, on the other hand, 'who being collected into towns, and accustomed to that exclusive corporation spirit which prevails in them, naturally endeavour to obtain against all their countrymen, the same exclu-sive privilege which they generally possess against the inhabitants of their respective towns'. We should pay serious attention to what Smith is saying here. He is suggesting that the country is morally superior to the towns and that merchants and manufacturers have a tendency to form themselves into a kind of faction which places the interest of one group before the interest of the nation. He repeats this theme again and again throughout his work, showing how the merchant class in particular uses its knowledge in order to trick the government (WN IV. i. 10). They regularly employ the 'sneaking arts of underling tradesmen'; they are characterised by 'mean rapacity', a 'monopolizing spirit,' self-interested 'sophistry' and a 'mercantile jealousy' of others (WN IV. iii. c. 8–10). 'As merchants,' he asserts, 'their interest is directly opposite' to that of the sovereign (WN, IV, vii. c. 103). They have a tendency to construct mean-minded, inhumane, prejudiced corporations which conjure up 'dazzling' images in order to deceive the public and their regulations are 'written in blood' (WN IV. vii. c. 26–33 and 106). Such corporations could rarely be trusted, and hardly ever to undertake public works (WN V. i. d). They constituted a faction which promoted 'the little interest of one little order of men' against the 'interest of all other orders' (WN IV. vii. c. 60).

Smith's treatment of the agricultural labourer versus his urban and industrial counterpart further emphasises the superiority of the countryside. It was a mistake, Smith argued, to look upon the 'common ploughman' as 'the pattern of stupidity and ignorance' (WN I. x. c. 24). Because agricultural production was not and would never be susceptible of the same division of labour as manufacturing, the inhabitants of the country were accustomed to a wider range of emotional and intellectual stimuli. As a result, their 'understanding' was clearly superior to that of individuals 'whose whole attention from morning till night is commonly occupied in performing one or two very simple operations'. This natural superiority, Smith firmly believed, would inevitably result in higher rank and wages were it not for the unnatural power of the urban corporations.[4]

Smith distrusted merchants, manufacturers, and the urban environment which gave rise to the corporation spirit. If anything, this distrust grew in the various additions which he made to *The Wealth of Nations*. He found the attitude of merchants and manufacturers towards the poor and helpless particularly unconscionable. In the 1784 edition, for example, Smith outlined the ways in which manufacturers encouraged the importation of a certain amount of cheap linen yarn in order to force poor spinners and weavers, who were scattered throughout the country, to lower the prices of their products (WN IV. viii. 4). Similarly, manufacturers, who were 'collected together in numerous bodies in all great cities' were able to oppress the graziers who were 'dispersed through all the different corners of the country' (WN IV. viii. 34).

Adopting a traditional rhetoric which would have been familiar to his readers, Smith compared these natural monopolists to an 'overgrown standing army' (WN IV. ii. 43). In parliament, he argued, they often formed a 'faction' which acted against the national interest (WN V. iii. k. 40). One result of this was that the English capital of a mercantile empire had become a mad 'scramble of faction and ambition' (WN V. iii. 90). Independent thought was increasingly the prerogative of those 'indifferent and impartial spectators' who lived at a distance from the corrupting metropolis. It was most characteristic of the provinces. 'The spirit of party,' as Smith tersely put it, 'prevails less in Scotland than in England.' The solution to such social corruption was to ensure that men of independent circumstances and prudential thinking held the reins of social and political power. And the best way to achieve such a state of affairs was to encourage an agricultural improvement, which would increase rents and farming income and establish the kind of competition in industry and commerce which could limit the profit, speculation and power of the merchant and manufacturing classes.

III

The well-known historian of Scotland, T. C. Smout (1990, pp. 1–21) has recently suggested that the ethical language of the late-eighteenth-century Scots has been overemphasised and that the Scottish upper classes were more inclined to hearken to the programme of economic improvement advocated in *The Wealth of Nations* than they were to the obtuse moralising of *The Theory of Moral Sentiments* (Smout, 1990, pp. 1–21; see also Chitnis, 1986, pp. 475–88 and the reply by Dwyer, 1988, pp. 325–33). If this is the case, then it behoves us to pay close attention to exactly what Smith meant by economic improvement rather than to construct a premature equation between rapacious Scottish landlords and the improving mentality. For Smith, genuine improvement was not a contributor to greed and luxury, but a natural control upon avarice and prodigality.

As Smith points out repeatedly in *The Wealth of Nations*, national improvement is most accurately measured in the price of primary foodstuffs which, in the case of Britain, meant the price of corn (WN I. xi. c. 35). Although agricultural production was not susceptible to the same division of labour as manufacturing, it was capable of remarkable progress. To Smith's way of thinking, agricultural and more general social improvement were not so dependent upon the rationalisation of holdings through enclosure, about which he says little, as it was to the security provided to the man who farmed the land. The stable laws and government of Great Britain, Smith argued, 'so favourable to the yeomanry, have perhaps contributed more to the present grandeur of England than all their boasted regulations of commerce taken together' (WN III. ii. 14).

British stability had stimulated the gentry and yeoman class to put more capital, largely in the form of wages, into the labour-intensive enterprise of agriculture. In response to the demand of the growing towns, moderate and tenant farmers began to plant marginal land, to drain the marshes, to experiment with crop rotation and the like. But a genuine agricultural revolution only occurred, argued Smith, when former pasture land became sufficiently scarce so as to push up the price of animal flesh. This made it profitable for farmers to engage in some form of a mix between grain production and animal husbandry. This phenomenon not only supplied the farmer with beasts who could aid in heavy labour, but their manure further enriched the soil and allowed it to produce more grain (WN I. xi. b. 10–12; I. xi. 1. 3; IV. viii. b. 29). The relative shortage and price of butcher's meat and dairy products made even the grasslands of England and Scotland valuable and increased the rents of proprietors. As all land became a valuable resource, there was no shortage of enterprising individuals who wished to lease it.

The union of 1707, argued Smith, had opened the market for Scottish beef to England and tripled the rents of highland landlords. The grasslands which were formerly worth little now became valuable. But this situation was anomalous and Scottish agriculture remained relatively unimproved in comparison with that of John Bull. In order for Scottish agriculture to experience more lasting improvement, it needed to follow the slow and steady process of capital injection which had transformed the English countryside. Improvement, in other words, needed to be 'slow and distant' (WN II. ii. 73). And the individuals who were best suited to carry out this capital accumulation and improvement were those who were 'prudent' and 'parsimonious'.

In both *The Theory of Moral Sentiments* and *The Wealth of Nations*, Smith consistently extols the virtues of frugality and industry (cf. WN II. iv. 1–3; TMS VI. i. 5–6). He repeatedly contrasts 'sober men' with 'prodigals' (WN II. iv. 15; IV. i. 16). What is more, he often equates 'prudence' with 'public spirit' (WN V. iii. 45).[5] To Smith's way of thinking, prudence was not an unusual virtue. There would always be many more prudent men in a state than there would be 'gluttons', 'beaus' or 'drunkards' (WN IV. iii. c. 8). There were always more people who would spend less than they could afford. In *The Theory of Moral Sentiments*, Smith was concerned to affirm the moral nature of prudence and propriety and its firm basis in the normative structure of the community; he developed this theme in relation to economic improvement in *The Wealth of Nations*. The morals of the vast majority of people, he asserted, were superior to those 'contrivers' who bustled for positions of state or power. It was necessary to maximise this moral character of the community throughout the nation. And one of the most effective ways of doing that was to avoid all unnecessary interference with the prudent behaviour of the average man and woman.

An economic system which encouraged capital accumulation was one which simultanously spurred 'prudence' and 'parsimony'. It was the 'frugal man' who established a fund for the employment of labour; it was the 'prodigal' man who diminished that same fund (WN II. iii. 14). The gentry and upper yeomanry had the habits best suited to this small-scale capital accumulation. Despite the fact that he believed that the real interest of all proprietors of land was identical with that of the nation as a whole, Smith could be extremely critical of the behaviour of the large landowners. Great proprietors, he suggests, had minds which were turned to ornament (WN III. ii. 7). Their eyes were typically 'larger than the belly' and their behaviour was often characterised by 'luxury and caprice' (TMS IV. i. 10).

Such individuals were not noted for their prudence. While there was nothing wrong with them subscribing to the public-spirited movement for economic improvement, their most proper contribution was the experimentation of crops on small parcels of land. They could most easily bear the inevitable losses and communicate important discoveries (WN IV. ii. c. 15). The independent country gentlemen and farmers, however, who constituted the moral backbone of the nation and were the least subject to the 'wretched spirit of monopoly', were the most proper supervisors of agricultural improvement (WN IV. ii. 21). But in a statement which reveals his commitment to a clearly *capitalistic* deployment of land, Smith remarked that a frugal merchant who had saved a little capital could also play the role of country gentleman and was perhaps 'fitter to execute, with profit and success, any project of improvement' (WN III. iv. 3).[6] His qualities of economy and attention to business, when detached from the corporation spirit of the urban and mercantile world, were well suited to the ethic of improvement.

The ideal agrarian capitalist was the product of unique historical forces. In his fascinating account of feudalism and the rise of towns, Smith focused on what he viewed as the single most important transformation of landed society in England. He suggested that a critical watershed in European history occurred when the proprietors of land began to switch from a reliance upon peasant to tenant farming. They provided tenant farmers with plots of land, encouraged the development of the specialised family farm, and allowed the prudence and initiative of the yeomanry to provide them with rents (WN III. iv. 17–19). It was the self-interest of the British nobility, not the constitutional development of feudal law nor a strengthened monarchy advocating order and legitimacy, that resulted in 'a revolution of the greatest importance to the public happiness' – the rise of the 'respectable' and 'independent' class of yeoman farmers (WN III. iv. 9–10). What particularly set England apart from other European countries was that it was the country in which 'the yeomanry has always been most respected' (WN III. ii. 14).

Although Smith was a firm believer in the importance of land and its relation to rank and subordination in society, he fully understood that Britain's social structure had historically allowed for a great deal of mobility. Moreover, he believed that this was no bad thing. To Smith's way of thinking, mobility meant that the most frugal and prudent men always played the dominant role in the social structure. Those who were unnecessarily extravagant or imprudent tended to fall down the social ladder. The one social institution that could interfere with this benign natural process, however, was monopoly. Monopoly allowed a few men an unnecessary advantage, eliminated the necessity for prudence, and established a small group of potentates who ruled in their own, rather than the public, interest. Such monopolies were not only the prerogative of merchants, but also existed upon the land in the form of the Corn Laws and entails. Smith advised against the first by pointing out that landlords, who lived on rents rather than profits, gained no advantage from a procedure which merely fuelled inflation and which left the real value of rents the same as it was before. But he regarded the second as a major obstacle to improvement because it locked up too much land and made remaining available land unnaturally expensive for the putative improver.

Smith's attack upon entails provides an insight into the kind of improving society which he advocated (WN III. ii. 6; IV. vii. b. 16–19). If land was no longer entailed, the price of land generally would drop within the reach of the yeomanry and minor gentry. This in turn would result in 'the multiplication of small proprietors' (WN III. iv. 19). Small proprietors, Smith believed, made the best improvers. 'A small proprietor, however, who knows every part of his little territory, who views it with all the affection which property, especially small property, naturally inspires, and who upon that account takes pleasure not only in cultivating but adorning it, is generally of all improvers the most industrious, the most intelligent, and the most successful.' Smith went on to suggest that, even where land was not the most profitable investment, some young men, who put happiness and independence above 'great fortune or great illustration' would always employ their stock of perhaps two or three thousand pounds in a small piece of land. But if primogeniture and perpetuities were eliminated, land would become a less sterile investment and attract individuals of moderate means and prudent character.[7]

Smith's model of a harmoniously functioning economy and society was one dominated by capitalist yeoman farmers. Clearly, such individuals were motivated at least in part by self-interest. But Smith was concerned to point out that the pursuit of rational self-interest among most men was not characterised by the acquisitive ego. Rather, the desire to better one's condition was typically 'calm and dispassionate'. Within it, the 'principle of frugality seems not only to predominate, but to predominate very greatly' (WN II. iii. 28). Frugality, in turn, implied prudent self-control, which was for Smith an essential characteristic of virtue and one which I would suggest counted for more in his way of thinking than the scales of justice. For, while Smith often praised that 'simple system of natural liberty' which removed the restraints upon level-headed and sober men, he appears to have been suspicious of any attempt to create an ideal constitution or what he termed 'the exact regimen of perfect liberty and perfect justice' (WN IV. ix. 28; IV. ix. 51). Those abstract theorists who sought to create a perfect polity or system of laws, Smith suggested, did not consider the character and resilience of man. 'If a nation could not prosper without the enjoyment of perfect liberty and perfect justice,' he continued, 'there is not in the world a nation which could ever have prospered.' But in a regularly ordered and secure society, one which avoided excessive interference with human nature, prudence naturally overcame prodigality.[8]

Clearly, Smith's model of a society of prudent farmers is quite distinct either from modern capitalism's understanding of economies of scale or economic historians' stress upon the increasing

primacy of trade and manufacturing. Moreover, Smith was concerned to underline such socio-cultural values as the naturalness
of man's attachment to the soil and the way in which the ownership
of land encouraged independent thought and personal development. He was even willing to suggest a practice which would be
anathema to those modern economic writers who revere the
marketplace. Because he believed that improvement was a 'slow
and distant' process, Smith was an advocate of long leases. He
argued that French leases had lately been extended to twenty-
seven years, 'a period still too short to encourage the tenant to
make the most important improvements' (WN III. ii. 16; IV. ix.
38). And he condemned the 'avarice and injustice' of European
landlords for destroying real and lasting improvements in their
search for higher and higher rents.

Not only was Smith critical of those members of landed society
who made a simplistic equation between improvement and high
rents, but he also attacked what he called 'vulgar' interpretations
of improvement. Any injudicious investment, he argued, took capital
away from the 'funds destined for the maintenance of productive
labour' (WN II. iii. 26). In effect, this meant that every 'injudicious
and unsuccessful project in agriculture, mines, fisheries, trade or
manufactures' was more than a mistake; it was an attack on the
nation. Its perpetrators were nothing less than 'public enemies'.
Smith was particularly scornful of those individuals who tried to
wear the mantle of the improver and who uttered cries of 'public
spirit' in defence of their fantastic schemes. Few eighteenth-century
moralists were more critical of the spirit of 'projection' and 'speculation' than was Smith. He regularly ridiculed those 'projectors' who
had lately 'amused the public with the most magnificent accounts
of the profits to be made by the cultivation of land' (WN II. v. 37).

IV

Smith made considerable use of the civic vocabulary in his attack
upon 'projectors' and 'prodigals' who live in their own overheated
imaginations, construct chimeras to delude the public and whose
extravagant schemes help to bankrupt nations. However, Smith's
conjunction of prudential and civic concerns are most clearly
evidenced in his treatment of money and banking.

In the third edition of 1784, Smith condemned an institution that
many economic historians regard as the *sine qua non* of capitalistic

development – the joint stock company (WN IV. i. e. 15f). Such companies, he argued, sinned against the public in so far as they were characterised by the 'spirit of faction'. Moreover, they rocked the very foundation of public security because they encouraged 'negligence and profusion' (WN V. i. e. 18). Smith used the examples of the South Sea Company and the East India Company in order to illustrate his argument, and his language is particularly interesting. He claimed that such companies were characterised by 'malversion', 'plunder', 'knavery', 'extravagance', 'injustice' and a general 'indifference' to anything but their own private interests. This 'indifference', Smith suggested, stemmed from 'irresistible moral causes' (WN V. i. e. 26). The sovereign, as a result of ignorance, had allowed such moral cancers far too much influence in affairs of the nation and the empire. Such companies had no concern for the well-being of the nations which they plundered or for the empire which they pretended to serve. Indeed, Smith suggested, 'as merchants, their interest is directly opposite to that (i.e. the sovereign's) interest' (WN IV. vii. c. 103).

There were two kinds of joint stock companies, however, which, if rightly supervised, posed no such threat to public safety and even served the public interest. These were banking and insurance. The reasons why banking and insurance were exempt from Smith's scathing indictment of joint stock companies were twofold. First, they were so obviously useful, a point to which I shall return in a moment. Second, the principles according to which they operated were sufficiently clear as to be 'capable of being reduced to strict rules' (WN V. i.e. 33). Since any departure from these strict rules would spell disaster for both the bank and its customers, it was relatively safe for the soverign to permit such institutions to operate under the protection of the law.

To Smith's way of thinking, the primary purpose of a bank was not the formation of fixed capital for investment. Its purpose was to provide credit and to aid in the circulation of money, which otherwise got tied up in the delay between the costs of a venture and the realisation of profit (WN II. ii. 39–41). Smith spent a great deal of space attempting to teach his readers the real value of money. He argued, for instance, that money had little intrinsic value; it made up only a very small part of a nation's wealth (WN IV. i. 17). Almost all of its utility consisted in its function as the 'wheel of production'.

The revenue of society consists altogether in those goods, and not in the wheel which circulates them. In computing either the gross or the net revenue of any society, we must always, from their whole annual circulation of money and goods, deduct the whole value of the money, of which not a single farthing can ever make any part of either. (WN II. ii. 14)

Smith constantly inveighed against the fetishism of money and gold, pointing out that it was productive labour rather than money which was the true source of wealth. So little did money constitute national wealth, that it could always be replaced either by barter or by paper currency whenever it was found lacking (WN IV. i. 15).[9]

The productive labour which interested Smith first and foremost was agricultural. The fundamental purpose of banking was to provide farmers with capital for agricultural improvement; it allowed them to convert 'dead stock' into 'active and productive stock'. 'The judicious operations of banking, by providing,' wrote Smith, 'if I may be allowed so violent a metaphor, a sort of waggon-way through the air; enable the country to convert, as it were, a great part of its highways into good pastures and cornfields, and thereby to increase very considerably the annual produce of its land and labour' (WN II. ii. 86).[10] It was for precisely this reason that both banking and 'the Daedalian wings of paper currency' were contrived.

But like all human inventions, banking and the issuing of paper currency were highly dependent upon the care and skilfulness of the operators. When bankers did not look beyond the real labour and productive capacity of the nation, they stood on reasonably firm ground; whenever they went beyond this, in schemes for imaginary improvement or 'projection', they not only lived in the realm of fantasy but they 'endangered the security of the whole society' (WN II. ii. 94). Smith's lengthy discussion of the inflation which followed upon the spread of paper currency in Scotland during the 1760s illuminates the danger to the nation when this spirit of projection replaced common sense and prudence.

Smith had nothing but praise for the early development of banking in Scotland. The Scots, he argued, invented the system of cash accounts characterised by regular repayments. Scottish bankers not only required frequent and routine repayments, but they typically refused to 'deal with any person, whatever might be his fortune or credit, who did not make, what they called, frequent and regular operations with them' (WN II. ii. 60). This system of punctual payments allowed prudent Scottish bankers to avoid issuing more paper money than 'what the circulation of the country could easily absorb and employ'. With its intimate knowledge of landed society and its constant face-to-face exchange with its clients, therefore, Scottish bankers reinforced a society of independent landed proprietors, whose improved estates in turn benefited the entire nation.

Smith believed that the halcyon days of Scottish banking had been over for more than twenty-five years. The slow decline began when 'traders and other undertakers' began to complain about the 'contracted views and dastardly spirit of the directors of those banks' (WN II. ii. 65). Then began the clarion call to much greater improvement and an 'extension of projects' beyond that which the nation could prudently bear. The amount advanced by the banks increased, and the 'stream of circulating bills' steadily advanced. 'Vast and extensive projects of agriculture, commerce or manufactures' were proferred without sufficient foresight. And, 'in the midst of this clamour', the Ayr bank was established on the principle of providing an even more liberal flow of funds for improvement.

Many of Smith's friends, including his student the Duke of Buccleuch, were implicated in the failure of the Ayr bank, and Smith was not unsympathetic to their public-spirited desire to improve the nation (WN II. ii. 72–4).[11] But such policies were wrong-headed in so far as they actually took money away from the most cautious and independent proprietors of land and placed it in the hands of 'projectors' and 'stock jobbers'. They made it increasingly impossible to distinguish between 'real' and 'fictitious' bills of exchange. And they perpetuated a vicious spiral of ever-increased borrowing to pay off debts which should never have been incurred in the first place. Whereas the original impulse of those behind the Ayr bank was the liberal plan to 'beautify, improve, and enrich the country', the sponsors actually 'increased the real distress of the country' which they meant to relieve.

Smith's analysis of the function of paper currency was certainly more advanced than that of some of his countrymen, who filled the Scottish periodical press and county meetings with lamentation during the 1760s and 1770s. Some of the latter regarded bank notes of any kind as an 'imaginary' or 'fictitious' form of wealth which should be entirely eliminated. Behind each and every paper bill, they saw 'pensioners', 'stock jobbers', 'harpies' and 'drones'.[12] But Smith was not so very far removed from writers like Lord Hailes, who blamed the spread of bank notes on 'crafty traders', or correspondents like 'Simplicious' who condemned the abuses of credit which resulted in that 'ideal wealth' and concomitant 'luxury' and 'debility' which destroyed the nations of the ancient world.[13] Although Smith was careful not to engage in a blunt and naive attack upon some abstract concept of luxury, his criticism of extravagance, projection and stock jobbing, as well as his concern to elevate the improving role of small and independent proprietors, suggests that he spoke within the same intellectual parameters as many of his fellow-countrymen.

Smith's contribution to the paper currency debate in Scotland also provides a fascinating instance of the emphasis which he could sometimes place upon the concept of public security. For one of Smith's arguments was that it was quite proper for the state to prevent the proliferation of paper currency by restraining the use of small bills or even promissory notes. This practice, he patronisingly suggested, would also put an end to the activities of 'beggarly bankers' who were the most likely to act irresponsibly and to suffer bankruptcy (WN II. iii. 90 and 94). While Smith readily admitted that such a practice was a clear 'violation of natural liberty', especially of private individuals with limited means, he deemed it absolutely necessary to the security of the nation. The proliferation of paper currency, he suggested, was like 'the communication of fire'. Its regulation was in the interest of public safety.

V

While Smith favoured slow and steady growth and attacked any practices or policies which reflected projection and extravagance, he did believe that agriculture was capable of greater investment of the prudential kind and that such a capital injection would be in the nation's best interest. 'Agriculture,' he maintained, 'is almost every-where capable of absorbing a much greater capital than has ever yet been employed' (WN II. v. 37). The primary obstacle to the judicious investment of capital was the fact that it was possible to make huge profits in trade. Commerce had been given an unfair advantage over agriculture, a superiority which was directly contrary to the natural order of things. Monopolistic traders had inverted economic growth and rendered the nation economically unstable. In the process, however, they had also inverted the ethical order by elevating speculation over prudence, spending over saving, and luxury over subsistence and simple comfort. These same 'moral causes' had transformed European nations into prodigals, which lived beyond their means, funded their own debts, and engaged in 'waste and extravagance' (WN V. iii. 5–53).[14]

One of Smith's chief aims, I would suggest, was that of redressing the balance in favour of agriculture whose independent proprietors simultaneously constituted the economic and ethical backbone of the nation. In order to achieve this end, Smith had to seek a mechanism for limiting the ever-increasing economic power of those engaged in commerce and industry. His solution was to devise a system which provided realistic rents and wages while it limited profit.

Early on in *The Wealth of Nations*, Smith remarks that a society characterised by high profits is a society in which credit is expensive (WN I. ix. 13). Farmers are necessarily impoverished by the interest which they have to pay, and landlords cannot demand high rents. Smith has no difficulty calling these interest rates usurious or suggesting that it was 'such enormous usury' that led to the 'fall of the Roman republic'. High profits were a much more serious threat to public security than high wages:

> In raising the price of commodities the rise of wages operates in the same manner as simple interest does in the accumulation of debt. The rise of profit operates like compound interest. Our merchants and master-manufacturers complain much of the bad effects of high wages in raising the price. They say nothing concerning the bad effects of high profits. (WN I. ix. 24)

Elsewhere, Smith made the distinction between wages, rent and profit even more sharply when he suggested that, while high wages and rents equated with 'the general interest of society', the highest profits were characteristic of 'countries which are going fastest to ruin' (WN I. xi. p. 10). High profits spelled 'private interest' and profusion, while high rents and wages supported the public interest.

There was nothing wrong with profits which were moderate, and Smith made an important distinction between 'creditable traders' and those 'projectors' whose wishes always exceeded their grasp. In the ideal system, however, the private interest of the men who live upon profit would be controlled. Any excessive promotion of 'the little interest of one little order of men in one country', Smith maintained, 'hurts the interest of all other orders of men in that country' (WN IV. vii. c. 60). A rise in the rate of mercantile profit, moreover, drew valuable 'capital from the improvement of the land' which was the chief support for all citizens. The monopoly of the colonial trade was particularly pernicious because it not only took investment away from wages and rents, but because any possible return to its native country was so slow and circuitous.

The only effective method for reducing profits was to allow free and unhampered competition. Such a competition would mean that many of those who lived within the precarious world of profit would be regularly ruined. But the private ruin of such men resulted in no danger to the nation. In any case, the capital which a country acquired through commerce and manufacturing was necessarily a 'very precarious and uncertain possession' (WN III. iv. 24). The men who acquired such capital were rarely the most solid citizens. 'A merchant,' Smith remarked, 'is not necessarily the citizen of any particular country. It is in a great measure indifferent to him from what place he carries on his trade.'

While the man who lived upon profit lacked the necessary independence and motivation which characterised the citizen, he was by no means a neutral influence. Not only did he often tap wealth which could be used to better purpose, but he could also strike at the very roots of national virtue. When his profits were high, the merchant or industrialist typically turned his back upon his former 'parsimony' and 'sober virtue', and began to adopt habits of 'expensive luxury' (WN IV. vii. c. 61). If he was an employer of men or women, his 'disorderly' and 'dissolute' lifestyle set a bad example for his servants and workmen.

In former times, Smith maintained, the main culprits for extra-vagance and profusion were the traditional nobility who wallowed in the 'wantonness of plenty' (WN III. iv. 15). But he believed that such characters were increasingly rare in a freer and more mobile society, where landed profusion invariably led to the alienation of land, the rise of the gentry and a more prudent proprietorship.[15] The modern agents of curruption were those commercial men whose 'profusion' and 'prodigality' set a bad example, or those individuals or 'upstart fortunes', such as the tax farmers of France, who engaged in 'foolish ostentation' and who had 'no bowels' for their fellow man and woman (WN V. ii. k. 73–4).

The comparable *parvenu* in Scotland was the 'nabob' who had made his fortune with the East India Company and whose wealth allowed him to play an increasingly important role in his native land. Henry Mackenzie's journal the *Lounger*, for example, characterised these 'mushrooms' as pernicious influences in Scottish landed society and as corruptors of its prudent and 'homespun' values.[16] His friend Smith did not speak about the 'nabobs' *per se*, although he had much to say about the company to which they formerly belonged. He believed that the East India Company was a disgrace (WN IV. vii. c. 103–8). Its operations were characterised by fraud and prejudice, and its employees were appointed by graft and influence. Its servants, even if they began as men of character, were subject to systematic corruption. They invariably obtained their fortune by trading upon their own account and oppressing the native population. Such individuals, Smith concluded, should never be allowed to act as sovereigns, nor should their counsel ever be given much weight in the state.

We should not expect a writer of Smith's penetration to construct his critique of the East India Company in terms of a simplistic condemnation of luxury and empire. Smith had read his Mandeville and recognised that it was virtually impossible to draw a strict line between a desirable 'conveniency' and a pernicious 'luxury' (WN III. i. 2; V. ii. k. 3). He also appreciated that the concept of luxury depended upon social definition, and that extravagance in one society could sensibly be regarded as respectibility in another. The linen shirts of contemporary British labourers, for example, were now considered to be 'decent' apparel. What is more, Smith followed in the footsteps of Hume in suggesting that the growth of both commerce and civil society was dependent upon the impulse to better one's position (WN III. iv. 4).[17]

One should be wary, however, of adopting the position recently advanced by Michael Ignatieff, who argues that Smith's ideal commonwealth is a 'marketplace of desires' as distinct from Rousseau's more recognisably civic 'republic of needs' (1986, pp. 187–206). Ignatieff not only caricatures Rousseau, who fully appreciated that the movement from the state of nature to civil society replaced simple needs with more complex desires. Moreover,

Rousseau understood perhaps more clearly than Smith that the essential character of this change was the substitution of 'justice for instinct' and the creation of the moral individual (1986, p. 15). But Ignatieff's attempt to fit Smith into the Procrustean bed of the acquisitive ego is even more misleading. He manages to ignore Smith's repeated repugnance towards a world characterised by limitless desire, as well as his ingenious attempt to construct a system which would prevent it.

Ignatieff suggests that the only check upon desire in Smith's ideal society was 'the Stoic self-command all too often displayed only by the "wise and virtuous few"' (1986, p. 203). In effect, however, Smith's economic programme's explicit purpose was that of outlining a number of such checks, some natural, some historical, and some artificial. Smith constantly asserted that, as far as most people were concerned, the desire for self-improvement tended to be cool and prudent rather than limitless. The common people, especially, were adverse to levity and luxury, and as long as they had an influence in the community they would seek to prevent its spread (WN V. i. g. 10–11).[18] Since there is no evidence that Smith ever envisioned any dramatic rise in the standard of living of the labouring people, this check was presumably constant. The middling gentry and yeomanry were by definition prudent, and in a society characterised by slow growth and realistic rents, they would remain so. The luxury of the traditional aristrocracy was controlled by the historical necessity of more prudent estate management. Moreover, it increasingly consisted in architecture, art and the patronage of letters – things which acted as public ornament for the entire society. The more foolish and private extravagance of those who lived upon profit would be drastically reduced by getting rid of monopoly and allowing free competition. Smith believed that such a practice would result in very low profits and restore thrift and prudence to their rightful hegemony in the panoply of mercantile and industrial values. Getting rid of entails would do much the same for their remaining counterparts among the landed elite.

Smith went a few steps further in order to fine-tune such checks and balances in his important and often overlooked discussion of taxation. Here, he adopted a working definition of 'luxuries' as all those items which were not physical necessities or 'those things which the established rules of decency have rendered necessary to the lowest rank of people' (WN V. ii. k. 3). Since the intemperate use of these items not only took capital away from the production of much more necessary commodities but also encouraged extravagance, Smith argued that these were the most appropriate to be taxed. Such taxes acted as 'sumptuary laws' and as controls upon 'dissolute and disorderly' behaviour. Taxes upon wine, tobacco and all spirituous liquors fell mainly upon the middle and upper classes (WN V. iii. k. 43–58).[19] Smith believed that such taxes were not only the most efficient, but also the most ethical.

It is quite possible, therefore, to read *The Wealth of Nations* as a moral as much as an economic text. Smith sought to create a model of society which supported native prudence while it circumvented the threat of luxury. It was a system in which extravagant profits were culled, not by the inefficient teeth of government legislation, but by the sharper fangs of competition. It was a fundamentally agrarian system in which independent landowners maintained their social and political hegemony. And, finally, while it may have been a system which accepted the importance of capital investment, it was anything but what Ignatieff calls 'the core of modern capitalism's defence of itself' (1986, p. 193). The very limited agrarian capitalism which Smith supported had little room for the fixtures of modern capitalism: economies of scale, an emphasis upon fixed capital, and the joint stock company. Moreover, as Smith's treatment of profit and paper currency suggests, his model was inimical to anything remotely resembling the fantasy world that was a 'republic of desires'.

VI

How optimistic was Smith about achieving the very limited form of agrarian capitalism which he so ardently advocated through the many pages of *The Wealth of Nations*? His concluding chapter 'Of Public Debts' must sound very strange to the ears of any who regard him as the optimistic champion of a recognisably modern system of commercial capitalism. It is equally foreign to those who would regard the work as a strictly economic treatise. For Smith pessimistically treats of the 'operation of moral causes' in the current 'commercial state of society' and concludes that there is reason to fear the worst (WN V. iii. 2–5). Commercial society ensures the 'regular administration of justice', but it brings in its train the most dangerous moral habits. Governments, like rich merchants, become spenders and borrowers, rather than prudent

administrators. When statesmen mimic merchants, the results are
even more disastrous to the public. The national debt continues to
grow, only partly offset by such new contrivances as the Sinking
Fund. The state itself rests upon the precarious foundation of debt
and perpetual funding. Increasingly, it drains the fund of productive labour in order to support its 'waste and extravagance', and
undermines the spirit as well as the 'frugality and industry of
private people' (WN V. iii. 49–53).

The state of Great Britain, like ancient Rome, has become
bankrupt, Smith lamented. Like ancient Rome, its resources were
wasted in supporting an increasingly 'debilitated and languishing'
empire (WN V. iii. 76). This empire was a fantasy; it existed 'in
imagination only' (WN V. iii. 92). It was not so much an empire
as it was 'the projection of a gold mine'. The final paragraph of
The Wealth of Nations reads very much like any other civic humanist
tract as Smith warns his readers against indulging in 'this golden
dream' and calls upon the rulers of Great Britain to 'awake from
it themselves, and endeavour to awaken the people'. And in a final
piece of advice which should be taken seriously by those politicians
who profess to admire him, Smith exhorted Great Britain to
'accommodate her future views and designs to the real mediocrity
of her circumstances'.

If anything, Smith became even more pessimistic as the century
wore on. By the time he came to write the final edition of *The Theory
of Moral Sentiments* in 1790, Smith no longer retained as much
confidence in the prudent behaviour of the British gentry and
yeomanry.[20] It was in this edition that Smith developed his theory of
conscience and finally and irrevocably replaced the real community
with an ideal 'spectator' within the individual breast as the final
arbiter of behaviour. It was also in this same edition that Smith
grew closer to the Stoics in his insistence on the priority of that
self-command which could only be practised by the 'wise and
virtuous few'. Finally, it was here that Smith delivered his personal
cachet to those historians and economists who persist in regarding
him as champion of modern capitalism and of the 'marketplace of
desires'. 'The great and most universal cause of the corruption of
our moral sentiments,' Smith insisted, was the 'disposition to
admire, and almost to worship, the rich and powerful' (TMS I. iii.
3. 1). Left unchecked, this disposition opened the gates of desire,
which led to nothing remotely resembling either a classical republic

or a just commercial polity, but to a fantasy world characterised by 'hypocrisy', 'vanity', 'intrigue', 'cabal', 'pollution' and 'defilement' (TMS I. iii. 3. 8). Once trapped in this world of 'imagination', the wretched individual invoked 'in vain the dark and dismal power of forgetfulness and oblivion'.

Notes

1. This is not to suggest, however, that the argument which follows has no relevance for an understanding of Smith's economic model. Indeed, Smith's attachment to civic humanist concepts helps to explain his otherwise puzzling desire to posit agricultural production as a special sector of the economy, his inability to regard rent as a commodity like any other, his virtual neglect of mechanisation (after the opening pages of his economic treatise) and his lack of consistency in applying the principle of the division of labour.
2. The significance which Smith attaches to agricultural production, and the problems which this poses for Smith's analytical model, have also been noticed by several economic historians, notably R. H. Campbell. See his comments in the introduction to WN, esp. pp. 45 and 57.
3. In his development of an abstract model of capitalism in Book II of *The Wealth of Nations* Smith certainly does make a distinction between fixed and circulating capital (WN, II. i. 25). But he downplays the function of fixed capital by suggesting that it is 'both originally derived from, and requires to be continually supported by circulating capital'. In his description of the actual workings of the English and other national economies, Smith virtually ignores the role of buildings, machinery and other forms of capital plant. The countryman of James Watt, he is surprisingly silent about such other forms of investment as the sponsorship of scientific research.
4. It is a revealing gap in Smith's analysis, however, that he did not deal with the issue of increasing alienation and dependency among rural wage labourers. Smith's support of enclosure and capitalist farming was one-sided; he was unconcerned about the decline of the very smallholders and the loss of that access to commons and pasture which made self-sufficiency possible. As a result, his flattering picture of the 'common ploughman' obscures the very real exploitation which was taking place upon the land and which Smith effectively legitimised.
5. Thus, the administration of Pelham was 'truly patriotic' precisely because it was 'prudent'.
6. The capital which Smith thought reasonable for setting up an estate was between 2,000 and 3,000 pounds sterling.
7. It must be said, however, that Smith's triadic distinction of rents, profits and wages, while it provided a mechanism for elevating land over commerce and manufacturing, provided no systematic distinction between those who received revenue in the form of rents. The abolition of entails and production for the market might have eliminated some of those aristocratic proprietors whose attachment

to luxury made them blind to their own self-interest, but it did not abolish the monopolistic and political power of the larger land-owners of Great Britain. Smith's intricate discussion of rent as a special case with relation to the market indicates that he was not ignorant of this fact. But Smith's primary agenda was to attack not the monopolistic tendencies of landowners but those of merchants and manufacturers. The problems in Smith's treatment of rent, of course, would eventually be illuminated by Ricardo.

8. Smith believed that France was such a society, despite the fact that it retained some tyrannical anachronisms, such as the taille and corvée, and lacked the constitutional liberties of Great Britain. See David McNally, *Political Economy and the Rise of Capitalism*, pp. 206–7.

9. Notice how this view of money conforms to the needs of a relatively small-scale agrarian economy in which circulating capital is limited, rather than a society which is characterised by large-scale enterprise. It also conforms to the real-life experiences of many provinces and colonies, where currency was often hard to get. The difficulties of cash flow and accumulation in the *ancien régime* society of New France during the early eighteenth century, for example, were not very far removed from those of lowland Scotland, where the role of the trader and commercial capitalist was submerged in a society that was fundamentally agrarian. See Alan Greer, *Peasant, Lord and Merchant: Rural Society in Three Quebec Parishes, 1740–1840*, chapter 6. It is always important to remember, however, that Smith was talking about capitalist farming and not the household economics or subsistence agriculture that characterised the traditional *ancien régime* society of New France. His ideal-type was much closer to the small-scale capitalistic farming community of colonial America. On that com-munity and the particular sort of agrarian capitalism which it espoused, see especially Daniel Vickers, 'Competency and competi-tion: economic culture in early America'.

10. See also R. H. Campbell and Andrew Skinner's footnote no. 73 which refers to Smith's use of a similar agricultural analogy in his other works and also cites Smith's fascinating comparison of roads and money. Smith's agricultural focus is further suggested by his comment that if 'we could find any way to save the ground taken up by highways, we would increase considerably the quantity of commodities . . .'.

11. See also Skinner and Campbell's notes 42 to 45. For a discussion of the cultural significance of the paper currency crisis in eighteenth-century Scotland, see 'Paradigms and politics: manners, morals and the rise of Henry Dundas, 1770–1784', *New Perspectives on the Politics and Culture of Early Modern Scotland*, ed. John Dwyer, Roger Mason and Alexander Murdoch (Edinburgh: John Donald, 1982), pp. 212 and 230f. For the economic background, see H. Hamilton, 'The Failure of the Ayr Bank, 1772' (1956).

12. *Caledonian Mercury*, 5 October 1764.

13. *Caledonian Mercury*, 5, 22 and 29 October 1764.

14. Smith could be very pessimistic about the historical fate of nations like Great Britain and its neighbours. He believed that their debts would 'in the long-run probably ruin all the great nations of Europe'.

Nations were in this respect similar to private individuals; once the process of corruption had begun, it was difficult to control.

15. Smith, of course, was deliberately blurring important distinctions here, since he fully realised that the rent of land was not controlled simply by economic forces but by the status of property and proprietorship in the minds of social actors and citizens. Therefore, the large proprietors of land would be cushioned from a truly free market in ways that merchants and industrialists would not. The ambiguities in Smith's economic doctrines provided ideological support for the landowning class generally and helps to explain their popularity in Great Britain and America where land would long remain the primary support of social and political power.

16. Henry Mackenzie was a friend of Adam Smith's and a younger leader of the Edinburgh literati. He was the leading figure in the Mirror Club, whose journals the *Mirror* (Edinburgh: Creech, 1779/80) and *Lounger* (Edinburgh: Creech, 1785/7) were significant successors to Joseph Addison's more famous *Spectator* (1711–14). The essays on Scottish nabobs can be found in *Mirror* no. 53 and *Loungers* nos. 17, 36, 44, 56 and 62.

17. Although Smith refers admiringly to Hume's essay 'On Luxury', his own position was far more pessimistic than that of 'le bon David'. See David McNally's perceptive comments in *Political Economy and the Rise of Capitalism*, pp. 201f.

18. A clear benefit of the natural prudence of the poor was that it encouraged the values of independence and respectability. The dangerous quality of this 'austere system', however, was that it was too easily manipulated by religious fanatics into antisocial behaviour. Smith, therefore, praised the Scottish system of church patronage which, he felt, checked simultaneously religious enthusiasm and personal extravagance.

19. In order to ensure that wealthy home brewers did not circumvent his proposal, Smith even advocated that the tax be placed upon malt.

20. For a fuller treatment of Smith's other important work *The Theory of Moral Sentiments* (1759; important revision 1790) see *Virtuous Discourse*, esp. chapter 7. Here I argue that such cosmopolitan factors as the French and American Revolutions cannot be seen as primary influences on Smith's increasing pessimism.

References

Brenner, Robert (1982), 'Agrarian Class Structure and Economic Development in Pre-Industrial Europe', in *Past and Present* (97), pp. 16–113.

Campbell, R. H. and Skinner, A. S. (1976), eds., *An Inquiry into the Nature and Causes of the Wealth of Nations* by Adam Smith (Oxford, University Press).

Chitnis, A. (1986), 'Agricultural Improvement, Political Management and Civic Virtue in Enlightened Scotland: An Historiographical Critique', in *Studies on Voltaire and the Eighteenth Century* (245), pp. 475–88.

Dwyer, J. and Murdoch A. (1982), 'Paradigms and Politics: Manners Morals and the Rise of Henry Dundas, 1770–84', in *New Perspectives on the Politics and Culture of Early Modern Scotland*, eds. Dwyer, J., Mason, R. and Murdoch, A. (Edinburgh, John Donald).

Dwyer, J. (1987), *Virtuous Discourse: Sensibility and Community in Late Eighteenth-Century Scotland* (Edinburgh, John Donald).

Dwyer, J. and Murdoch, A. (1988), 'Henry Dundas Revisited but not Revised', in *Studies on Voltaire and the Eighteenth Century* (256), pp. 325–33.

Greer, A. (1985), *Peasant, Lord and Merchant: Rural Society in Three Quebec Parishes, 1740–1840* (Toronto, University Press).

Haakonssen, K. (1981), *The Science of a Legislator* (Cambridge, University Press).

Hamilton, H. (1956), 'The Failure of the Ayr Bank, 1772', *Economic History Review*, second series, VIII, pp. 405–17.

Hont, I. and Ignatieff, M. (1983), 'Needs and Justice in the *Wealth of Nations*' in *Wealth and Virtue: The Shaping of Political Economy in the Scottish Enlightenment* (Cambridge, University Press), pp. 1–44.

Ignatieff, M. (1986), 'Smith, Rousseau and the Republic of Needs', in *Scotland and Europe, 1200–1850*, ed. Smout, T. C. (Edinburgh, John Donald).

Lindgren, J. R. (1973), *The Social Philosophy of Adam Smith* (The Hague, Martinus Nijhoff).

McNally, D. (1988), *Political Economy and the Rise of Capitalism: A Re-interpretation* (Berkeley, University Press).

Phillipson, N. T. (1986), 'Adam Smith as Civic Moralist', in *Wealth and Virtue*, pp. 179–202.

Pocock, J. S. G. (1975), *The Machiavellian Moment: Florentine Political Thought and the Atlantic Republican Tradition* (Princeton, University Press).

Robertson, J. (1983), 'Scottish Political Economy Beyond the Civic Tradition: Government and Economic Development in *The Wealth of Nations*', *History of Political Thought*, IV, 3, pp. 451–82.

Robertson, J. (1985), *The Scottish Enlightenment and the Militia Issue* (Edinburgh, John Donald).

Rousseau, J. J. (1968), *The Social Contract and Discourses*, ed. Cole, G. D. H. (London, Dent).

Smout, T. C. (1990), 'Problems of Nationalism, Identity and Improvement in Eighteenth-Century Scotland', in Devine, T. M., *Improvement and Enlightenment: Proceedings of the Scottish Historical Studies Seminar, University of Strathclyde, 1987–88* (Edinburgh, John Donald).

Teichgraeber, R. (1982), 'Rethinking Das Adam Smith Problem', in *New Perspectives*, pp. 249–264.

Vickers, Daniel (1990), 'Competency and Competition: Economic Culture in Early America', *The William and Mary Quarterly*, XLVII, 3–29.

Winch, D. (1978), *Adam Smith's Politics: An Essay in Historiographic Revision* (Cambridge, University Press).

10

Political economy: Adam Smith and his Scottish predecessors

ANDREW S. SKINNER

Over thirty years ago, Alec Macfie addressed the question of the 'Scottish tradition in economic thought'. He sought to isolate a number of characteristic features of the Scottish approach and in so doing drew attention to the sociological, philosophical and historical dimensions which Adam Smith, together with his predecessors and successors, had brought to the study of economic phenomena. In particular, Professor Macfie gave prominence to a certain penchant for systematic argument, and to an approach which was 'more concerned with giving a broad, well balanced comprehensive picture, seen from different points of view than with logical rigour' (1967, p. 22). While one might hesitate to describe these approaches to the study of political economy as particularly or even exclusively Scottish, there is no doubt that all are characteristic of the work done by three major figures of the Enlightenment, David Hume, Sir James Steuart and Adam Smith.

Adam Smith proved, in the event, to be the most influential figure; the writer whose choice of 'model' (and there were choices to be made) did most to establish the shape of the early classical system as Alfred Marshall would have known it. Yet there is a sense in which we can claim that each of the writers named not only shared common intellectual interests, but also produced work of lasting value. It may also be true that we can only attain a true perspective on the measure of Smith's achievement by pausing to review the contributions of his immediate predecessors, both of whom he knew. It is, in any event, certain that we cannot attain an accurate understanding of the tradition which Macfie identified by considering the contribution of Adam Smith in isolation. There is, besides, the intriguing fact that Hume's *Political Discourses* profoundly influenced two writers who were to produce systematic treatises which were quite markedly different in character from his own.

This chapter is divided into four main parts. In Part I we consider Hume's contribution. In Parts II and III we examine the different ways in which Steuart and Smith may have reacted to the lead provided by their friend. In Part IV we consider the advantages of the Smithian system and examine the consequences of his dominance as the founder of classical economics, especially as this affected the interpretation of the past. But it is not the intention in this place exhaustively to review the work done by these major figures, and far less to consider in detail their analytical contributions. Rather, our concern is with the broad perspectives adopted; our concern is with what might be termed the 'shape' which these writers gave to their studies.

I

David Hume's *Political Discourses* (1752 later included in *Essays, Moral, Political, and Literary*) contain nine essays on economic topics which were conveniently collected and most helpfully introduced by Eugene Rotwein in 1955. The essays cover such subjects as money, the balance of trade, the rate of interest, public finance, taxation and population. The topics were treated as *essays*; a fact which makes it difficult to recover Hume's intention if not his meaning. But as Professor Rotwein has shown, the essays are marked by a unity of purpose and of method. They also enable us to identify a number of particular and interdependent themes.

The first theme is broadly methodological and arises from Hume's conviction 'that all the sciences have a relation, greater or less, to human nature, and that however wide any of them may seem to run from it, they still return back by one passage or another' (*Treatise of Human Nature*, Intro., para. 4). The study of human nature was thus to be based upon empirical evidence: as Hume himself made clear, the *Treatise* constituted an attempt to introduce the 'experimental method of reasoning into moral subjects'.

The approach allowed Hume to state a proposition which was profoundly influential in the eighteenth century, namely that: 'It is universally acknowledged that there is a great uniformity among the actions of men, in all nations and ages, and that human nature remains still the same in its principles and operations' (*Inquiry Concerning Human Understanding*, Section viii). Among these 'constant principles', Hume was to include a desire for action, for liveliness and, of particular interest to the economist, avarice or the desire for gain: a constant principle of motion which allows the commentator to offer scientific generalisations, at least in the sphere of political economy (*Essays*, pp. 112–13).

A second major theme in the *Discourses* relates to Hume's employment of historical materials. From one point of view this perspective is straightforward in the sense that the study of history is an 'invention' which 'extends our experience to all past ages, and to the most distant nations' (*Essays*, p. 566). But from the point of view of our understanding of economic phenomena broadly defined, the picture which was to emerge from the 'economic writings' was in fact a complex one.

If Hume did argue that the principles of human nature were constant, he also appreciated that the way in which they found expression would be profoundly affected by the socio-economic environment which may happen to exist, and by habit, customs and manners. While this theme runs throughout the essays, perhaps two examples will suffice for the present purpose.

In the long essay 'Of the Populousness of Ancient Nations', a work which has scarcely received the attention it deserves, Hume addressed a proposition which had been advanced by both Montesquieu and Robert Wallace to the effect that population levels had been higher in ancient as compared to modern times (*Essays*, pp. 378–9, Note 2). In deciding in favour of modern society, Hume drew attention to the use of slavery in the classical period as 'in general disadvantageous both to the happiness and populousness of mankind' (*Essays* p. 396), pointing also to the incidence of military conflict and of political instability. But perhaps the most striking aspect of the argument is the attention given to the point that 'Trade, manufactures, industry were no where, in former ages, so flourishing as they are at present in Europe' (*Essays*, p. 416). Population is ultimately limited not just by political factors, but also by the food supply, and this in turn by the type of economic organisation prevailing.

The same basic theme emerges in the essay 'Of Money' where

Hume rejected the conventional wisdom that money can be regarded as wealth (*Essays*, p. 281) and stated the famous relationship between changes in the money supply and the general price level: a relationship which remained substantially unchallenged until the twenties of this century (Schumpeter, 1954, p. 396).

Less familiar is the point that Hume consistently contrasted the situation of a primitive economy with a more sophisticated version. It is, he argued, 'the proportion between the circulating money, and the commodities in the market which determines the prices' (*Essays*, p. 291). In the primitive economy, 'we must consider that, in the first and more uncultivated ages of any state, . . . men have little occasion for exchange, at least for money, which, by agreement, is the common measure of exchange' (*Essays*, pp. 290–1). But in the stage of commerce, in contrast, 'coin enters into many more contracts, and by that means is much more employed' (*Essays*, p. 291).

On the other hand, the changed form of economic organisation had given a greater scope to individual effort and must therefore massively increase the supply of commodities which are subject to exchange. Hume therefore concluded that although prices in Europe had risen since the discoveries in the West Indies and elsewhere, these prices were in fact much lower than the extent of the increase in the money supply might of itself suggest: 'And no other satisfactory reason can be given why all prices have not risen to a much more exorbitant height, except that which is derived from a change of customs and manners' (*Essays*, p. 292).

The technique which we have just considered is essentially an exercise in comparative statics in the sense that it enables us to contrast and compare the operation of certain economic relationships in different institutional environments. But there was another dimension to Hume's historicism which, if loosely articulated, is none the less more explicitly dynamic in character.

The theme of historical dynamics is addressed primarily in the essays 'Of Commerce' and 'Of Refinement in the Arts', where it is noted that:

> The bulk of every state may be divided into *husbandmen* and *manufacturers*. The former are employed in the culture of the land; the latter work up the materials furnished by the former, into all the commodities which are necessary or ornamental to human life. As soon as men quit the savage state, where they

live chiefly by hunting and fishing, they must fall into these two classes though the arts of agriculture employ *at first* the most numerous part of the society. (*Essays*, p. 256)

It was Hume's contention that there had been a gradual progression to a situation where the two main sectors of activity are fully interdependent, supported by merchants: 'one of the most useful races of men, who serve as agents between those parts of the state, that are wholly unacquainted, and ignorant of each other's necessities' (*Essays*, p. 300). The argument is rooted in Hume's deployment of a favourite thesis of the eighteenth century, namely that men have natural wants which gradually extend in a self-sustaining spiral.

The tone is best expressed in the essay 'Of Refinement in the Arts' where Hume also contrasts the form of government found in 'rude and unpolished nations' with that likely to be associated with the modern state. In passages which are likely to have caught the attention of both Smith and Steuart, Hume observed that 'where luxury nourished commerce and industry, the peasants, by proper cultivation of the land, become rich and independent; while the tradesmen and merchants acquire a share of property, and draw authority and consideration to that middling rank of men, who are the best and firmest basis of public liberty' (*Essays*, p. 277): a development which may be expected further to encourage the rate of economic growth.

The final major theme in Hume's thought relates to the problem of international trade: a theme which, here as elsewhere, unfolds on a number of levels. To begin with Hume drew attention to the general benefits of foreign trade. In the essay 'Of Commerce', for example, he made the point that if 'we consult history, we shall find that in most nations, foreign trade had preceded any refinement in home manufactures, and had given birth to domestic luxury'. In the same context he drew attention to induced changes in taste and to the point that imitation leads domestic manufactures 'to emulate the foreign in their improvements' (*Essays*, p. 263–4). Hume continued to note that the encouragement of domestic industry would further enhance the opportunities for trade and economic growth (*Essays*, pp. 327–8).

The second aspect of Hume's argument supports his repeated claim for freedom of trade on grounds that are essentially technical. Building upon the analysis of the essay 'Of Money', Hume examined the case of two or more economies *with no unemployed resources* with a view to demonstrating the futility of the mercantile preoccupation with a positive balance of trade. Against this, Hume contended, a net inflow of gold would inevitably raise prices in the domestic economy, while a loss of specie would reduce the general price level elsewhere – thus improving the competitive position in the latter case and reducing it in the former. In the essay 'Of the Balance of Trade' Hume concluded that 'money, in spite of the absurd jealousy of princes and states, has brought itself nearly to a level' (*Essays*, p. 314) just as 'All water, wherever it communicates, remains always at a level' (*Essays*, p. 312).

The third dimension to Hume's treatment of foreign trade is much more complex. It is based upon the premise that countries have different characteristics and different rates of growth, thus opening up a different and distinctive policy position as compared to those so far considered. The argument effectively introduced what Dr Hont has described as the 'rich country/poor country debate' (Hont, 1983, chapter 11). Dr Hont has identified no fewer than twelve aspects of the argument (1983, pp. 274–5). But for the present purpose, perhaps we may be permitted to approach the matter in a slightly different way.

While critical of Montesquieu's thesis regarding the role of physical factors, Hume was nonetheless conscious of the fact that different countries could have different factor endowments and aware that climate could have some influence upon economic activity (*Essays*, p. 267). But there is also a sense in which the rich country/poor country thesis reflects strands of thought which we have already identified in dealing with the comparative static and dynamic branches of Hume's argument.

In this context it is worth recalling that the comparative static technique involves the *comparison* of *different* economic types, while the dynamic element draws attention to the importance of individual effort and to an accelerating rate of change as institutions and manners themselves change. On the one hand the reader is reminded of the phenomenon of a 'diversity of geniuses, climates and soil', while on the other attention is drawn to the point that the extent to which men apply 'art, care and industry' may vary in one society over time and between different societies at a given point in time. Other factors which will affect the rate of growth and cause variations in rates of growth in different communities include the form of government, and the degree to which public policies such as trade regulations, taxes and debt are deployed with intelligence.

Hume illustrated this new phase of the problem by referring to the issue of regional imbalance (a concern which he shared with Josiah Tucker), citing the case of London and Yorkshire (*Essays*, pp. 354–5). The regional dimension is just as relevant to the rich country/poor country debate as is the international, although it was upon the latter that Hume chose to place most emphasis.

Hume's treatment of the performance of the modern economy, especially in the context of the essays 'Of Money' and 'Of Interest', implies an increase in productivity which may give the developed economy an advantage in terms of the price of manufactures (Oswald to Hume, 10 October 1749, *EW*, pp. 190–96). He also recognised that an inflow of gold in the context of a growing economy need not generate adverse price effects (Hume to Oswald, 1 November 1750, *EW*, pp. 197–99). But he clearly felt that rich countries could lose their competitive edge, in noting that England feels 'some disadvantages in foreign trade by the high price of labour, which is in part the effect of the riches of their artisans, as well as of the plenty of money' (*Essays*, p. 265). It was thus recognised that advantages may be eroded, causing the loss in turn of *particular* industries, (*Essays*, p. 330), *unless care is taken to preserve them.*

Hume also seems to have felt that the tendency for the price of labour and provisions to rise over time could lead to a *general* loss of markets and that this could involve a policy of protection to support employment levels: a situation which he contemplated with calm objectivity, noting that 'as foreign trade is not the most material circumstance, it is not to be put in competition with the happiness of so many millions' (*Essays*, p. 265).

Hume concluded in the essay 'Of Money' that 'there seems to be a happy concurrence of causes in human affairs, which checks the growth of trade and riches, and hinders them from being confined entirely to one people' (*Essays*, p. 283). The point was to be elaborated in correspondence with Lord Kames (4 March 1758) and reflects an old preoccupation with the thesis of 'growth and decay' (*EW*, pp. 109–202).

II

Sir James Steuart cited more than fifty authorities in the *Principles of Political Economy* (Skinner, 1966, pp. 739–40) in a list which includes Cantillon, Mirabeau, Montesquieu and Hume. It is not difficult therefore to identify Steuart's sources of inspiration in matters of *doctrine*. But it is sometimes forgotten that Steuart faced an acute problem of *organisation* in writing the *Principles* (cf. Skinner, 1966, pp. 5–6); a problem which was largely solved by his adoption of the broad methodological perspectives associated with Hume. While Hume was said to have been critical of the 'form and style' of the *Principles*, it is not difficult to understand his pleasure when first he read the work in manuscript form (Skinner, 1966, p. xlv).

Perhaps the use of the historical approach provides the most striking parallel especially as applied to political subjects where Steuart ascribed to economic development a gradual but fundamental change in the patterns of authority and dependence, deducing that 'modern liberty' had arisen from the 'introduction of industry, and circulation of an adequate equivalent for every service' (Skinner, 1966, p. 209). The change in the balance of power which was the reflection of the same process also led Steuart to the conclusion that 'industry must give wealth and wealth *will* give power' (Skinner, 1966, p. 213). As an earnest of this position Steuart drew attention (in his notes on Hume's *History*) to the reduced position of the Crown at the end of Elizabeth's reign; a revolution which appears 'quite natural when we set before us the causes which occasioned it. Wealth must give power; and industry, in a country of luxury, will throw it into the hands of the commons' (Skinner, 1966, p. 213n).

There is an equally obvious parallel between Steuart and Hume in respect of the treatment of population where in effect the former sought to extend the analysis of Hume's essay and to place this topic at the centre of his treatment in Book I. In so doing, Steuart stated that the first fundamental principle of population is generation, the next is food (Skinner, 1966, p. 31) from which it followed that where men live by gathering the fruits of the earth (the North American model), population levels must be determined by their extent (Skinner, 1966, pp. 36–7). Where some effort is applied to the cultivation of the soil (the agrarian stage) Steuart recognised that the output of food, and therefore the level of population, would grow. But here again he drew a distinction between cultivation for subsistence and the application of industry to the soil, as found in the modern situation, where all goods and services command a price and where the potential for economic growth (and therefore population) is enhanced – especially in a situation where the major sectors of activity are fully interdependent (Skinner, 1966, p. 42). It was for these reasons that Steuart was able to side with Hume's judgement against that of Montesquieu and Wallace.

Steuart's account of the stage of commerce also includes a statement which Hume would have instantly recognised when it was noted that:

> we find the people distributed into two classes. The first is that of the farmers who produce the subsistence, and who are necessarily employed in this branch of business; the other I shall call the *free hands*; because their occupation being to procure themselves subsistence out of the superfluity of the farmers, and by a labour adapted to the wants of the society, may vary according to these wants and these again according to the spirit of the times. (Skinner, 1966, p. 43)

The whole process, it was then noted, would be facilitated by the use of money as the means of exchange and further 'by an operation by which the wealth or work, either of individuals or of societies, may, by a set of men called merchants, be exchanged for an equivalent, proper for supplying every want, without interruption to industry, or any check upon consumption' (Skinner, 1966, p. 146).

Hume would have had little difficulty in appreciating these points or the broadly optimistic assessment which Steuart offered with regard to economic growth within this institutional framework. It is readily apparent that Steuart saw no reason to doubt the potential for economic development in the context of the *exchange* economy. Here, and for the first time in an *institutional* sense: 'Wealth becomes *equably distributed*; . . . by *equably distributed* I do not mean, that every individual comes to have an *equal* share, but an equal chance, I may say a certainty, of becoming rich in proportion to his industry' (Steuart, *Works*, 1805, ii. 156). Steuart also argued that the potential for economic growth was almost without limit or certain boundary in the current 'situation of every country in Europe' (Skinner, 1966, p. 137). An equally dramatic confirmation of the general theme is to be found in the chapter on machines, which he considered to be 'of the greatest utility' in 'augmenting the produce or assisting the labour and ingenuity of man' (Skinner, 1966, p. 125).

Again in the manner of Hume, it was Steuart's contention that the modern economy had encouraged new forms of demand and new incentives to industry. In a passage reminiscent of Smith's *Theory of Moral Sentiments* (which he may have read), Steuart drew attention to man's love of ingenuity and to the fact that the satisfaction of one level of perceived wants tends to open up others by virtue of a kind of demonstration effect (Skinner, 1966, p. 157). The general point is best caught by his earlier (but recurring) contrast between the feudal and modern systems: '*Men were then forced to labour because they were slaves to others; men are now forced to labour because they are slaves to their own wants*' (Skinner, 1966, p. 51). But Steuart was to offer further applications of the thesis and in ways which recall Hume's concern with variations in rates of economic performance in different communities.

In the second book Steuart dropped the assumption of the closed economy and proceeded to examine the issue of international trade. Characteristically, he traced the interrelationship between developed and undeveloped nations in terms of the distinction between active and passive trade, which had already been established by Malachy Postlethwayt but in the context of a problem already addressed by Hume. Steuart was clearly preoccupied with variations caused by 'natural advantages' such as access to materials, transport and the nature of the climate (Skinner, 1966, p. 238), as befits a close student and admirer of 'the great Montesquieu' (Skinner 1966, p. 121). To these he added the form of government in arguing that 'trade and industry have been found to flourish best under the republican form, and under those which have come nearest to it' (Skinner, 1966, p. 211). But equally important for Steuart were the spirit of a people and 'the greater degree of force' with which 'a taste for refinement and luxury in the rich, an ambition to become so, and an application to labour and ingenuity in the lower classes of men' manifested themselves in different societies at any one point in time and over time; a thoroughly Humean perspective.

Steuart was acutely conscious of the sheer variety of economic conditions and indeed noted early in the book that: 'If one considers the variety which is found in different countries, in the distribution of property, subordination of classes, genius of people, proceeding from the variety of forms of government, laws, climate, and manners, one may conclude, that the political economy of each must necessarily be different' (Skinner, 1966, p. 17). The number of possible 'combinations' opened up by the proposition that growth rates and other characteristics will vary is virtually endless. In recognition of this point Steuart employed three broad classifications, all of which may derive from Mirabeau's *Friend of Man* (1756): the stages of infant, foreign, and inland trade. This generalisation and clarification of Hume's position reminds us of a further characteristic of Steuart's argument, namely his concern with economic policy.

The duties of the statesman in the economic sphere are clear: having defined the essence of the exchange economy as involving a 'general tacit contract', Steuart went on to note that 'Whenever . . . anyone is found, upon whom nobody depends, and who depends on everyone, as is the case with him who is willing to work for his bread, but who can find no employment, there is a breach of contract and an abuse' (Skinner, 1966, p. 88). As in the case of Smith, the justification for intervention is market failure, although Steuart's position with respect to the functions of the state in fact arises directly from the areas of analysis and policy with which he was primarily concerned.

It is appropriate to recall Steuart's interest in the model of primitive accumulation and in the *emergence* of the exchange economy. Steuart's concern with society in a process of transition is reflected in his attempt to formulate policies designed to deal with the problems generated by *historical* developments: developments which had caused cities to expand, and feudal retainers to be dismissed. It is in this context that the statesman is invited to consider the employment of redundant nobles and of the 'multitudes of poor' together with the all-important issue of the means of communication (such as good roads). Steuart suggested that the historical and contemporary record would provide an invaluable guide to the problems which would confront a statesman who adopted a self-conscious policy of economic *and therefore* of social development. It was Steuart's contention that in many cases the transition from a state of 'trifling industry' and subsistence farming (which could be described as the primitive version of the stage of commerce) could not occur without the interposition of the sovereign (Skinner, 1966, p. 108).

Steuart also gave a great deal of attention to policy with respect to international trade, in emphasising the need for protection in particular cases and freedom of trade in others. The position is conveniently summarised by reference to the 'stages' of trade. *Infant trade* represents an undeveloped economy where the ruling policy must be one of protection (Skinner, 1966, p. 262) – although he also noted that: 'the scaffolding must be taken away when the fabric is completed' (Steuart Works ii. 235). In the case of *foreign trade*, taken as representing the attainment of a competitive stage, the policies recommended are designed to retain the capacity of an economy to compete. The ruling principles are: 'to banish luxury; to encourage frugality; to fix the lowest standard of prices possible; and to watch, with the greatest attention, over the vibrations of the balance between work and demand. While this is preserved, no internal vice can affect the prosperity of it' (Skinner, 1966, p. 263). *Inland trade*, on the other hand, represents a situation where a developed nation has lost its competitive edge. Here the basic preoccupation must be the maintenance of the level of employment. Steuart recognised the importance of the balance of payments in advocating a restrictive monetary policy, and concluded: 'I will not therefore say, that in every case which can be supposed, certain restrictions upon the exportation of bullion or coin are contrary to good policy. This proposition I confine to the flourishing nations of our own time' (Skinner, 1966, p. 581).

Two additional points are worth making before we conclude this sketch. First, we should recall Hume's distinction between the loss of particular markets in international trade and the situation where an *economy* finds itself in an uncompetitive position. Exactly this point was made by Steuart in commenting upon the fact that his 'stages of trade' may apply to economies, or regions, or indeed to particular industries. As he noted: 'we are not to suppose the commerce of any nation confined to any one of the three species. I have considered them separately, according to custom, in order to point out their different principles. It is the business of statesmen to compound them according to circumstances' (Skinner, 1966, p. 265). Secondly, we should note that Steuart's policy recommendations are always related to *circumstances*. He contended that economic intervention could only be justified in cases of perceived economic necessity. For example, in a passage which applies to nations as well as to sectors or regions within a nation he observed: 'Were industry and frugality found to prevail equally in every part of . . . great political bodies, or were luxury and superfluous consumption everywhere carried to the same height, trade might, without any hurt, be thrown entirely open. It would then cease to be an object of a statesman's care and concern' (Skinner, 1966, p. 296).

III

It is now recognised that Smith owed much to Hume (and to Francis Hutcheson) in his approach to ethics, at least in the sense that he employed mechanisms which involved the use of sympathy, reason and imagination in an argument which greatly developed the concept of the spectator. A distinctive feature of the approach is the role ascribed to self-interest, where Smith took the opposite view to Hutcheson in suggesting that a 'regard to our own private happiness and interest . . . appear upon many occasions to be very laudable principles of action' (TMS VII. ii. 3. 6).

Smith's analysis placed much emphasis on man's desire for approval: a desire which finds many illustrations in the economic sphere, where Smith suggests that the basic drive to better our condition is rooted in the pursuit of status, and further supported by a desire to acquire the imagined conveniences of wealth. These passages in *The Theory of Moral Sentiments* reflect the tone of Hume's essay 'Of Refinement in the Arts' regarding the benefits of economic growth, and provide a good illustration of Smith's use of the basic thesis of man's insatiable wants. Smith was also at one with Hume in his calm assessment of Bernard Mandeville's provocative argument that private vices were public benefits (see above, ch. 7).

> If the love of magnificence, a taste for the elegant arts and improvements of human life . . . is to be regarded as luxury, sensuality and ostentation, even to those whose situation allows, without any inconveniency, the indulgence of those passions, it is certain that luxury, sensuality and ostentation are public benefits; since without these qualities upon which he thinks it proper to bestow such opprobious names, the arts of refinement could never find encouragement. (TMS VII. ii. 4. 12)

If Smith followed Hume in offering a moral dimension to his system, he agreed with both Hume and Steuart in applying a sociological perspective to his treatment of history; a treatment which is marked by an interest in the link between economic organisation and patterns of authority and dependence. Smith also shared the same interest in the association between economic development and the changing distribution of political power which, in the case of England, had led to the House of Commons assuming a position of dominance *vis-à-vis* the House of Lords.

But Smith gave the 'history of civil society' a distinct status built in turn upon a distinctive thesis – that of the four stages which he developed in its complete form (Meek, 1976). One example of Smith's historical writing is to be found in the treatment of public jurisprudence in the *Lectures on Jurisprudence*. A further illustration, possibly of more direct interest to the student of economics, is found in *The Wealth of Nations*, Book III, where Smith set out to trace the rise and fall of the feudal system: a process which culminated in the emergence of the 'present establishments' in Europe.

Following a general description of the feudal state, Smith's account of the process of transition begins with the emergence of the city as a means of establishing a countervailing power *vis-à-vis* the great landed magnates. Smith argued that royal policy had in effect created self-governing institutions with the right to defend themselves, thus establishing an environment within which economic growth was possible (WN III. iii. 12). In a compact analysis remarkable for its formality, Smith proceeded to argue that economic growth must initially be supported by foreign trade. This would be based on the exchange of domestic surpluses in primary products for foreign manufactures. This in turn would be followed, he suggested, by an attempt to introduce manufactures at home based upon foreign materials and, finally, by the gradual refinement of manufactures based upon domestic output (WN III. iii. 20). It will be noted that the argument gives prominence to a point emphasised by Hume, namely the role of imitation. It is also noteworthy that the whole process depends upon the assumption that trade initially took place between societies at different stages of development, and that the pattern of trade will change as domestic development unfolds in the manner suggested by Steuart in his analysis of what he (unlike Smith) took to be a central problem in international trade.

As is now well known, Smith proceeded to show that the emergence of new forms of activity and of wealth would impinge upon the interests of the great proprietors until a situation was reached where they became 'as insignificant as any substantial burgher or tradesman in a city. A regular government was established in the country as well as in the city, nobody having sufficient power to disturb its operations in the one, any more than in the other' (WN III. iv. 15). Smith thus established a link between commerce and liberty, and in so doing acknowedged a debt to Hume as the 'only writer who, so far as I know, has hitherto taken any notice of it' (WN III. iv. 4). In the manner of Steuart and Hume, Smith had established that the modern economy is a two-sector case within which all goods and services command a price, but by a more formal route.

Smith's students would undoubtedly have understood that his treatment of economic questions was to be seen against the background provided by the ethics and by the historical analysis. But when Smith turned to political economy he also made it possible to see this subject as separate and distinct – thus emulating the achievements of Hume and Steuart, while departing from Hutcheson whose analysis of economic questions is integral with his theory of jurisprudence (cf. Teichgraeber, 1986). But at the same time Smith followed Hutcheson in respect of the *organisation* of his argument, featuring as it does a consideration of the division of labour, money, and the analysis of price and allocation (Taylor, 1965, p. 14; Scott, 1900, ch. 11).

While Smith differs from Hutcheson in respect of trade policy, it is perhaps in this area that he shows some debt to Hume. He cited Hume's authority in connection with the doctrine of the specie-flow (cf. Eagly, 1970), while in addition there is a strong Humean flavour in the claim 'that Britain should by all means be made a free port, that there should be no interruptions of any kind made to foreign trade . . . and that free commerce and liberty of exchange should be allowed with all nations and for all things' (LJ(B), p. 269). At the same time, the *Lectures on Jurisprudence* were innocent of a clear distinction between factors of production and categories of return. Absent too was 'the fundamental analysis . . . of saving, investing, capital and money which was to become the central pillar of the classical macro-economics' (Hutcheson, 1988, p. 353). These deficiencies may well have been corrected as a result of Smith's contact with the Physiocrats in 1766, and especially by his knowledge of Turgot's *Reflections on the Formation and Distribution of Riches* (cf. Skinner, 1979, ch. 5).

As far as the purely economic analysis is concerned, the familiar tale need not detain us. It is sufficient to be reminded that in *The Wealth of Nations* the theory of price and allocation was developed in terms of a model which made due allowance for distinct factors of production (land, labour, capital) and for the appropriate forms of return (rent, wages, profit). This point, now so obvious, struck Smith as novel and permitted him to develop an analysis of the allocative mechanism which ran in terms of interrelated adjustments in both factor and commodity markets. The resulting version of general interdependence also allowed Smith to move from the discussion of 'micro' to that of 'macro' economic issues, and to develop a model of the 'circular flow' which relies heavily on the distinction, already established by the Physiocrats, between fixed and circulating capital. These terms, which were applied to the activities of individual undertakers, were transformed in their meaning by their application to society at large. Working in terms of period analysis, Smith represented the working of the economic process as a series of activities and transactions which linked the main socio-economic groups (proprietors, capitalists and wage-labour). In Smith's terms, current purchases withdraw consumption and investment goods from the circulating capital of society: goods which are in turn replaced by virtue of productive activity in the same time period.

Looked at from one point of view, the analysis taken as a whole provides one of the most dramatic examples of the doctrine of 'unintended social outcomes', or the working of the 'invisible hand'. The individual undertaker (entrepreneur), seeking the most efficient allocation of resources, contributes to overall economic efficiency; the merchant's reaction to price signals helps to ensure that the allocation of resources accurately reflects the structure of consumer preferences; the drive to better our condition contributes to economic growth. The argument is also buttressed by a series of judgements as to *probable* patterns of behaviour and *actual* trends of events. It was Smith's firm opinion, for example, that in a situation where there was tolerable security, 'The sole use of money is to circulate consumable goods. By means of it, provisions, materials, and finished work, are bought and sold, and distributed to their proper consumers' (WN II. iii. 23). In the same way he contended that the savings generated during any (annual) period would always be matched by investment (WN II. iii. 18): a key assumption of the classical system which was to follow. If such a model enabled Smith to isolate the causes of economic growth, with the emphasis now on the supply side, it is also informed throughout by what Terence Hutcheson has described as the 'powerfully fascinating idea and assumption of beneficent self-adjustments and self-equilibration' (1988, p. 268).

Joseph Schumpeter may have been correct in his assertion that 'the *Wealth of Nations* does not contain a single analytical idea, principle, or method that was entirely new in 1776' (1954, p. 184). But what is important is the presence of a *system*; the fact that Smith gave political economy a distinctive analytical *shape* which was a dramatic step forward. Looked at from this point of view it is apparent that the concept of the analytical system as a kind of imaginary machine is entirely apt as a description of Smith's contribution, and that his particular 'machine' went well beyond those of Hume and Steuart in terms of organisation and content. Smith's contribution made it possible to proceed from one area of analysis to another in a clear and logical order; to proceed from the analysis of price to that of distribution, from distribution to the concept of the circular flow and hence to the treatment of dynamics. Moreover, it is apparent that Smith advances through the work by dealing with distinct logical problems in a particular sequence which successfully illustrates the interdependence of economic phenomena.

The quality of *system* was appreciated by some contemporaries such as Dugald Stewart who noted that 'it may be doubted . . . if there exists any book beyond the circle of the mathematical and physical sciences, which is at once so agreeable in its arrangement to the rules of a sound logic, and so accessible to the examination of ordinary readers' (Stewart IV. 22). This is a compliment which Smith would have appreciated, conscious as he was of the 'beauty of a systematical arrangement of different observations connected by a few common principles' (WN V. i. f. 25). As in the case of Steuart, there is also a policy dimension which reflects the author's areas of interest. But the dimension is now very different and based, in the main, on a series of judgements of an analytical and empirical nature. Smith was concerned essentially to formulate policies which would *facilitate* the operation of an economy based on exchange. It was of course in this context that he advocated abolition of all impediments to the working of the allocative mechanism and, in the interests of growth, the repeal of regulations in respect of trade.

This feature of Smith's work is evident in his concern that the state should organise services which would ensure an appropriate and secure *environment*: services such as justice and defence. As is well known, Smith defended the view that the state should encourage public works and institutions designed to facilitate the commerce of society and which were 'of such a nature, that the profit could never repay the expense to any individual or small number of individuals, and which it, therefore, cannot be expected that any individual or small number of individuals should erect or maintain' (WN V. i. c. 1). Education, including military education, was later added to the list. But there is also another characteristic dimension to the argument which reminds us of the institutional structure which Smith had in mind; his concern that public services be *organised* in such a way as to *induce* efficient delivery (cf. Rosenberg, 1960; Peacock, 1975). It was in this context that Smith argued that public services should, where possible, be paid for by the consumer. He further suggested that public services should be so structured as to respect the point that in every trade and profession 'the exertion of the greater part of those who exercise it, is always in proportion to the necessity they are under of making that exertion' (WN V. i. f. 4).

While the reader interested in this branch of Smith's thought can do no better than to consult Jacob Viner (1927), one further point should be noted here on the ground that it reflects Smith's understanding of the nature of the economy with which he had to deal. Smith was well aware that the modern version of the circular flow depended on paper money and on credit: a system of dual circulation involving a complex of transactions linking producers and merchants, retail dealers and consumers. He was aware that such transactions would involve cash (at the level of the household) and credit (at the level of the firm). It was in this context that he was willing to regulate the small note issue in the interests of a stable banking system, and objected to the use of the optional clause (WN II. ii. 94; cf. Checkland, 1975). In the same context, Smith advocated control of the rate of interest, set in such a way as to ensure that 'sober people are universally preferred to prodigals and projectors' (WN II. iv. 15). The latter proposal was to call down the wrath of Jeremy Bentham (1787), who believed that this particular suggestion was inconsistent with Smith's defence of natural liberty. Apparently Smith remained unconvinced.

IV

This chapter has attempted to illustrate in general terms the point that Hume, Steuart and Smith all produced works which are important in their own right and which amply illustrate the qualities which A. L. Macfie ascribed to the Scottish Tradition especially in the form in which that tradition was established in the Age of Enlightenment.

Hume in particular shows a typical interest in the principles of human nature and thus 'deserves to be remembered . . . for his more fundamental attempts to incorporate economics into a broader science of human experience' (Rotwein, 1955, p. cxi). As we have noted above, the approach is also dominated by Hume's awareness of the variety of human experience over time and by his use of the historical method in dealing with purely economic issues: a point which explains Terence Hutchison's contention that he was 'too deeply committed to historical relativism to accept a single model' (1988, p. 214).

The same feature is to be found in Hume's concern with variations in economic performance; a problem which manifests itself in the *Political Discourses* in the form of an analysis of the rich country/poor country relationship. On this view of the economics process, policy prescriptions must always be related to the circumstances prevailing. Hume thus emerges as 'the writer who always insisted on the variability of man and the relativity to time and place of all policies; the one who was completely free from the paralysing belief, that crept over the intellectual life of Europe, in practical principles that claim universal validity' (Schumpeter, 1954, pp. 293–4, commenting on Galiani).

It has also been contended that Sir James Steuart's connection with Hume, and the influence of the latter upon him, have been unduly neglected, and further that Steuart may well have organised his *Principles of Political Economy* along lines suggested by the *Political Discourses*. There is certainly the same preoccupation with the social and political implications of economic growth, the same emphasis on the role of natural wants, the same style of treatment in the theory of population and when considering the nature of the exchange economy. But Steuart carries the argument further, not just in terms of the analysis of specific problems such as price theory or the theory of money (Vickers, 1960), but also in the sense that he explicitly addresses the issues presented by a socio-economic system in a process of transition. Not for nothing did he make the point that he proposed to follow the historical 'clue' (Skinner, 1966, p. 29) or draw attention to the fact that the process of economic development was causing a wonderful ferment in the remaining fierceness of the feudal constitution. Steuart's is perhaps the only example in the writings of the Scottish Enlightenment of an attempt to address what Perelman (1983) and Kobayashi (1967) have described as the problem of primitive accumulation, and as such is deserving of attention.

Steuart went further than Hume in addressing the problems presented by variation in rates of growth both regionally and internationally: an analysis which resulted, as we have seen, in the generalised statement of three 'stages' of trade. As with Hume, the implication is that economic policy must always be related to the circumstances which prevail. To this extent Steuart would have agreed with the Italian economist, Galiani, in his contention that 'Policy is a matter of detail. It must always be concerned with particular cases. If it is made universal, it makes for confusion: in particular circumstances, it produces good' (quoted in Hutchison, 1988, p. 270). In drawing attention to Steuart's lack of confidence in self-regulating mechanisms and to his corresponding fear of unemployment, Professor Hutchison concludes that his stylistic faults were 'brought about by his intellectual virtues, and by his persistent resistance to oversimplification . . . It is easier to write clearly and engagingly when one has a simple system to expound' (1988, p. 350).

When we turn to Smith it is not difficult to find marked parallels with his predecessors in respect of the style of approach. There is clear evidence of similarity in his interest in social psychology and, above all, in the fact that Smith also addressed the historical dimension in a way which elucidated the processes which had generated the exchange economy and explained changing patterns of dependence and a changing distribution of political power. The analyses and the conclusions are strikingly similar to those offered by Steuart and Hume; especially noteworthy is Smith's (rare) acknowledgement of a debt to the latter in this area of thought.

But there were differences: differences in the degree of formality
and of completeness; a difference in the fact that Smith allows us
to think of philosophical history as a distinct subject.

Smith also differs from Steuart and Hume in respect of his use
of the historical method. In Smith's hands, the history of civil
society is essential to our understanding of the exchange economy
and of the social and political environment which it may produce,
but it is now the *preface* to political economy rather than integral
to the treatment. In the event, Smith did not use the historical method
in dealing with economic questions – a point noted by Eugene
Rotwein in his discussion of Hume:

> one may say that, despite its pronounced emphasis on econo-
> mic development, Smith's approach to its more general
> aspects is less basically genetic or evolutionary than Hume's.
> . . . With regard particularly to his treatment of the theoretical
> issues of political economy, Smith clearly exhibits the tend-
> ency to abstract from the historical influence which was so
> characteristic of Ricardo and the later classical economists.
> (1955, p. cix; cf. Hutchison, 1988, pp. 213–14)

Smith also differs from Hume and Steuart in that he did not
address the problem of the primitive version of the exchange
economy, but rather concentrated on a relatively sophisticated
model of a capital-using system. While admitting that rates of
growth may vary both in Book III of *The Wealth of Nations* and in
his analysis of the American colonies (cf. Skinner, 1979) this is not
a major feature of his treatment of international trade.

Smith had chosen a different path and had given political
economy a different shape; a shape which was consistent with
analytical completeness and clarity and with a policy prescription
which was deceptively simple and attractive. While sharing common interests in the approach to the study of man in society, the
contrast with Hume and Steuart in terms of the choice of analytical
strategy could hardly be more complete. It was perhaps for this
reason that Smith scarcely acknowledged Hume's work as an
economist and chose to ignore entirely Steuart's *Principles of political
Economy*. This was hardly an act of generosity (cf. Raschid, 1982;
Skinner, 1988). As Steuart's biographer noted shortly after his
death, 'We cannot help lamenting that he should have passed over
the *Political Oeconomy* without once bestowing upon it a single mark
of public attention' (quoted in Skinner, 1966, p. lii). But the real

blow to the reputation of his predecessors came not so much *from* Smith, as from those who were to find *in* Smith the inspiration for a new classical orthodoxy.

The two pillars of Smith's success may be represented as the analytical system and the broad advocacy of free trade. Yet as Richard Teichgraeber has shown, success was not immediate. In a convincing argument, Professor Teichgraeber has indicated that Smith's advocacy of freedom of trade did 'not register any significant victories during his life time' (1987, p. 338), echoing a point already made by Salim Raschid (1982, p. 83). Indeed Raschid has argued that when success did come, it was largely because Smith's policy prescriptions were peculiarly relevant to British interests (1982, p. 82). In the same vein, Teichgraeber's research suggests that although there were contemporary admirers (such as Dugald Stewart), there 'is no evidence to show that many people explored his arguments with great care before the first two decades of the nineteenth century' (1987, p. 339). He concluded: 'It would seem that at the time of his death Smith was widely known and admired as the author of the *Wealth of Nations*. Yet it should be noted too that only a handful of his contemporaries had come to see his book as uniquely influential' (1987, p. 363).

But if Smith's analytical contribution was understood only by a few at the time of his death, the situation was soon to change. The point is implied in Hollander's exhaustive work (1973) and further elaborated in Dennis O'Brien's excellent account of classical economics (1975). In a later work, O'Brien has noted the *longevity* of Smith's paradigm (1976): a point also made by Boulding (1971) who found in Smith's work the basis of modern economics. It was this perception on the early nineteenth century which did most to consign the work of Smith's predecessors to oblivion precisely because it led to the belief that the history of the discipline dated from 1776.

Acceptance of the *Wealth of Nations* as shaping the analytical base would appear to have been accompanied by the acceptance both of Smith's definition of the mercantile system and his critique of its alleged deficiencies. Even where the flaws of Smith's account have been noted (cf. Thomas Pownall, 1776 for an early example), there was acceptance of Smith's point that there was an identifiable system. There was also general acceptance of the basic proposition that:

> No regulation of commerce can increase the quantity of industry in any society beyond what its capital can maintain. It can only divert a part of it into a direction into which it might not otherwise have gone; and it is by no means certain that this artificial direction is likely to be more advantageous to the society than that into which it would have gone of its own accord. (WN IV. ii. 3)

Economic historians have long argued that Smith's account of the mercantile system was a straw man, an invention (Coleman, 1969) and little more than free trade propaganda (Hecksher, 1965, ii. 332). A. V. Judges has also argued that, following Smith, the classical economists established a dummy dragon which, 'articulated and endowed with organic functions by its indignant creators, had the fire of life breathed into it by the avenging angels themselves' (1969, p. 36). In the event, acceptance of the view thought to be that of Smith led to a situation where regulation of trade and industry was deplored and, by implication, generally thought to be unenlightened. At best this perception has caused some commentators to view with mild embarrassment the occasional failings of Hutcheson, Hume – and indeed Smith himself, whose views on the functions of the state are nothing if not complex (cf. Skinner, 1986). At worst the conventional interpretation generated a situation where Steuart was roundly condemned as a mercantilist (cf. Anderson and Tollison, 1984) – thus neatly illustrating Hume's contention that we frequently produce fallacies where a 'collateral effect is taken for a cause' (EW, p. 46). This was a view which made it difficult on occasion for economists to appreciate the perspective of the economic historian which contends that 'an understanding of the contemporary economic situation may be a better guide to contemporary recommendations than a criticism of policy' (Coleman, 1967, p. 15). This is exactly the view which would have been taken by Hume and Steuart.

Other problems followed from the development of a new orthodoxy. As Hutchison has eloquently argued, from an analytical point of view 'the losses and exclusions which ensued after 1776, with the subsequent transformation of the subject and the rise to dominance of the English classical orthodoxy were immense' (1988,

p. 370). Among these losses were many of the issues identified by Hume and Steuart. The use of the historical method in addressing theoretical issues was one such loss; so too was the concern with unemployment and the model of primitive accumulation, while in addition the classical orthodoxy showed little interest in the problems of differential rates of growth or of undeveloped economies. If there is a line from Hume to Steuart and from Hume to Smith, the path followed by Steuart was to emerge, for a time at least, as a cul-de-sac to which the analysis of undeveloped economies was also consigned.

Ironically, the conventional perception of *Smith's* contribution also suffered as a result of the developing orthodoxy at least in later years. Here attention might be drawn to Smith's concern with *processes* of adjustment rather than with equilibrium states, and to his emphasis on uncertainty. It may be suggested that the rigorous logic of the classical system as developed by Ricardo unintentionally (for Ricardo expected serious students to read *The Wealth of Nations*) helped his successors to lose sight of Smith's broad perspective on the working of the economy. The reference is again to the issue of shape – in this case to Smith's concept of the circular flow with its focus on process analysis, where all magnitudes are dated and set in the context of an environment where all sectors and socio-economic groups are horizontally and vertically integrated.

More serious still was the fact that the classical orthodoxy made it possible to think of economics as quite separate from ethics and history, thus obscuring Smith's true purpose. In referring to these problems Terence Hutchison, in a telling passage, has commented that Adam Smith was unwittingly led by an Invisible Hand to promote an end no part of his intention, that 'of establishing political economy as a separate autonomous discipline' (1988, p. 355). Professor Macfie made a related point when noting that: 'It is a paradox of history that the analytics of Book I, in which Smith took his own line, should have eclipsed the philosophical and historical methods in which he so revelled and which showed his Scots character' (1967, p. 21). While a version of Smith's work vigorously survived, Macfie was suggesting that major aspects of the Scottish tradition did not, as least for a season: that tradition which Hume, Steuart and Smith had done so much to establish in their different ways.

The elements of the 'tradition' which Macfie identified do not disclose habits of mind which are exclusively Scottish, as he was well aware. They find some expression in the work of the German Historical School, in the contributions of the American institutionalists, and in the work of Englishmen such as Alfred Marshall. Marshall's work especially shows how much he was influenced by contemporary work in philosophy, history and biology. The *Principles* (1890) in particular exhibits real sensitivity to the complexity of economic phenomena seen in a wider social setting, causing Keynes to describe his work, significantly, as 'a mine rather than a railway', the fruit of 'Marshall's learning and ripe wisdom' (1951, p. 213).

Like Smith, Marshall's concern with realism presented problems for subsequent commentators, leading to Samuelson's claim that the 'ambiguities of Alfred Marshall paralysed the best brains in the Anglo-Saxon branch of our profession for three decades' (1967, p. 109). Hutchison recorded only a matter of fact in pointing out that the work done in the 1920s and 1930s reflected another victory for the mathematical model and the application of 'more rigorous academic standards of logical and terminological tidiness and precision' (1953, p. 315).

As in the case of the immediate post-Smithian period, there were gains in terms of theoretical elegance and precision, but losses to be measured in terms of realism and relevance (Skinner, 1986b). Smith, with his acute understanding of the role of the subjective in science and of the competing claims of the theoretical and the practical, would have been quick to understand such developments, but it may be fitting to leave the last word with a central figure in this story, David Hume, who commented with wry humour:

> though men are commonly more governed by what they have seen, than by what they foresee, with whatever certainty; yet promises, protestations, fair appearances, with the allurements of present interest, have such powerful influence as few are able to resist. Mankind are, in all ages, caught by the same baits: The same tricks, played over and over again, still trepan them. (EW, p. 104)

Note

This chapter originally appeared in the *Scottish Journal of Political Economy*, vol. 37 (1990), under the title of 'The shaping of political economy in the Enlightenment'. It is reproduced with the kind permission of the Scottish Economic Society.

Abbreviations

David Hume's *Writings on Economics*, edited by Eugene Rotwein, (1955) are cited as EW.

Hume's *Essays Moral Political and Literary*, edited by Eugene Miller (2nd ed. 1987) are cited as *Essays*.

Sir James Steuart, *Principles of Political Economy* (1767), edited by A. S. Skinner is cited as Skinner, 1966.

Dugald Stewart's 'Account of the Life and Writings of Adam Smith' is cited as Stewart.

References

Anderson, G. M. and Tollison, R. D. (1984), 'Sir James Steuart as the Apotheosis of Mercantilism and his Relation to Adam Smith', *Southern Economic Journal*, vol. 51.

Bentham, J. (1987, 1790), *Jeremy Bentham's letters to Adam Smith*, in the *Correspondence of Adam Smith*, ed. E. C. Mossner and I. S. Ross (Oxford, 1977).

Boulding, K. (1971), 'After Samuelson, Who Needs Adam Smith?', *History of Political Economy*, vol. 3. Reprinted in Wood (1983), iii. 247–55.

Checkland, S. G. (1975), 'Adam Smith and the Bankers' in *Essays on Adam Smith*, eds. A. S. Skinner and T. Wilson (Oxford).

Coleman, D. C. (1969), ed. *Revisions in Mercantilism* (London).

Eagly, R. (1970), 'Adam Smith and the Specie Flow Doctrine', *Southern Journal of Political Economy*, vol. 17. Reprinted in Wood (1983), iii. 240–6.

Hecksher, E. (1965), *Mercantilism* (London).

Hollander, S. (1973), *The Economics of Adam Smith* (Toronto).

Hont, I. (1983), 'The Rich Country–Poor Country Debate in Scottish Political Economy', in Hont, I. and Ignatieff, M., *Wealth and Virtue: The Shaping of Political Economy in the Scottish Enlightenment* (Cambridge).

Hume, David (1987), *Political Discourses*, included in *Essays Moral, Political and Literary*, ed. Eugene Miller (2nd edn, Indianapolis).

Hume, David (1874–5), *Treatise of Human Nature* and *Inquiry Concerning Human Understanding* both included in *The Philosophical Works of David Hume*, ed. T. H. Green and T. H. Grose (London).

Hutchison, T. W. (1953), *A Review of Economic Doctrines, 1870–1929* (Oxford).

Hutchison, T. W. (1988), *Before Adam Smith: The Emergence of Political Economy, 1662–1776* (Oxford).

Judges, A. V. (1969), 'The Idea of a Mercantile State', in Coleman (1969), 92–117.

Keynes, J. M. (1951), *Essays in Biography* (London).

Kobayashi, N. (1967), *Sir James Steuart, Adam Smith and Friedrich List* (Tokyo).

Macfie, A. L. (1967), *The Individual in Society* (London).

Meek, R. L. (1976), *Social Science and the Ignoble Savage* (Cambridge).

O'Brien, D. P. (1975), *The Classical Economists* (Oxford).

O'Brien, D. P. (1976), 'The Longevity of Adam Smith's Vision', *Scottish Journal of Political Economy*, vol. 23. Reprinted in Wood (1983), iii. 377–94.

Peacock, A. (1975), 'The Treatment of the Principles of Public Finance in the *Wealth of Nations*', *Essays on Adam Smith*, ed. A. S. Skinner and T. Wilson (Oxford).

Perelman, M. (1983), 'Classical Political Economy and Primitive Accumulation', in *History of Political Economy*, vol. 15.

Pownall, T. (1776), *A Letter from Governor Pownall to Adam Smith*. Reprinted in *Correspondence of Adam Smith*, eds. I. S. Ross and E. C. Mossner (Oxford, 1977), appendix A.

Raschid, S. (1982), 'Adam Smith's Rise to Fame: A Re-examination', *The Eighteenth Century, Theory and Interpretation*, vol. 23.

Rosenberg, N. (1960), 'Some Institutional Aspects of the *Wealth of Nations*', *Journal of Political Economy*, vol. 18. Reprinted in Wood (1983), ii. 105–20.

Rotwein, E. (1955), *David Hume: Economic Writings* (Edinburgh).

Samuelson, P. A. (1967), 'A Modern Theorist's Vindication of Adam Smith', *American Economics Association, Papers and Proceedings*, vol. 67. Reprinted in Wood (1983), iii. 498–509.

Schumpeter, J. A. (1954), *A History of Economic Analysis* (London).

Scott, W. R. (1900), *Francis Hutcheson* (Cambridge).

Skinner, A. S. (1966), *Sir James Steuart; Principles of Political Economy* (Edinburgh and Chicago).

Skinner, A. S. and Wilson T. (1975), eds. *Essays on Adam Smith* (Oxford).

Skinner, A. S. (1979), *A System of Social Sciences: Papers Relating to Adam Smith* (Oxford).

Skinner, A. S. (1986), 'Adam Smith: Then and Now', in *Ideas in Economics*, ed. R. D. C. Black (London).

Skinner, A. S. (1986b), 'Edward Chamberlin: The Theory of Monopolistic Competition', *Journal of Economic Studies*, vol. 13.

Skinner, A. S. (1988), 'Sir James Steuart, Economic Theory and Policy', in *Philosophy and Science in the Scottish Enlightenment*, ed. P. Jones (Edinburgh).

Steuart, Sir James (1805), *Works, Political, Metaphysical and Chronological* (London).

Stewart, Dugald (1793), 'Account of the Life and Writings of Adam Smith, LL.D', included in *EPS*.

Taylor, W. L. (1965), *Francis Hutcheson and David Hume as Precursors of Adam Smith* (Durham, NC).

Teichgraebar, R. (1986), *Free Trade and Moral Philosophy: Re-thinking the Sources of Adam Smith's Wealth of Nations* (Durham, NC).

Teichgraeber, R. (1987), 'Less abused than I had reason to expect': The Reception of the *Wealth of Nations* in Britain, 1776–1790', *The Historical Journal*, vol. 30.

Vickers, D. (1960), *Studies in the theory of Money, 1690–1776* (London).

Vickers, D. (1975), 'Adam Smith and the Status of the Theory of Money', in *Essays on Adam Smith*, eds. A. S. Skinner and T. Wilson (Oxford).

Viner, J. (1927), 'Adam Smith and Laisser Faire', *Journal of Political Economy*, vol. 35. Reprinted in Wood (1983), i. 143–67.

Wood, J. C. (1983), *Adam Smith: Critical Assessments* (London).

Index

abstraction, in language, 25–6, 45–6
adjectives, 31, 40
adventitious rights, 174, 175, 176
Advocates, Faculty of, 168–9
aesthetics, xi
  beauty, 67
  dancing, 71–2, 76
  fashion, 66
  harmony, 71
  Hume, 64
  imitative arts, 17–18, 59, 68–70
  music, 17–18, 71–7
  opera, 61, 74–5
  style, 60
  taste, 65, 67
  The Theory of Moral Sentiments, 64–7
agrarian capitalism, 192–4
agrarian roots, capitalism, 192–3
agriculture
  in history, 175
  improvements, 193, 197, 198, 204, 206
  and industry, 193, 195
  and trade, 194
Alembert, Jean le Rond, 23
ambiguity, 40, 44
ambition, 15, 153
anomalous motions, astronomy, 85
applied ethics, 119
approval, desire for, 154–5, 157, 229
Aquinas, Thomas, Saint, 128
art
  as intellectual pleasure, 59

and effect, 70
  painting, 68, 69–70
  see also aesthetics
Arthur, Archibald, 1–2
astronomy, 85–91
Astronomy, The History of (Smith), 79–80
  psychological approach, 91
  systems, 85–91
attribute expressions, 27, 31–3
authority, in family, 176
autonomy, and moral experts, 137–8
auxiliary verbs, 33

banking, 202–6
Beattie, James, 73
beauty
  intrinsic, 67
  of language, 8–9
  of style, 10
  and utility, 64, 151
  see also aesthetics
Beauzée, Nicolas, 24
beneficence, 158–9
Bentham, Jeremy, 235
Berkeley, George, Bishop of Cloyne, 162
biographies, of Adam Smith, 93–5, 101–2
Blacklock, Thomas, 50 (n25)
Blackwell, Thomas, 42
Boswell, James, 9–10, 13, 98
Bouhours, Dominique, 8
Bouillaud, Jean Baptiste, 88